THE LAST HUSTLE

THE LAST HUSTLE

A True Story

We can never know what will lead to our freedom

KENNY JOHNSON
as told to Shanti Einolander

NON-DUALITY PRESS

C.1 921
Johns

THE LAST HUSTLE

First edition published July 2011 by NON-DUALITY PRESS

Cover portrait by Adam Shemper: www.shemperphoto.com

NON-DUALITY PRESS | PO Box 2228 | Salisbury | SP2 2GZ
United Kingdom

ISBN: 978-0-9566432-8-5

www.non-dualitypress.com

This book is dedicated to all those incarcerated, whether in prisons of brick and stone or prisons of the mind. If you are earnestly looking inward for the key to eternal freedom, you will be rewarded. This is the truth.

Throughout my 23 years of incarceration, there were many moments, often in the middle of the night, when I would cry out to my Lord, the only one I knew, and ask to be given a simple life. I sincerely prayed to let this cup of bitterness, confusion, and the insanity of repeatedly going in and out of prison be taken from me.

My prayers in these moments were not eloquent or specific to any certain set of circumstances. I just wanted to be a normal person, a man who was respected and who respected others. This desire was deeply embedded in my heart, and my heart would be searched and read by my creator and dispensation granted.

Yet while my heart was saying one thing, my actions would be telling an altogether different story. As soon as I'd get out, I would be faced with the need to survive and so inevitably go back to the only world I knew. Crime.

That is, until the awakening ...

It was not easy recounting this story, and in no way is the writing meant to glorify a life of crime. Rather, the goal was to recapture the vibrant and seductive energy of the culture of those times.

I humbly ask forgiveness from all those men and women, families and business owners, whose lives were affected by my greed and disconnectedness as a thief, robber, con man, and pimp.

All praise and thanks be to all the saints, teachers, and lovers of truth who gave and are giving their lives in service to the liberation of all. For if you all had not drunk from the cup of illusion, there would be no redemption for any of us.

May all beings know peace.

Table of Contents

Part 3 — Muddy Waters

Part 4 — Belly of the Beast

Part 5 — Higher Ground

Part 6 — Freedom Behind Bars

Part 7 — Fire of the Unknown

*"All our personal stories,
however complex and multi-layered,
however deeply implanted in our genetic structure,
are only stories.*

*"The truth of who we are is not a story.
The vastness and the closeness of that truth
precedes all stories.*

*"When we overlook the truth in allegiance to some story,
we miss a precious opportunity for self-recognition."*

—Gangaji

Prologue

Steel shackles cut into my wrists and ankles and I had to take a piss. Would this bus ride ever end? Did I want it to? Truth was, I was scared shitless. I was scared to death.

We'd been riding for eighteen hours straight, crisscrossing the countryside, dropping men off at one institution and picking others up at the next. The moonless night outside my window revealed nothing but blackness, a blackness that did nothing to ease the growing panic inside my heart.

It was January 1980, the dead of winter, and there was no heat on the bus. The only thing warming my sorry ass was the fire raging along my nerves and inside my head. Even my bladder was on fire.

It's too damn much time! my mind screamed into the darkness. *This place is crazy dangerous. What if I never make it out?*

I was thirty-two years old and facing the longest stretch of time in all my years of hustling, an unthinkable forty years. I would serve a minimum of ten before ever laying eyes on a parole board. All the time I'd been in the game, all the different jails I'd seen the inside of, somehow I'd never really believed I'd be headed here, the "butcher shop," what every prisoner dreaded the most. What a helluva name to hang on a prison. Finally the worst was upon me.

The men were making their usual racket, chattering away and yelling back and forth. Sweat and stink, pain and fear, oozed from every pore, filling the inside of the bus with an acrid stench like old cigarette butts. I had no idea who the guy shackled next to me was and I didn't care, lost as I was in my own private nightmare.

I felt it long before I saw it, that hellhole of a prison. Its heavy energy of despair emanated for miles outside the razor-wired walls and armed guard towers. Rounding that last bend in the woods I looked up past the driver and got a glimpse of what was to be my new home, Lewisburg Federal Penitentiary, well known as one of the most dangerous maximum-security prisons in the nation. Same as every other prison, high-intensity lights defined its perimeter, flooding the countryside for miles in unnatural brightness.

My lips and tongue felt as dry as an old cowhide left on a cracked desert floor; my chest constricted, so I could only suck in little sips of air at a time. Taking a deep breath didn't seem like a good idea anyway. That might make me relax, and this surely was no time for relaxing. All my senses were winding up into a fever pitch of self-preservation.

Suddenly the whole of the prison came into focus. *Shit!* I couldn't believe what I was seeing. Looming above us was Dracula's castle, huge, ancient, and sinister. The memory of every scary movie I'd ever seen as a child came rushing back at me. Given the amount of fear I'd been generating for the last eighteen hours, Barbie and Ken's plastic toy home would've looked like a monster house. Almost imperceptibly, the conversations of the men around me began coming into focus.

"Man, they got guys in there who'll just walk up to you and start stabbing," one guy was saying. My eyes traced the long white scar traveling from the side of his nose to the nape of his neck. He looked like he knew what he was talking about.

"Gotta get you a knife," he went on. "Gotta be ready to protect your ass."

My already crazed mind shifted into overdrive. *Somebody's gonna try and stab me? I don't know nobody here! How am I gonna get a knife?*

"Yeah," another chimed in, "they got mobsters in there who'll eat lesser cons for lunch."

But I'm just a little ole chili pimp! A sneak thief. Plus I'm out of my home territory. They're gonna eat me alive!

Intense light suddenly flooded the inside of the bus. The lines of fear and tension etched on every man's face jumped out in stark relief. Eyes wide, we were a herd of captive animals frozen in the prison's headlights. Like a Polaroid snapshot, that instant of collective emotion would be forever branded onto the desolate field of my heart—anger, fear, frustration, doubt, anxiety, hopelessness, faith, prayer, wishing, hoping, wanting to cry, wanting to yell, wanting to scream, wanting to . . .

My jaws clenched. My fists clenched. The muscles in my shoulders corded up like old vines. I stopped breathing.

I felt like I was being squeezed ten miles deep in an ocean of dread, drowned in an infinite, mind-freezing fear of the unknown.

Looking out.

Seeing nothing.

PART 1

Stealing The Key

"Open the door to my cage,"
said the wild man to the prince.
"The King has forbidden it," said the prince,
"and I cannot even if I wish,
for I have not the key."

"It lies under thy mother's pillow,"
said the wild man.
"Thou canst get it there."

—from *Iron John*, The Brothers Grimm

Peaches 'n Sweets

What path had led me to be trembling before the gates of hell? I'd have to say it all began with a hunger for sweets and the desire to impress a girl.

My first act of thieving was in rural Arkansas, living in my grandmother's house. It was 1955, so I must have been seven years old at the time. We called it the "shotgun house." Reason was, if you took a shotgun and fired it through the front door, the buckshot would go clean out the back, hitting nothing cause it was just a straight box, one big 20-by-20 foot room smelling of old bacon grease.

Four corner cinder blocks held the house two feet off the ground, leaving plenty of room for the chickens to run back and forth underneath. I used to watch them through the cracks in the bare wood floor. Newsprint papered the walls from floor to ceiling, both for insulation and to keep the bugs out. Grandma used to catch the mice that ran up our walls and drown them in a bucket. A big potbellied stove stood dead center of the room.

In the back was Grandma's bed where we slept together nights. Grandma always slept on her back with her knees propped up. I did the same. I mimicked everything Grandma did. I wanted to have tiny Benjamin Franklin glasses that sat on the end of my nose just like hers. Grandma was also known to carry a pistol in her waistcoat. Eventually I would grow up to do the same. She was our protector, and the pistol was just part of her wardrobe.

In Grandma's day, white racist men lynched and killed niggers on a regular basis, yet Grandma, known to the rest of the world as Ollie Ashford, had little fear of white folks. I once heard a story about my grandmother walking down a country road with my mother and me as a toddler. Some young white boys had driven by in a pickup truck, yelling "Niggers!" at which point Grandma promptly turned around, pulled her dress up to show them her butt, and told them to kiss her black ass.

I'd been living with Grandma since I was four. I didn't know where my mother was, nor my brothers and sisters, nor why I wasn't with them. Only later would I find out that while I'd been living down in Arkansas with Grandma, my momma had been living up north in Kansas City, as had my auntie, Equator Gold. A lot of people had moved up north from Arkansas to try and make a better life. Apparently, I'd stayed with Grandma because I was the oldest and because she needed somebody to help her.

Saturday mornings I'd get up and go straight to Peaches and Pumpkin's house to watch Tarzan or cowboy movies on the TV. Peaches was a little older than me, and I was sweet on her. I was always stealing glances on her, admiring her dark, curly hair, and the way it shined like silk. Pumpkin was my age. I loved looking at their skin with its high yellow tones, Peaches, a light caramel with just a hint of blushing red, and Pumpkin, the deeper orange of a pumpkin. I wished I could live with them.

The fact that they had a TV was just one of the stark differences between our house and theirs. One day it dawned on me: *Wait a minute; these people got a picture box, whereas we don't have S-H-I-T at our place. Not even a radio.* That's when I realized we were poor.

All down our dirt road stood beautiful white houses with big front porches. Even Cousin William across the road had cows and chickens. He had a cotton field and pecan trees, which by local black standards made him rich. All we had were some chickens, Grandma's vegetable garden, and a pond with thousands of mosquitoes and the pointy heads of water moccasins skimming the surface. The grown-ups said that just one tiny bite from a water moccasin could strike you dead, but that never kept us kids from swimming on a hot day. Our water came from a well in the yard with an old big-handled pump. It took all my weight to bring that handle down.

Peaches, Pumpkin, and I had to walk a mile or so down the dirt road to the highway to catch the school bus over to our one-

3

room black school. We didn't own a car. Anywhere we wanted to go, we had to walk.

Next to the bus stop stood a little candy shack, Buck's Country Store, and here's where the thieving comes in.

One day I went into Grandma's purse and lifted one of her silver coins. It was a quarter. I didn't know what a quarter was or how much it could buy, but I knew I loved candy. Plus it was a way to impress upon Peaches and Pumpkin that I was worth having around. Little did I know it would become the genesis of a lifetime of stealing, always driven by the desire not only to have something of my own, but also to feel like I was somebody important.

Stealing from Grandma's purse became routine. It was exciting because it was my little secret. It felt innocent. There was no guilt or fear. All of that would come later on.

One day when I couldn't find any silver coins in Grandma's purse, I took a green. That was the day I got caught.

We ran all the way to the store where I laid the money up on the counter and told the clerk, like I always did, "Give me some candy."

"All right, Kenny Dale," he said, same as he always did, only this time he gave me back a huge pile of candy, a bunch of "greens," and some change. That's when I knew I'd gone too far. We all knew it. I started feeling panicky, trapped just like one of Grandma's rats.

I shoved the money at Peaches because she was the oldest. I thought she'd know what to do with it. Peaches ran home and straightaway gave the money to Grandma. Next thing I knew she was packing me up.

We walked in silence all the way down to the Greyhound bus station at the end of the road, a little boy, with a tiny little suitcase, holding his Grandma's hand. It was clear that Grandma loved me, but she had boundaries, rules and regulations, and this obviously was the consequence of breaking them. She simply stuck me on a bus to Kansas City, Missouri, no trial, no discussion, my first conviction and sentencing for thieving.

I was devastated. I didn't know how to broach what had happened, and so we never talked about it. As a kid I kept everything inside. I didn't even know how to cry.

I never left my seat on that long bus ride, nor talked to a single person. I was a little boy, and I was all alone.

Hobo Stick

"Yes Jesus! Praise the lord! Glory! Glory! Glory!"
There she goes again! I thought, shivering and peeking into the kitchen from the safety of my little add-on bedroom.

The mysterious force moving inside my mother on Sunday mornings was my first indoctrination into spirit. I would awaken to the sounds of pots rattling in the tiny kitchen and Momma softly singing her gospel music. Mahalia Jackson was her favorite singer, *Amazing Grace* one of her favorite songs.

That Sunday morning had started with a gentle *Just a Closer Walk with Thee...* Next thing I knew it was "Yes Lord! Thank you Jesus!" yelping out of her like she was happy just to be alive, grateful for all that she had. Whenever us kids heard that, we'd know there were a lot more "yes Lords" on the way. I braced myself cause I knew Momma was getting ready to "get happy."

Within seconds she was gone, all her words rushing out in one long fusion of religious fervor. "Yes Lord! Hallelujah! Thank you Jesus! Glory! Glory! Glory!"

Whenever my mother got happy, she might throw herself down on the floor. She might scream or cry. She would be reaching a place inside her soul where there was nothing but happiness that Jesus was in charge.

Her complete infusion with the Holy Spirit scared us. We didn't understand why she was jumping up and down being thankful when she was the only person in the room. I'd seen it in the church house, when the preacher would preach the people into a frenzy of emotion. The women would suddenly flip out and go running down the aisles blurting out their hallelujahs. Eventually they'd fall out on the floor right in front of the preacher, legs kicking the air in a riot of silk stockings and petticoats flying everywhere.

All of that was crazy enough, but when Momma started doing it all alone in the kitchen, we just didn't know what to do.

Normally the ushers were right there to grab and hold on to her. I was always afraid she might not come back from that place she was visiting inside herself and we needed her.

After a while she started to wind down, getting quieter and quieter. I knew what was coming next: "Kenny Dale, get up boy and get ready for church!"

My mother, Mrs. Geraldine Scott, never took to dressing frilly except on Sundays, when she'd break out her fanciest hats, gloves, purses, and perfumes. Those hats were a woman's signature piece back in the day, gigantic and colorful, with ribbons, bows, swirls, feathers, and all manner of plumage.

Most of the time, day or night, Momma could be found in the kitchen in her turquoise polyester pants and maroon blouse, cooking, canning vegetables, or brewing up some honey wine. To me her Sunday morning transformation from a poor, hardworking mother and cook into this beautiful woman I hardly recognized was almost beyond belief.

Momma was short and round, and although I'm not short, everybody always said I was the spitting image of my mother. I was never stoic like her though. Except for those occasions when she was feeling infused with the Holy Spirit, Momma had that same reserved manner Grandma Ollie did. I knew she loved me, but hugging and physical affection were never a part of the picture. It never even occurred to me that I could hug or kiss on her.

My mother was a paradox. Anyone looking at her would mostly see this warm, loving, God-fearing woman. But if I made a mistake, a stern, cold, unyielding side would come out, and I was terrified of it.

Momma loved us in her own way. She loved us by cooking for us. She loved us by giving us a house. She loved us by disciplining us. But the physical love I so desperately craved was just not there.

Why was my mother so serious? Day in and day out she had plenty of worries on her mind. There were seven of us kids. I was the first, then came Cynthia and Lemuel, who had a different father; then Reggie, Lashonda, Maurice, and Robin, all belonging to my stepfather, Bob Scott.

Momma was completely dependent upon my alcoholic stepfather to bring home a paycheck. The many days he came home drunk usually ended in a fight. On those days he'd be so drunk he'd park nose into the curb, ass out on the street. We could always tell by the quality of his parking how difficult our night was gonna be.

From the day I first arrived in Kansas City at the age of seven to the day I got sent away again at fifteen, the one constant in our lives was the AME, the African Methodist Episcopal Church, where Momma kept us going every Saturday, Sunday, and Wednesday.

The church bus came and picked us up every Sunday morning, even those mornings Momma had already gotten happy, 'cause she never got so happy she couldn't get ready for church.

I was in all the church plays, and one Easter Sunday my part in the play was to read a single verse from the Bible: Timothy 2:15. On stage that day I experienced a rare moment of total happiness. I felt good about myself because I had memorized that verse, and I knew I'd be able to repeat it. The stage felt like home, as if I belonged up in front of people, speaking The Word. The clapping of the audience was my confirmation. It was the crowning moment of my childhood, and the only time I'd ever felt my mother and I were on the same page. In that moment, I was a servant of the Lord.

Out of all the stuff she had yelled at me, beat into me, and tried to get me to do or not do, the one golden nugget I was left with was that passage from Timothy 2:15—*Study to shew thyself approved unto God, a workman that needeth not to be ashamed, rightly dividing the word of truth.*

I've always had this image in my mind of a hobo leaving home with his little sack on a stick. In that sack was a nugget of food, which for me was that one passage from Timothy. I didn't particularly understand its meaning at the time, yet it still resonated somewhere deep inside. Out of the hundreds of passages I studied as a youth, this was the one I know helped shape the man I am today. In my mind "rightly dividing the word of truth" would come to mean the same as "right discrimination."

Throughout my life I would attempt to separate things out in my mind, to divide the circumstances of each situation according to what felt right and what felt wrong. Often it had more to do with intuition and self-preservation than any particular moral direction. I admit my interpretation of right from wrong could get pretty creative, because, after all, I was gonna be rightly dividing my way through thirty years as a hustler, thief, and pimp. I somehow conveniently left out the first part of that verse, which was: *Study to shew thyself approved unto God, a workman that needeth not to be ashamed.*

All the same, my sorry-ass idea of rightly dividing stood me in good stead in the next decades of thieving, pimping, and hustling. I knew I couldn't rob women, I knew it would be dumb to shoot the gorilla pimps who wanted to take over my girlfriend, and I knew I had to stay away from heroin. Somehow this little nugget I carried with me sustained me in small ways, kept a spark of conscience alive, until I was ready to understand the real meaning of right discrimination.

The Hood

"**O**h my Lord, look at this!" my mother cried, rushing through the front door waving a piece of paper in her hand. Her face was ashen, uncertain, like the ground was shifting under her feet with not a thing in sight to grab onto.

I thought for sure something bad had happened, like the day my cousin Larry had stepped into a pile of burning coals and just about burnt his foot off. Momma, Auntie, and Grandma had cried and run around wringing their hands from the sight of his bulbous ankle and burnt flesh.

On this day, however, it was only a matter of seconds before a smile split her dark face and laughter clear and bright as the first day of spring filled the room. Other than gettin' happy in the Lord, it was one of the rare moments I'd ever seen my mother truly rejoice. A $10,000 check had just come in the mail.

My mother's ex-husband, a military man, had just passed away, and his pension had been awarded to Cynthia and Lemuel, my little half-sister and brother. Since they were still underage, that put the money in my mother's hands to do with the best she could.

At that time $10,000 was all it took to buy us a ticket out of the projects and into a white, middleclass neighborhood on the other side of the tracks; the kind of neighborhood where big beautiful trees lined the streets and everybody had a nice front porch.

African American families with a little bit of money had begun migrating over the tracks in droves. It seemed like every week a white family was moving out and a black family taking its place.

Before that we'd been living in the projects on Independence Avenue, a group of dingy one-bedroom apartments surrounding a central courtyard. My brother, sister, and I slept on the foldout couch in the living room. All the kids played together in the courtyard while the adults clustered around in pods, telling jokes that us kids weren't privy to.

Moving over to 44th and Montgall was like getting a whole new life. Our new house, built in the 1920's, had three bedrooms instead of one. After a while we added a fourth bedroom off the back. It was just ten feet by ten, but to me that little room was nothing short of a palace. For a while I even had it to myself. It had a window looking out over the back, and I could see into the yards of the Edwards' and the Grants', retired black couples on either side of us who'd also just moved in.

Though we had definitely moved up in the world, other than acquiring that little piece of real estate, nothing much had changed. We were still dirt poor. Anything we wanted, we had to beg, borrow, or make from scratch. Bicycles, sports equipment, you name it; we'd somehow manage to come up with it. Once I even built a go-cart out of an old lawnmower engine I'd found in a lot behind our house.

On the one hand our whole neighborhood was like family, all the adults taking part in watching out after each other's children. On the other hand the women gossiped viciously behind each other's backs. Nevertheless, if anybody ever got sick, injured, or down on their luck, the whole neighborhood would come together to pitch in and help out.

There were no school buses at the time in Kansas City, which meant everybody had to walk to and from school. Our block was one of the main thoroughfares for all the high school kids. When we first moved in, these were mostly the children of white doctors, lawyers, teachers, and preachers.

Though I wouldn't be going to high school for another year, I studied those kids from head to toe, day after day, observing how they acted and how they dressed, so I could try to emulate them. I made note of which ones wore leather coats, and which had the bright letterman's jackets signifying Lincoln, Central, or Paseo High, the school I'd soon be attending. I especially loved to watch the girls walk by in their big petticoats, a sight that most definitely got a rise out of my burgeoning male libido.

The next year I'd see those same kids driving down Montgall

11

in their '57 Chevys, with the baby moon hubcaps so shiny you could see your face in them or comb your hair.

If I had to name one single influence in my childhood that might have driven me toward becoming a professional thief, I'd have to say it was watching all those well-dressed kids parade past my house, day in and day out, reminding me of just how poor we were. I knew there was no way I was ever gonna have what those kids had. Not even close.

My stepfather, Bob Scott, was a cool guy, at least that's how I saw it, because he never really gave me much trouble, except for the fact that he was always drinking and beating on my mother. They'd be fighting in their room, and all I could do was stand and listen to her screams and pleadings, my fists curled up in silent protest. Rushing in there and trying to get him to stop would mean nothing but disaster for my butt, and most likely make matters worse for my mother.

I never met my father, nor even knew who he was. I knew my brothers and sisters had a father, but nobody ever talked about mine. I never even asked about him until I got to be fifty-seven years old, and by then he was dead. I don't know why my mother never talked about my daddy, where he was or what he thought about me. Only one time had she ever spoken about him, and all she'd said was that he was a twin, he lived on the other side of the tracks, he was educated, and his parents had money. My mother's family was poor sharecroppers. When she'd told him she was pregnant with me, he'd denied he was my father.

I've often wondered how those words of rejection may have reached me in my mother's womb, and what affect they might've had on her. Could it be that she was so deeply wounded on that fateful evening that she never again wanted anything to do with men, including me? Did I in that moment determine that it was every man for himself, don't love or take any responsibility?

To this day I have never seen a picture of my father. How did he look? How did he dress? Do I look like him? I may never know.

What I do know is that there were no male role models in my

family life who could show me how to be a man, how to let love and compassion be the ruler of my actions, and how to put into practice that nugget from Timothy, "rightly dividing the word of truth."

Lil' Blue

The year I was sent away to Little Blue Boys' Home was the year of my initiation into violence. It was 1963, I was fifteen, and I'd been busted for joyriding in a stolen car.

Boys at Lil' Blue punched and tormented each other on a daily basis. Seems like all we did was fight, and I, for one, got beaten up repeatedly. This one guy in particular, Box-Head Nash, had this thing about seeing if he could knock a guy out with one punch. He practiced on me a lot. He had a deceivingly sweet baby face and arms that stretched past his knees.

After hearing what was happening over at Lil' Blue, my old Boy Scout Leader, Mr. Bernard, took me aside one day. "Kenny," he said, "if you face a bully seven days a week and fight him seven days a week, one of those days you're going to beat him. From that day on you're going to have confidence in yourself, and that bully's going to become your friend." He was the only man in my life who had ever taken a real interest in me, so I took his advice to heart.

Gradually I learned how to fight, how to bob, weave, slip, slide, and fake. Eventually I won my first fight and the word went out. After that my confidence grew quickly until it was me slapping guys upside the head or kicking them in the butt. The only way to not get beat up was to start pushing other guys around. The only way to stop being the victim was to start being the perpetrator. From that time on the violent nature that got activated at Lil' Blue would slowly escalate until one day it would just about destroy my life, and my mother's life as well.

But the truth is Lil' Blue was not the first time I'd been exposed to violence. Not by far. Blue was just the magnifier.

The community I grew up in was aggressive and loud. Hitting each other was the way we related, the way we communicated. I witnessed everybody beating on everybody. I liked my friends, and even though I didn't understand why they kept hitting me, after a while I quit thinking about it. Violence was simply part of the fabric of our culture. We didn't hold hands. We didn't hug. I never hugged anyone until I was a grown man and my daughter came to visit me in prison. My own daughter had to teach me how to hug and hold in a genuine way. Many years later, when I met my spiritual teacher and was introduced to a spiritual community, I finally got comfortable hugging people. You can tell a lot about a person by the way they hug.

When it came to my mother, "Don't this and don't that" was her main style of communication. If I disobeyed her, I got beat, period. I came to understand that, as slaves, my black ancestors had been beaten into submission, and when I was a child that programming was still operating in our culture. I was taught that in order to communicate and get your point across you had to thrash somebody's ass, just as the slave owners had beaten the slaves in order to keep them in line. Eventually we had gone on to treat each other the same.

I've heard that slave mothers would beat their male children as a way of teaching them to never get uppity with white men and put themselves in danger. Looking back, I can see it in the way my own mother raised me. If she beat me, it was her way of saying, "Kenny Dale, don't you go and bring shame upon our family, and don't you get yourself killed!" At the heart of all her rigid discipline was her love for me and the desire to protect me.

"Boy, don't you go near that white man," my momma would often say; "don't you look at that white woman." Having sex with a white woman was a goal most black men secretly aspired to, most likely because it had been beaten into us that we couldn't have that.

I can't remember my mother or Bob Scott or any of the adults around me ever talking to me in any kind of meaningful way. Unless I'd done something to get in trouble, my presence was barely acknowledged. As fate would have it, it was the street people, the "hoodlums," as my mother called them, whom I would eventually come to feel seen and embraced by.

Our culture of the streets was undeniably violent and crazy, our main concerns being hustling, scheming, and conning. It was a world in which I was destined to be the giver and the receiver of much pain. Even so, the world of players was the world I would eventually end up gravitating towards, because it was the first world in which I had felt acknowledged.

Does my heart still harbor resentment from the patterns of behavior my mother and other adults passed on to me? I can honestly say that I have forgiven them. I know my momma did the best she could to raise us. She always stayed true to what she thought was the right thing to do.

Now, when I look back on all the violence, I see how it helped to prepare me, to shape me, and eventually to drive me toward wanting to find a deeper meaning to life. It was God's little set-up. We can never know what will lead to our freedom.

My mother and I have such a deep connection now. She does not know what really happened to me while in prison or how I found freedom from within. All she knows is that her son is doing good, not worrying her, sends her money, tells her how beautiful she is, and hugs and kisses her—even if it does sometimes feel uncomfortable for the both of us.

I can see how back then she knew that if I stayed on the path of hanging with the hoodlums all was going to end badly. This is what she knew from the Bible and from her years of experience as a parent and an adult.

I did not get a chance to be beside my mom as she worried herself to a nub about me and the life I was living. But life has a strange way of giving us the chance to learn and revisit situations where we once behaved in an ignorant way. Now my grandson is in jail and my beloved daughter worries herself silly over his state of affairs. Each day I have to listen to her fears and judgments of herself as a mother. Now I am witnessing each thought and emotion that a mother endures when one of their precious creations goes astray. Recently I even asked her, "Why are you so worried about him?"

16

"He's my son," she said, "and I don't want him to get killed in there, or to be raped, or to get into trouble." She couldn't understand why I even needed to ask the question, but I wanted to know her thinking and feeling because years ago my own momma was in the same situation and I was the one in jail. Bless you Momma, I just didn't understand—but now I do.

The Arrangement

The catalytic event that threw me into a life of crime, the activity from which I would not deviate for another thirty years, happened just after I got out of Lil' Blue.

It was the summer of 1965, and I was sixteen. My mother was hell bent on trying to get me to do the right thing. I wanted that too. I didn't want to get sent back to Lil' Blue where I had to fight all the time. Momma had been talking to a neighborhood contractor, Conrad Robinson, and they had come up with a plan. The agreement was that I would work all summer with Conrad, live with him, baby-sit his kids, and he would pay me at the end of the summer. I was to be his painting apprentice, and he was going to teach me his trade.

I'd seen this kind of arrangement work well with my younger sister Cynthia. My mother had sent her across the street to be raised by Miss Helen and her family.

Miss Helen, a short little black woman resembling my mother, was teaching my sister how to play the violin. Cynthia got her own bedroom, and she got to go on trips with them. I saw that my sister was blossoming over there, so I hoped that this new arrangement with Conrad would work for me too. I wanted the money to buy school clothes. I was tired of looking all ratty-ass and poor. My mother couldn't buy clothes for all seven of us, and neither could she buy us schoolbooks. All of my clothes were second-hand, most of them stained or ripped. My shoes, if I had any at all, were always hand-me-downs.

My stepfather, Bob Scott, could only afford so much on his chef-cook's salary. When payday came, we knew we were either gonna get shrimp fried rice that evening or hamburgers. That was the one day of the week we were gonna live good. I might even get to eat a big ole Wimpy Burger or a tenderloin sandwich. Just that one day, and then we'd be back to eating commodity meat and commodity cheese out of a can.

My mother, being the great cook she was, could make a lot of different dishes out of that meat. We never had to worry about going hungry, but a little bit of food in our stomachs and a place to sleep was about it. Anything extra I was gonna have to go out and get on my own.

Conrad Brown was a straight up kind of guy, a clean-shaven, tax-paying, educated businessman who pronounced all his words correctly. He had a sincere way of looking that made you want to trust him. I was fond of his wife, Lois, and all three of his kids.

Conrad taught me how to paint, how to hammer nails, and how to lean and lay on the back of his motorcycle. It all felt great. It was a chance to turn my life around.

One day I was on a ladder painting the outside of the Wimpy Burgers restaurant, the orange paint stinging my eyes. The sun was hot that day, "hotter than little sister's pussy," as my uncle Melvin loved to say. I never knew what he meant by that, but it sounded cool. I was still a virgin at sixteen and wanted so bad to brag about sex like the other boys.

As I was reflecting on that topic, my old gang from juvenile hall, Pete Mallory, Dan Haywood, Pop Jaws, and Reggie Cummins, came walking up the street, all four looking sharp as tacks as they swaggered in to get themselves some burgers. I stopped my painting and studied them. They all looked like a million bucks and it was just high noon. Each one had on brand new shoes and Sansabelt slacks, silk shirts, nice straw hats, and gold teeth in their grill.

From my ladder I called out, "Hey, man, how do ya'll dress so well? Where do you get all that money?"

Showing off, each of the guys pulled out a wad of greens. "If you want some of this," Pete said, "just come hang out with us."

My mind skipped back to the day before when I'd seen a white man at the Kresge's Soda Fountain pull out a wad of cash. I wanted to be like that white man with all that money in his hand. I wanted the life he had, not mine. I hated being poor.

These guys with their rolls of cash had the air of princes who

19

knew exactly where they were going and could make money at will. The image of the way they looked that day was burned into my brain. For the time being, however, I was set on doing right.

"Naw, man," I said, "I'm learning to paint right now. I'll get my money later on at the end of summer."

I kept painting and working with Conrad, and I was happy and proud to be doing it.

Finally summer ended, and it was time to get paid. Conrad and I went to his office, and he got out his checkbook. He started listing how many hours I had put in and how much I'd made. Then he went on to list all the deductions. I didn't understand any of that, and I didn't care. All I wanted was my money.

After he got through with all his adding, subtracting, and multiplying, he wrote me out a check for $32.00. At first I just looked at it in shock. Then I got confused. Did the check say $32, $320, $3,200 or what? I could see for myself where the dot was, but my mind was simply refusing to believe it. I didn't say anything, however, I didn't question him, and that would become a trait of mine in the years to come. People would do or say something that demanded correcting on the spot, and I wouldn't be able to find the courage inside to say what was really on my mind. That day with Conrad I just took the check home and gave it to my mother, who was chopping onions at the kitchen table.

"Look what he did Momma!" I howled, throwing the check on the table in disgust. "I don't understand! I worked all summer for *THIS?*"

Picking up the check, she peered at it. Amazingly, her face registered not the least bit of surprise. "Well, son," she replied with her usual stoicism, "the Lord knows best. You did learn a skill this summer, and he did give you a paycheck today. Apparently, you must've ate up all your pay."

"But that wasn't the deal!" I shouted, stomping my feet and waving my arms around the tiny kitchen in exasperation. "That's not what we agreed on!" Now I was arguing with Momma, when Conrad Robinson was the one I should've been arguing with.

"Kenny Dale, we'll just have to take that check down to the bank and cash it, then we'll see what we can do with it."

"Momma," I cried, "we can't do nothin' with *that!*"

I was devastated. Obviously she had no intention of going over to Conrad's and fighting for me. She never did fight for me. A heavy swell of hopelessness washed over my teenaged soul. I wanted her to march into his office and demand to know what was going on. I wanted her to get right up in his face and scream, "You had an agreement with my son, and you didn't live up to it!"

Momma just went back to chopping her onions. I finally gave up and quit arguing with her. I felt like Sonny Liston after going seven rounds with Cassius Clay and losing every round. I slogged back over to Conrad's house, got my clothes, and moved back in to my mother's. I felt hurt, dejected, and utterly disillusioned. The fact that I'd learned a skill was no longer relevant. I could've cared less about working as a painter. It was the last time I ever took my mother's advice or took stock in anything she said.

A few days later, after the dust had settled and my emotions had calmed a bit, I remembered that day several months earlier when Pete and the guys had come walking up the street with their fine clothes and plenty of money. I got Pete's number from my sister Cynthia and called him up.

Initiation

L et's walk, man" was all Pete said, standing on my doorstep looking sharp in a new Dobbs hat and dark sunglasses. It was the Monday after the first week of school, September 1965, and I was desperately in need of some money to buy clothes.

This was gonna be my first time out, and I had no clue what was about to come down. I had never stolen any money other than from my grandmother's pocketbook. I knew this was the beginning of my training, and I wasn't afraid. I was eager to follow Pete's lead. I'd be playing with a real sneak thief, and we weren't gonna be stealing no potato chips off the Frito Lay truck.

Pete and I had first gotten hooked up at Lil' Blue when he had become sweet on Cynthia. One day in the visiting room he'd asked, "Is that your sister, man? Oh, she's fine. Can I write her?"

Sisters were usually how us boys met girls. Practically the first thing out of a guy's mouth was, "You got a sister?" and most guys did. I was eager to hook Pete up with Cynthia. He had always been one of the cool cats. Pete was the one who'd first taught me how to fight, and that's when the other guys had finally started leaving me alone.

The day I'd called him he'd promised, "I'll be over to your house Monday 'bout nine. We'll take off walking. Make sure you're wearing your Hush Puppies." A sneak thief always had to have soft-sole shoes so he could be silent as a cat and run just as fast.

Sure enough, there he'd been as promised, his two gold teeth glistening in the sun.

Pete was the color of a manila envelope. You'd never know he was only five-foot tall cause he carried himself like a full seven. Pete wasn't trying to be like a white man. Pete was proud of being Pete. I was envious of that. I wasn't proud of being Kenny.

Pete always carried a screwdriver, which on this day he had shoved inside his back pocket. From that day forth, I would do the same. The screwdriver would be our main working tool.

Back in the sixties, cash register tills were made of wood. Pete taught me how to angle my screwdriver between the lock and the edge of the drawer and pop it open, catching the drawer and easing it out nice and slow to keep the little bell from ringing.

We walked one block up from my mother's house to Prospect Avenue, the main drag running straight through the black section of Kansas City, Missouri.

Prospect Avenue was like the river of life in our part of Kansas City. The street was lined with supermarkets, hardware stores, beauty salons, pharmacies, clothing stores, barbershops, and the Fairyland Amusement Park. Loffler's supermarket was there too, where as kids we'd once bought candy so old that worms were living inside it; yet that didn't keep the old man who owned it from selling at the regular price.

It was nine o'clock in the morning, and Prospect Avenue was bustling. We were like two little lions on the prowl, looking for something to eat. I had no idea exactly what we were looking for, but I knew Pete did, and I was gonna follow his lead.

"Let's go to the hardware store," Pete said, gesturing further up on Prospect.

First we walked by the store, glancing through the windows and casing the place. "Kenny," Pete whispered intently, tugging on my arm, "when we go in, grab that lady clerk and pull her all the way over to the corner. Say something that will keep her busy and talk loud 'til I leave."

"You got it, man," I agreed, but I was already sweating. Here was my chance to prove up and I already wanted out. *Shit, I've never done this before!* I worried to myself. *What am I gonna say to her?* Nevertheless, I walked in while Pete stayed just outside the door.

"I'd like to buy a hammer," I told the lady clerk, "but it's a special kind." Then I started describing a hammer I'd seen at Conrad's, one with a little ball-peen on one side of the head. She took me over to the corner where the hammers were displayed. I

23

kept up some discussion about whether I thought that particular hammer would do the job or not. I had to keep her attention focused on the hammers and not on the door.

Out of the corner of my eye I saw Pete come in and whip behind the sales counter. Now I was getting excited because I was doing my part, Pete was doing his, and we were working as a team. In my excitement my voice went up a couple of notches, then I forgot to keep the clerk engaged with the hammers. She followed my gaze just in time to see Pete rushing out the door.

"Hey boy!" she hollered. "You come back here! Hey! Hey!" Then she took off running after Pete, out the door and down the street. I ran after them both.

"Stop! Stop!" she kept screaming. Everybody on the street had stopped to stare and point. Finally I passed her, and as soon as I caught up with Pete, we cut across the busy street, dodging the cars that zipped back and forth. Pete clutched his red felt hat up against his chest. We turned north off Prospect toward Brush Creek Park, and without missing a beat Pete ran straight off into the briar bushes. I followed, both of us stumbling through the brush, getting all poked and cut up. We could hear the lady clerk behind us, screaming and cussing as she hit the briars. Finally she gave up on chasing us. We turned back around, raced down the hill toward the park, and kept on running all the way to my mother's house five blocks away. We charged straight through the house to my back room. Closing the door, we both bent over panting heavily, hands on knees, trying to catch our breath. Leaves and sticks stuck out all over our clothes. Pete opened the hat, and all I saw was coins.

"Oh man," I groaned, "there's nothing here but a bunch of change!"

"But it's all quarters man!" Pete cried triumphantly. Then we counted out $147 in quarters. We were rich! I couldn't believe it. We split our little heist 50/50, then I went and bought me some wine and headed home to my room to celebrate by myself. I was barely seventeen.

Coming in through the front door I stopped short under the piercing gaze of my mother, who was sitting on the couch. My stepfather sat across from her in his big, overstuffed chair, a customary pint of Christian Brothers in his hand. Bob Scott loved his alcohol, usually straight up out of the bottle.

On many an evening my momma, Bob Scott, and my auntie and uncle would gather in that same living room, drinking hooch and smoking cigarettes. Us kids performed for them, mostly dancing to "You Can't Sit Down" by the Dovells. It was my job to DJ. This night, however, was not about having fun.

Momma started right in, her eyes narrowing in on me like laser beams, "Kenny Dale—"

Whenever she called me "Kenny Dale," I knew there'd be nothing good coming.

"Where you been today boy?" she demanded.

"School, Momma." The confrontation already had my stomach bunched up in knots, plus I was queasy from the wine.

"You wasn't at school today boy," she accused.

"But I was," I stammered, playing lame, which is what I always did in the face of trouble. I searched her face, trying to decipher what it was she knew.

"Don't you lie to me boy!" she scowled, eyebrows cinched together and eyes blazing. She was getting angrier by the second. Momma was always in complete control of herself, like a pit viper coiled and ready to strike. She never got hysterical. Her eyes just kept steady on mine, seeking to burn the lie right out of me.

As usual our bodies carried on a silent conversation that spoke volumes. Momma had a way of sitting or standing when she was mad—head thrust forward, the muscles around her mouth corded up tight as purse strings, her arms folded across her chest, making sure I knew she meant business. Everything about her body language said, *Kenny Dale, I taught you better boy!*

"Momma, I been to school all day!" I whined. "I just got home!"

"Quit lying!" she shrieked, her finger jabbing the air between us. "Miss Helen said she saw you and that little hoodlum Pete Mallory running down Prospect Avenue."

Shit! That damned Miss Helen!

"Boy, whatever you went and did, I'm not having that stuff in my house!"

Suddenly, I got very calm. Somewhere inside my almost adult body a decision was being made. It was time to assert my independence. I came right out and admitted it.

"Okay, Momma, you're right," I stated matter-of-fact. "Me and Pete did some stealing, and I got some money."

Bob Scott was suddenly interested in the conversation. "How much you get boy?" he asked.

"About $75 dollars. You want some of it Momma?"

"I don't want that money!" Momma shrieked. "That's the devil's money!" But I could tell by the look on Bob Scott's face that he was into it. I had an ally.

Right there was the moment I "stole the key from under my mother's pillow." That was the break. I was outta there. I was ready to be my own man. I had admitted it to her straight out, "Yes, I'm a thief. Yes, I stole that money." After that, I never lied to her again about my thieving.

There's a German fairy tale, *Iron John*, about a wild man who gets locked up in a cage by the King and is kept in the courtyard as a curiosity. One day the prince is playing in the courtyard with his red ball, and it accidentally rolls between the bars of the cage. The wild man says he will only give the ball back if the prince will steal the key to open the cage. "You will find it under the Queen's pillow," he promises. The prince is reluctant at first because he is afraid. Eventually he builds the courage to steal the key and set the wild man free.

The story is a metaphor for the moment when a young man takes back the power he has always given to his mother to be in charge of his life. That day I stole the key to what I thought was my freedom. I became my own man. No longer would I be beholden to the whims of my mother's purse strings.

In the meantime Momma was still being Momma, and she continued to rant and rave and read me the riot act about how I was a bad person, how I was going to hell, how I was just like the rest of them hoodlums, how I had to get myself a real job, and on and on. It couldn't have landed on deafer ears. I had proven I could go out in the world and make my money a lot faster than any regular job could provide. I had made more in that one day than my stepfather would make all week. It was a no-brainer. It was the final break not only between my mother and me, but also from me trying to lead a straight life. I felt freed, liberated, empowered. I had proven I could do it. All I needed was my screwdriver and to be walking up and down the streets looking for something to steal.

That was the day my career into thieving got officially launched, a career that would last more than three decades. After that first hustle, the die was cast. Now I knew how to feed my belly and buy clothes for myself, and I wasn't looking back. If I needed to sneak into somebody's back room and steal some money, I would. From that day forward I would be in and out of prison, mostly in, for next thirty years until that miraculous day in September, 1995, when an angel would walk into the federal penitentiary at Littleton, Colorado, and change my life forever.

The Game

*A man who stands for nothing
will fall for anything.*

—Malcolm X

Lil' Red Rooster

Sophomore year was my last year of high school; after that the hustling got too good. Not only was the game more alluring, the racial tension at Paseo High had become so thick you could cut it with a knife, and that's pretty much what we did. It was the early sixties, and the Civil Rights Movement was reaching the boiling point. Packs of kids roamed the halls during breaks, looking for somebody to jump. Sometimes we went to school just to fight.

Even though we were living in a better neighborhood, our house bigger and our street prettier, the atmosphere had become so racially polarized that my brothers and I were forced to fight all the time. Blacks at my school were definitely in the minority. There wasn't a single African American teacher. I was casual friends with a number of white boys and girls at school, but if a race riot broke out, which happened on a regular basis, it was automatically whites against blacks and everybody fending for themselves.

Guns weren't so much a problem back then, but the knives, chains, and brass knuckles we used on each other inflicted serious damage. Every once in a while, somebody got killed.

Somehow during those first couple years of high school, I managed to keep from getting seriously hurt. Nevertheless, getting home from school was running the gauntlet, the biggest danger being the no man's land at Brush Creek Park. Whites would come cruising over from other schools looking to "get a nigger." A number of days found me running for my life up to some poor woman's house, screaming at the top of my lungs for her to let me inside. It got so bad that white boys were beating up on our young women, striping off their clothes, humiliating them, and sometimes even raping them.

Getting an education had become the last thing on my mind. Typically I'd show up at school in the morning, hang out to see what was happening, then go off to a hooky party and make out with the girls. If that didn't pan out, I'd hit the streets, day or night, attending my own kind of school.

Hooking up with Pete also meant hooking up with a whole new crowd. I got introduced to Fat Reggie, Bernard, Benny, Rat, Popjaws, and Lil' Dan, who all became my crew. They, too, had been initiated into hustling and were already living on their own. My desire was to be like them, to live free taking care of myself, and to be somebody that the other guys respected.

Looking back I can see that most all my actions throughout those years were driven by my aversion to poverty and an ego that craved respect. I was tired of never having my own money. My hustling peers had cars, new hairdos, new hats, and new shoes. My quest became about acquiring those things that would give me a sense of respect, both from others and from myself. It was this continual wanting that caused me much suffering throughout my life.

Within a month I had hustled enough money to leave my mother's house and rent my own apartment. My leaving hurt her. She felt helpless, like all her efforts in trying to raise me right were for nothing. She had said her piece, of course, warning me I was going to hell and all that, but I believed I knew better what was best for me. As far as making money went, I knew I was far better off than any of the grownups around me.

Every night 'til dawn found me hanging out on 31st and Prospect, watching the show of hustlers and players. I became a regular fixture at the after-hours clubs. Pete and I studied the prostitutes rolling their tricks, the pimps pimping their women, and the gamblers rolling their dice. The diverse cast of characters coming through night after night was the best entertainment I'd ever had.

Baby Lawrence, this one gay black pimp out of Texas, loved to have Pete and me sit on his lap while he told us outrageous stories about the game. We knew he was lying, but we enjoyed listening anyway. Everybody knew Baby Lawrence was homosexual, but he was a killer too, big, tough, and very, very black.

One night a group of us concocted a plan to go hustling at daybreak. As the night wore on, guys started drifting away to catch some sleep. I never wanted to go home, so I sat on the curb all night mesmerized by this new life of hanging out with players, pimps, and murderers. All the players loved me. Their women loved me too. No one ever told me to go home. They even bought me food. It was paradise. I had died and gone to heaven.

Every player had to make a name for him or herself by pulling off some crime that impressed the other players. That was how you attracted the best players to hustle with you. Then you learned from each other, sharpened each other up. The next morning was the day I finally won the respect of the guys.

I copped a bus downtown and started cruising the stores I'd already staked out, like a trapper going to check his traps. I cruised by each one daily to see if a safe was open here, a money drawer accessible there, whatever I could find.

That Saturday morning I took the elevator to the third floor of Macy's where a big neon sign—CASHIER—welcomed me like a kid at a carnival. Walking by the cash window, I couldn't believe what I was seeing. Shoebox after shoebox was lined up along the counter, filled to the brim with cash, and nobody around. *Oh my God look at that! Look at that!* I sang to myself. Adrenalin shot along every nerve.

Okay, be cool now, I coached myself, eyes rapidly scanning the department floor and finding nobody around. *Holy shit! This is it! Here we go!*

I walked quickly up to the cashier's window and saw it was formed by two glass sliders with a little latch on the inside. I dashed into a nearby locker room, snatched a coat hanger, untwisted the top, and bent one end over into a hook. Back at the window, I stuck the hanger through the gap between the sliders and raised the latch, easing the window aside. Heaving my chest up over the counter, I grabbed all the money in the closest box and shoved it down my pants. I always wore a big elastic belt for moments just like this. At the bottom of the box lay credit card receipts and checks, which at that stage of my career were useless, so I left them in the box.

Stashing the shoebox behind some merchandize, I headed down the stairs and out onto the sidewalk.

I couldn't believe my luck! I wanted to do the Twist, the Kansas City Kick, the Jerk, and the Twine Time all at once right there on the sidewalk. But I had to be cool. I didn't know how much money I had. What I did know was that it was more than I'd ever had in my life. In my excitement, I hadn't even thought to do what my buddy Vic would have done, which would've been to jump right over the counter and take *all* the money.

Back on the bus I headed straight for the back seat where I laid out the money, stacking it into little piles. Unbelievable! I had copped $847!

Immediately I went to a car lot and bought me a black 1959 four-door Oldsmobile for a hundred bucks. It was missing the center console, but that was no problem. The guy threw in an old motorcycle seat to use as an armrest.

I couldn't wait to find Pete Mallory and the gang and tell

them what I'd just pulled off. By 11:00am I was cruising down Prospect in my new car, and sure enough, there they were, standing in front of the Byron Hotel where all the players loved to hang. I pulled up to the curb and leaned on the horn, completely enjoying the shocked looks on their faces when they saw it was me behind the wheel. Most of us had never had a car. I was the king of the world.

They all piled in. "Kenny, man, where'd you get this ride?" Pete asked.

I felt so damned cool. Dropping deep into my seat, I smoothly answered his question.

"Man, I just hit a lick downtown. It was sweet, a real bird's nest on the ground. You should've seen me. Let's go down to the Pancake House. It's all on me."

That $847 went a long way back in the day. It got me a car, an apartment, breakfast for my friends, new clothes, and a shiny new wig for my girlfriend India. I was rich, and now everybody wanted to hustle with me. Pete was grinning from ear to ear, and I knew I'd earned his respect. I'd shown him he'd taught me well. I was riding such a huge high that I even gave him some of the money.

Night after long night I'd been hanging out with thieves, listening to them brag on and on about their hustles, craving that same success for myself. I'd wanted the same Cadillacs, the same diamonds dripping off my fingers, the same fine women. More than anything I'd wanted to make a name for myself, and when I'd come back that day with some real money and a car, my reputation as a hustler was finally solidified. Not only in the eyes of my hustling buddies, but also in my own. I was on my way, and nothing could stop me. I knew that not only could I do it, I could do it on my own.

That very same night Reggie, Pop Jaws, and I went to a Temptations concert. After it let out, we went cruising around in my new car. Next thing we knew, the cops were pulling us over for no reason at all, a common occurrence whenever cops saw a carload of black teenagers out at night. I had no papers for the car, no driver's license, and no other identification to prove who I was. Neither did any of the guys. We were all just seventeen.

They took the car, impounded it, and hauled us off to jail for questioning in conjunction with another investigation. They kept us overnight. Not wanting the police to know about the money I had on me, I hid what was left of it in the lining of my hat. We all went to sleep that night in one cell, on tiny steel bunks, in the midtown Kansas City jail. There were no blankets. I rolled my jacket up for a pillow, and placed my hat on my chest. I woke the next morning to find my hat on the floor and the money gone.

My great success had lasted but a day. The car was gone, the money was gone, and I knew one of my hustling buddies had taken it, most likely Reggie.

Later in life I learned a valuable lesson: Never become over-joyed at good fortune, neither grieve over misfortune; they are both impermanent. Another way of looking at it, as we said on the streets: "The same thing that made you laugh will make you cry."

Since I obviously couldn't trust the guys I was hustling with, I decided to keep hustling by myself. If I couldn't find any cash to steal, I boosted clothes, especially suits, shoes, and hats. I'd walk by the door of a Rothschild's or a Wolfe Brothers, spy a rack of cashmere suits, put one on, and walk out the door. Same with shoes. Florsheim wingtips were my favorites. Sometimes I'd ball up two or three high-priced Dobbs hats and stick them down my pants, then go across the street to the pool hall and sell them quick. I only stole things I knew I could turn over fast or that I'd like to keep for myself.

Walking into jewelry stores and having a look around, I'd eventually come across a situation where some employee had left one of the drawers open. Then I'd just reach over the counter, grab a handful of jewelry, and split. Sometimes it was a handful of watches.

At the same time I was always rightly dividing, or so I thought of it at the time. As a friend would later point out, it was more like "wrongly dividing." At that time, however, it meant considering my options and working out the best way to make money and gain respect. I learned that hustling by myself wasn't always working out. I was missing too many opportunities. Consequently, I sometimes went back to hustling with Pete, Vic, or Daniel, because I knew they wouldn't burn me. I didn't hustle with Bernard and Ronnie because they were too rough and couldn't be trusted. They were "dishonest thieves," just like Chancy, who'd always try to get to the money first, hide some for himself, and burn you without thinking twice.

I didn't want to hustle with most other guys because drugs had already come onto the scene, and I didn't know who was strung out. A lot of players were getting hooked on heroin and cocaine, which made them desperate to feed their habits. I didn't have that kind of habit. My habit was stealing. I knew several guys who'd become drug addicts in Vietnam and were on the streets living hand to mouth. I wasn't okay with that, and I didn't want to end up that way.

India

India Walker was the first girl I ever had sex with. I'd met her briefly back at Lil' Blue because she was the sister of my buddy Otis Lee.

A slim, flirtatious girl, India had huge eyelashes and an attractive way of shaking her ass when she walked. The giant smile that came easily to her face was like an open invitation. She had this short, kinky hair that sprung out all over her head, nothing like most of the other girls, who would go to any lengths to straighten their hair, the fashion for black women at that time. India had a natural way of being, like she was comfortable just being India, and I admired her for that.

Some months after our encounter at Lil' Blue, I saw her laughing it up with her girlfriends in a booth at the F.W. Woolworths soda fountain. As I walked up to the counter in my stylish straw hat and Stetson shoes, I strategically ordered milk, not soda, because I wanted her to think that Kenny was a wholesome, clean-cut kind of guy rather than the little sneak thief I really was. Little did I know that her filled-to-the-brim shopping bag held all the clothes she'd boosted downtown that day.

I didn't have the nerve to say anything to her. My heart was hammering too hard in my chest. Instead I followed her onto the bus and all the way home so that I could see where she lived. When she got off the bus, I waved to her and she waved back. That was all I needed. The door was open. I got her number from Pete, then, talked his sister Dee into calling her to tell her that I liked her. That evening we talked on the phone, and the next day found me on my way to 2922 Wabash St.

It was an Indian summer evening and my first opportunity to really court a girl. I had on my Fabergé cologne, and a lot of it. My Stetsons were shined, and my straw hat was new. My skin tingled from the perfect summer night and the clear premonition that something special was about to happen.

I turned the corner onto Wabash and caught my first sight of India's tiny white house with the dark green trim around the eaves. I was busy opening the gate and double-checking the address when I heard a soft easy voice that sounded like dripping honey, "You got the right house."

I looked up to the porch, and there she was sitting on a swing. A gentle golden light from the living room window illuminated her slim figure and soft Afro. *She's been waiting for me!* I realized.

That night we talked easily for hours. She kept eyeing me and laughing at my awkwardness. It was obvious that we liked each other.

I was in heaven. I could've sat there all night, but eventually it was time to leave. We made plans to see each other the next day downtown. When we stood to say goodbye, she leaned over, grabbed my face, and kissed me right on the mouth. In that moment I knew that she was my girl. We both knew it.

I floated off the porch. She stood at the door watching me walk down the street. A block away, I could still see her big white smile.

India.

I was a big grinning kid walking home from his first real date. I was seventeen and still a virgin, but not for long.

The next day we were back on the phone, talking for hours on end. The day after that had us back at India's house, making love. I hadn't known a thing about sex, and India became my educator. She was damned good at it and never made me feel bad for lacking experience. The world of sex was electrifying and unending.

I felt like I had come into my manhood that year. I had learned how to hustle and I'd gotten my first woman. India was two years younger than me, but she already had more life experience. She was a fantastic clothes thief. We were young and full of our power.

"I want a baby," she said one day shortly after we'd gotten together, and she wouldn't let up. I wasn't surprised. All of her little girlfriends were pregnant, and she wanted to be pregnant too. She was fifteen years old. Three weeks later, she was pregnant. I was so proud of myself and so happy for her. I'd given her what she wanted.

Now I knew I had to step up my game, I needed to make a home for India and the baby. The day of the Macy's theft, I'd managed to rent us a tiny apartment. Now here it was five months later, and I was broke. I grabbed my trusty screwdriver, my Hush Puppies, and my big brown coat with all the pockets. Then I hit the streets.

On that day, I never came home.

Young Buck Zales

That first day going to prison is always the hardest. It's scary. It's confusing. An actual greeting committee is there to welcome you, but you have no idea what you're being welcomed into. The committee can be real nice, a total one-eighty from the attitudes of the guards and staff once you're inside.

It was October 1966, and I was being booked into the Hutchinson Correctional Facility outside of Hutchinson, Kansas. I had just turned eighteen years old. The crime, a jewelry heist, had occurred when I was seventeen, but the authorities had wanted to make an example of me, so they had waited to convict me until I was eighteen and could be sentenced as an adult.

In the eleven months between the time of my arrest and my incarceration at Hutchinson, our little girl, Chanette, had been born. I'd also gotten arrested and out on bond a half-dozen more times, with charges ranging from vagrancy to theft to robbery to transportation of a stolen vehicle across state lines.

Hutchinson was a "reformatory." Reformatories had much higher rehabilitation rates than prisons because they focused on reforming youths through vocational training and education. Reformatories also introduced the concept of indeterminate sentences, such as 5-10 years, which was how inmates could get their sentences shortened by showing good behavior.

The heist had been Daniel, Vic, and me. I had felt honored to be hustling with Vic because he was considered the best hustler in Kansas City at the time.

I'd heard stories about a lone bandit copping twenty-five thousand dollars on a bank robbery; a solitary thief sneaking into a store and stealing thirty thousand dollars worth of jewelry; a robber scaling a wall like Spiderman and running off with two sacks of money from a store's safe. We all knew these stories were about Vic. He hustled alone, so to find myself alongside him, learning his game and watching the way he operated, had felt like extraordinary luck.

As we'd left the jewelry store that day, the store clerk had been in hot pursuit, beating on the car. Unbelievably, he'd thrown himself spread eagle onto the hood of our car. We'd peeled out, swerving back and forth down the street trying to shake the guy off, but he'd just kept hanging on, all the while screaming and hollering at the top of his lungs.

"Look at that stupid motherfucker!" I'd yelled from the back seat. "Can you believe this shit?"

Right then a cop had come out of another store, his mouth dropping in disbelief at the spectacle of the sales clerk swishing back and forth across our hood. He and his partner had jumped into their police car and chased after us.

Daniel was a horrible driver. Plus he'd been scared to death, so he'd whipped into the Greyhound parking lot to hand the wheel over to me. But the chase had been over for me before it'd even gotten started. While I'd been struggling to get out of the back seat, Daniel had run away, Vic had run away, and the cops had already had their guns trained on me. They'd hauled me off to jail and charged me with grand theft larceny, carrying a sentence of one-to-five years.

At Hutchinson, I was known as "Young Buck Zales" because Zales was the store I'd gotten caught stealing $10,000 worth of jewelry from. That first time in the joint was exciting. I was all over the place like some kind of wild man, crazy as a monkey in a cage.

Even within prison walls I was known as a thief. Nobody trusted me. At Hutchinson I stole food from other men's cells and took it back to mine. I didn't care because I knew I was the only one looking out after me, and if you're a thief, you're a thief, in prison or out.

At one point I got locked up in solitary confinement for thirty days for stealing a man's cookies. The only things in my cell were a toilet and a steel bunk four inches off the floor with a sheet of plywood and thin mattress on top. It was always dark in solitary, so I read my books by sticking them outside the bars into the hallway. In solitary you read anything you can get your hands on.

Not even the punishment of solitary confinement could stop me. As soon as I was back in the prison population, I just kept on stealing. I wasn't getting any money from home, and I hadn't yet gotten that sophisticated with money crimes or learned the skills of hustling in prison like gambling or loan sharking. I was still known as a rough hustler. There was little finesse in my game. I simply took, period.

In prison danger could flare up at any moment. Once I saw a bunch of homosexuals fighting and stabbing each other over rights of possession. I came to learn that whenever a man got "turned out," meaning raped by another man, he was termed "punk," then considered that man's personal property. After that, he could be pimped out for cigarettes, drugs, and other contraband.

One cold morning in December, the sounds of commotion on a tier below mine drifted up to my cell. I lay on my top bunk trying to make sense of the hubbub. It didn't sound like the usual breakfast move.

The sounds grew louder, so I got up and found guys rubber-necking all up and down the railing, trying to see what was going on down below. I caught snatches of their conversation.

"... killed... crawled down from the fourth tier to the flag-stone and stuck him with a knitting blade... dead."

Instantly my mind cleared, and I became focused on one thing only: getting more information. I had only been at Hutch a few months and there it was already—what I had heard so much about but had yet to see—one convict killing another. Of course I wanted to know why and what happened. Whatever it was that the guy had done to lose his life, I wanted to make sure I didn't repeat it. Information was my God, not a deeper wisdom, and no one could tell me anything different. Thinking that I was in full control of things was the illusion of my youth.

The day that inmate was murdered at Hutchinson served to sober me up a little. It snapped me out of any illusion that prison was a fun, exciting place to be. I realized that if I kept fooling around, if I kept stealing from other inmates, I could get myself killed. I had to play it cool, which meant keeping to myself, and for the first time I began to get a glimmer of the harsh reality of loneliness in prison.

Lord's Got a Work

My aunt, Equator Gold, was warm like the equator and big and soft from eating all those pies, cakes, peach cobblers, and fried chicken she loved to cook and still does to this day. She was always bringing something over to our house to eat, then taking us kids up in her arms and smothering us in hugs, kisses, and flattering words. Her cheeks, chubby and sweet, were just the kind you'd like to pinch, but she was the one always doing the pinching. Like any other boy I'd try to squirm away, yet secretly I loved her attention.

Every time I got out of jail, Aunt Equator told me, "Kenny Dale, the Lord must have a purpose for your life, cause he keeps saving you." At the same time, the guys were always calling me Reverend because of my hat. Me and my hustling buddies, Little Pete, Fat Reggie, and Bernard, used to get all dressed up in our fancy clothes, the Masterflex Oxford shoes with the white stitching, the Sansabelt pants, the cashmere coats, and our big hats. The hat I liked to hang out in was the Homburg, big and black with a wide brim like the church reverends of the day.

Though I wasn't hearing it, the message was all around me. On one side I had guys calling me Reverend, and on the other side I had my auntie whispering in my ear, "The Lord's got a work for you, son."

Throughout all my years of hustling, no matter how much I aspired to fame and success in that world, those words of Aunt Equator's were always subconsciously wedged into the back of my mind. From time-to-time I would find myself wondering, *If the Lord has work for me, then what is it? I'm still robbing and stealing, and I can't see any other way to make my life worth something.*

We would all know our life's purpose if only we'd listen to those around us. They are constantly pointing us to our true destinies.

Yet no matter how successful I became, no matter how much

money I made as a hustler and later on as a pimp, deep down I always had this nagging feeling that I didn't fit in. Even in the prison world I felt different from most men because I was interested in reading intellectual material. I would gravitate to the smartest guys in prison, the most interesting, whether they were Marxists, Masons, Black Muslims, or whatever. I wanted to be smart too. I wanted to know things. I believed that being smart could somehow get me free.

Was there a longing for God at the time? I can't honestly say that there was. Even twenty-five years later, when I finally did find God, or, more accurately, when God found me, I wasn't consciously aware it was God I was looking for. I only knew I wanted *freedom*.

An unwavering desire for freedom had always been my guiding compass, my true north, my holy grail, however crazily my definition of freedom shifted over the years. Up until I actually found freedom, and by freedom I mean *unconditional* freedom, I thought that freedom meant not only being out of prison, but also living freely in society as a black man with plenty of money and prestige.

When I first left home I wanted to be free of my parents and free from poverty. Then, whenever I got thrown in prison, all my energy would pour into studying law so that I could beat my charges and be free of prison. By the grace of God, I would one day desire even to be free of the hustling crowd.

Throughout it all, I would from time to time ask myself, *Why do I keep doing these things? Why do I keep putting myself deeper and deeper into these holes? How do I always manage to dig myself out only to jump right back in?*

It seemed as though something was constantly sabotaging both my efforts as a player and my desire to do the right thing. I'd go three steps ahead, two steps back, one step ahead, then fall on my ass.

In prison I listened to black revolutionaries making their speeches on the news at night. Those brothers could put together a complete thought and I wanted to be like them. I wanted to be a part of the black revolution any way I could, and since I was in prison, that meant reading books by revolutionaries.

During my thirty-two months at Hutchinson Reformatory I went on a reading rampage. The first book I ever read in prison was *The Autobiography of Malcolm X*. Malcolm X had wanted to improve his vocabulary, so he'd started studying the dictionary from A to Z. I began doing the same. I committed myself to learning at least one new word every day.

Malcolm X was also an ex-con, a hustler who'd had a spiritual experience in his cell one night and then found his way out, both out of prison and out of the game. He became my hero. Though I didn't fully recognize it at the time, reading his story planted seeds that would one day germinate into my own radical transformation.

I went on to read H. Rap Brown, Stokely Carmichael, Eldridge Cleaver, Huey Newton, Angela Davis, James Baldwin, Richard Wright, Frantz Fanon, and Ayn Rand.

Lady Chatterley's Lover, by D.H Lawrence, was to me the best book in the world. Man, could that guy write about sex! He knew the art of sensuality backwards and forwards. That cat could take a bare glimpse of a woman's well-turned slightly dimpled ankle and build it into a full-blown orgasmic explosion. I couldn't get enough of that book.

Six months into my time at Hutchinson I met Buford, an old con out of Wichita, Kansas, and my only real friend. Standing five-foot-seven and a scrawny 160 pounds, what struck me most about Buford was his huge gorilla-like hands all out of proportion with the rest of his body.

Buford took me under his wing. He started educating me about prison and taught me how to gamble, which at this particular prison was playing poker with dominos instead of cards. Cards weren't allowed. He cautioned me to stay away from hardcore gamblers, homosexuals, and drugs, even though he was doing all those things.

Buford was also part of a secret society called the Freemasons, a brotherhood of men who watched out after each other. A lot of the guards, captains, lieutenants, and prison staff were Freemasons.

"There are two kinds of Masons," Buford told me one day. "You got the Scottish Rite, and you got the black version founded by an African American named Prince Hall, both of which adhere to the belief in a Supreme Being." More than a hundred years ago, Scottish Rite Freemasons were among the first to fight racial prejudice. Any black man of good character was welcomed into their secret society.

"They are a family," Buford said, "a family that will come to the aid of their brother." I had never experienced being part of a family like that. I had never felt I could put my trust in anybody, not my hustling buddies, not my women, not even my biological family. I wanted to know that somebody cared if I had a problem and would come to my aid. I'd always had one problem or another, and nobody ever came to help bail *me* out. One way or another everyone had always abandoned me. The only person I had ever felt I could trust was Pete Mallory.

This whole idea of a secret brotherhood of men was magical to me. I was attracted to the mystery and the power that these men emanated. The next thing Buford said shot an arrow straight through my heart.

"To join the Freemasons you have to be sponsored by somebody who is already a Mason, and you can't have a criminal record." Finding out I couldn't become a Mason was a crushing blow.

Looking back I'd say that encountering the Masons was probably my first awakening of sorts. I came to understand that they were a brotherhood of conscious men guarding unconscious men, and this caused me to realize something critical about the world. Conscious people were consciously running things, or at least that's how I saw it at the time. It was the first time I'd ever had any desire to be a part of something conscious or to realize a deeper part of myself. Knowing about the Freemasons gave me something to aspire to. It was the very beginning of my search for a more positive way of being in the world, something other than the track I'd been on as a criminal. According to Buford, the Masons had secret knowledge of the arts, the sciences, mathematics, geometry, and all the religions. I wanted that knowledge.

"The Freemasons aren't the only people running things behind the scenes," Buford went on to say. "There are other secret organizations on the outside that control the world banking system, the big corporations, politics, and the military. People out there on the bricks are also in prison; it's just that most of them aren't aware of it. They're in a prison of their own ignorance, with other men consciously calling the shots. Don't think that once you're out of this prison you're a free man, because the world is being run by secret organizations that most people know nothing about.

"How they control things is through that boob tube hanging on the wall over there," Buford said, pointing to the television mounted up in the corner of the room, "so don't believe a thing that the media tells you because they're not telling you the real story. Whatever they choose to show people is designed to keep them unconscious."

All of this was fascinating to me, because up until that time I had believed everything I'd seen on the news. That day in the rotunda, Buford was lacing my boots so that I wouldn't get caught up in believing all the hype of politics and the media. He taught me how to rightly divide what I was seeing and hearing from what was not being said.

In the meantime, a longing to get out of prison and get home began to fill my days. My daughter had just been an infant when I'd gotten sent to Hutch. I needed to know her. I needed to get out and stay out.

I kept reading and studying. I played saxophone in the prison band and learned how to read music. I was also learning woodworking and enjoyed carving African figurines to send to my family.

Rightly dividing had continued to be a force in my life. There were crimes I had been willing to commit and other crimes that I hadn't. For example I refused to rob women. I had learned how to snatch purses and it was a good hustle, but I never felt good about it, so I stopped it before I even got started. I knew what felt right and what didn't. I knew where to draw the line and I was able to stick to it. One day, I thought to myself, *Okay Kenny, how do you want to make money? What does feel right?*

I had met other players in prison who stole only money, never things, and I realized that this was the direction I wanted to go. I wanted to learn how to steal money rather than clothes, jewelry, and cars. It was the obvious next step. As the time of my release grew closer, my thoughts started gravitating from doing the "right thing" to "how can I do a better hustle?"

Jimmy Campa, a well-known player in my time, used to say: "If you want food, go to a Safeway. If you want money, go to a bank." This made perfect sense to me. If I wanted to get money, some real money, I had to start stealing from banks, and that was exactly what I began planning to do just as soon as I got out. Thus began my career of stealing the money rather than the merchandize.

I became a money dog, as well as a honey hog. That's right, getting paid was still part of getting laid. Some things change and some things just don't.

Merry-Go-Round

When you get out, they give you gate money. Back then it was about thirty dollars. I caught the bus to Kansas City, Missouri, and the first thing I did was to go see *Goldfinger*, the new James Bond movie at the time. It was a big thing because the black woman in the movie had just been on the cover of *Playboy*.

After the movie I went straight to my mother's house, which was always the case when I first got out of prison. I'd live in her back room until I could get some money together.

What I loved most about my mother was that, as long as I carried my own weight, I always had a house and a meal to come home to. Throughout the long years I was in and out of prison, there was many an occasion I took refuge in that.

As usual, my mother was hoping I would change. I'd put up a front like I was going job hunting, but I was really trying to put my hustle back together and make enough money to get out on my own again.

The old man next door to Momma's, Mr. Grant, called me over to his house one day. I found him sitting on the front porch in his old rocker, wearing his favorite floppy straw hat, and smoking his pipe.

"Kenny Dale," he said, "come over here and sit next to me, boy," gesturing to the chair next to him. "I've been around the world, so I know a few things, and I know you're gonna go back out there and do your thing. I don't have no problem with that. I've done a few things in this life and but for the grace of God I could've been to jail myself. So son, here's my advice: If you're gonna be doing something illegal, leave town and do it. Whatever you're doing, take it on the road. You'll stay free longer, and you'll learn more."

"Yes sir," I agreed. I'd heard the same advice in the joint. His rheumy old eyes looked sincere, and I appreciated that he cared. Then I got up off his porch, went right back down to Prospect

Avenue, and started pulling hustles in my old neighborhood.

Mr. Grant was right in his way, but his was worldly wisdom. The kind of wisdom I needed to turn my life around was both of this world and not of this world. To find the real freedom I was seeking, and to learn the true meaning of rightly dividing, I would need the wisdom of love, and real love had not yet come to find me.

Consequently, I made a couple of weak attempts to get a job but with no success. The reality was I had no money, but I knew how to steal. Plus my old buddies were calling me on the phone every day and inviting me over. I got hooked back up with India. She was still boosting, and all her friends were boosters. India's thing was lifting clothing from Saks Fifth Avenue, Macy's, and other fine stores. She had good taste and could steal four to five women's knit suits at one time. She wore a girdle and simply wrapped them tight as hell and stuffed them in the girdle. Winter or summer, she always wore big coats so that by the time she left the store she looked pregnant, except that the bump on her belly was clothing.

Even though India and I had gotten back together, it wasn't a good coming together. While I'd been in prison, she'd gotten pregnant by another man, this time with her second baby, Lisa. Our own little girl, Chanette, was four at that time.

I went to visit India in the hospital after she'd given birth. I was at her bedside talking to her and who walks in but Gary, the father of the new baby. We ended up leaning over India's bed arguing with each other.

"What are you doing coming in here to see India!" I yelled at Gary, leaning all the way over India's bed to get in his face. "She's with *me* now!"

"I ain't coming to see India, you asshole. I'm coming to see my baby."

"Well the baby ain't in here; it's down the hall."

"Fuck you motherfucker!" Gary cursed, shaking his fist at me. The spittle flying from his lips created a chain of dark spots across India's blue hospital sheets.

"Stop!" India finally screamed, the dark circles under her eyes showing her exhaustion. "Both of you get the hell out of here!"

We never did come to blows, most likely because we'd both been in the penitentiary and we were each leery of the other.

It was hard getting out and knowing that India had been with another man, but now that I was out, she wanted to be my woman again. Whenever I was out, India was always my woman, and I was always her man.

Usually when a man goes to jail, he figures his woman is supposed to live in a vacuum. He expects her to do time like he's doing time. She's not supposed to look at other men, talk to other men, or have sex with other men. She's not supposed to do anything but stand still in time because that's what it feels like he's doing. This clashing of opposing realities is the crux of why so many men go crazy in prison or try to kill themselves. Men often beat or even kill their women when they get out. They want to punish them the same way they feel they've been punished. Truth is if a man doesn't do anything to change himself while in prison, time might as well be standing still. He'll walk back out the same person he was when he went in.

My way of thinking was that India was my woman and she was supposed to be there for me totally. I expected her to remember to write me every day, talk to me on the phone every day, send me all the pictures she could send me every day, think about me every day, and that was that—case closed.

Of course India never did any of these things, but in my book of forgiveness and forgetfulness, I held no grudges. In our world, the rules were simple: "Do whatever it takes to survive." When I got out, I had to wake up to the reality that she was pregnant, she was having another baby, someone else's baby, and there wasn't a damned thing I could do about it.

I knew that India cared for me and would not hesitate to be there for me, provided I was on the bricks. Getting out and getting back with India seemed like the most natural thing to do.

She was the mother of my daughter, and it was our obligation to try to be together as parents. Though to be brutally honest, not a real bone in my body wanted to take on the obligation of raising two little girls. The streets were still calling my name, and I knew I was only paying lip service to what in my mind was the "sucker life." Apparently it was the best I could manage at that stage.

The honeymoon out of prison was short-lived. I never even had a chance to try to move back in with India and Chanette. Within six months I was busted again, this time for robbing a Savings and Loan office along with my buddy Tyrone. They threw us in the county jail and kept us there for another six months. I fell into a bad depression. More than anything I was pissed at myself. I knew that this time I'd be going in for a long, long time. I ended up getting sentenced to three and a half years. It seemed I just couldn't win.

The Life

Why do convicted criminals become repeat offenders? Truth is, until you *know* better, you don't *do* better. I didn't know any better. It was the only life I knew. The resources available to me, educationally and financially, were little to none. How does a young man with a 9th grade education and no money or skills turn his life around? I had to figure out some way to survive in the world, and there was no one around to give me any real guidance.

In prison there would always be talk about getting out and getting square, but in the end it was really just lip service, fool's gold, it didn't truly come from the heart. There was always a chance I could make a living, that I could reform, but honestly, the biggest part of me at the time was deeply conditioned to forever be striving for that big score. I thought I could buy my way out of the game. We all did.

Like most people I was ego-driven to be "somebody," somebody successful, somebody at the top of their game, in the only world I had ever known. In my world, real success as a man meant driving down the street in a long Cadillac, diamonds dripping off my fingers. That self-image was what attracted me the most. Getting a job washing dishes for $1.25 an hour was not too appealing. I had learned the summer of my painting apprenticeship that if you worked the square way for a square, you got fucked by that square. I was determined not to let that happen again. The way I saw it, I was gonna go out and fuck the squares before they fucked me. Why would I want to make $100 a week when I knew I could be making thousands a day? The math just didn't add up. Yet the math I wasn't doing was to add up the days, weeks, months, and years I was spending in prison.

Now I know that only one force can ever truly intervene on that type of mindset—the grace of God and a sincere prayer to change—and God's grace was not gonna be penetrating my heart for some time to come.

In the meantime, all my energy was put into striving to be like those hustlers I looked up to. They were my heroes, my modern-day legends. It wasn't just about survival; I wanted to be a legend too. Word on the street was that Jimmy Campa had just robbed a Safeway for $200,000 dollars. Another crew had robbed a jewelry store and gotten away with half a million in jewelry. They were my superstars. These types of victories were all I wanted to hear about. Whether in the joint or on the bricks, those were the bedtime stories I went to sleep repeating to myself.

When the movie *Superfly* hit the silver screen, India and I could not wait to go see a brother pull the ultimate con. The fantasy of getting one over on everybody and walking away untouched was what kept us going. India and Kenny Dale also wanted to go down as legends of the streets.

I was still young, only twenty-two years old. I thought I was invincible, that I could bounce back from anything they threw at me. Once I'd gotten through my first sentencing and out again, I was no longer even all that afraid of prison. Sure, I'd get sad sometimes, I'd get depressed, but I knew that I could make it through, so my mind was always busy calculating my future success as a hustler.

I loved India in my own distorted way, but the pull of the streets was always stronger. That was the real love of my life. Every single day was an adventure filled with exciting or even death-defying events. Cops shot at us on a regular basis. We got drunk and crashed up stolen cars. Visits to the emergency room were accepted as part of the game.

One day I woke up with glass embedded in my head. My face was swollen, my hands shredded. I wondered what all the glass was doing in bed with me. Slowly it dawned on me that Russell, Purtle, and I had crashed the car the night before. Purtle had lost an eye in the crash, but I remembered nothing. It was my first concussion. How did I get home? I didn't know. The mind has a marvelous way of shutting out horrific events.

Whenever I went stealing or robbing, I stole a car to do it in. One day it was a 1954 Chevy, a stick shift, which I didn't know how to drive too well. I thought of it more as a wild bronco I had to tame or else.

I had parked it around the corner from India's house. When I went to use it, I put it in what I thought was reverse, stepped on the gas, and smashed head-on into a brick wall. The metal car horn cut into my teeth and gums. I sat there stunned, bleeding, staring at the wall, the motor racing on. Then I walked back to India's house in shock. In those days there was no going for chiropractic, no physiotherapy. You just had to walk it off. Lying in bed next to India was the only medicine I had.

The "streets" was its own culture. We were a family. Each time back in prison I was greeted by many of my old buddies—Pete, Reggie, Tyrone, and more. It was a reunion. Plus there were always bigger and better connections to be made. Forty-two months gave me plenty of time to refine my game and formulate a plan. We were all scheming together because many of us would be getting out and hitting the bricks at the same time.

Crossing the Line

I got transferred three times during that forty-two month sentence for the Savings and Loan robbery, first to Moberly Correctional Center in Moberly, Missouri. It was 1968, and I was twenty years old.

At Moberly I immediately went back to reading and studying. I picked up the saxophone again, played racket ball, jogged, and walked the yard. I worked at the prison laundry washing clothes. I even had me a little hustle going on. Guys would pay me to put their clothes through the wash out of turn.

It was also at Moberly that I got caught up in my first prison riot. This particular one got started because a white homosexual cheated on his white boyfriend with a black man. When his white boyfriend found out about it, he stabbed the black guy, and the yard immediately exploded with whites and blacks attacking each other. Men broke out windows. Guards fired shotguns. The whole melting pot of testosterone turned into a firestorm of rage. I had never been so scared in all my life.

As soon as the riot started jumping off, I ran and hid behind some buildings. I had read about prison riots, and I'd heard about them on the news. This one, however, was for real.

At Moberly there was this group of old white guards that we referred to as the KKK. When the riot started they were suddenly all over the place with their shotguns. The sounds of gunfire boomed and echoed off the prison walls. They were actually shooting *at people*. No one was killed, but a few guys got wounded. As soon as the coast was clear, I ran back to my cell.

Finally they managed to lock everybody down and started bringing food around. At three in the morning, when everyone was finally settled and sleeping, my door suddenly flew open. Looming in the doorway was what looked like Darth Vader in full riot gear—helmet, face shield, rip-proof suit, baton—the whole shebang.

I hadn't participated in the riot whatsoever, and I thought, *Shit, I don't know what you're up to, I don't know who gave you my name, but I want no part of it. Leave me alone. I didn't do nothin'.*

"Name?" demanded the voice behind the headgear.

"Kenny Johnson," I replied, backing a couple steps deeper into my cell.

"We got Kenny Johnson here," he yelled behind him to another guard who was standing in the corridor with a clipboard.

"What's your number Johnson?"

"Twenty-seven forty-nine."

"Criminal twenty-seven forty-nine Johnson," he shouted into the hall, never taking his eyes off me for a second. "Are you injured?"

"No sir." That's when I realized they hadn't come to take me away; they were only making count.

"All right then Johnson, go to bed."

They continued on, cell-by-cell, snatching guys up here and there and sending them to the penitentiary over at Jefferson City, Missouri. I had no idea how they were making these determinations. When they finally opened the prison back up a week later, a lot of guys I'd known were gone. It was a whole new prison.

Not long after, I was transferred to Renz Farm, and a year after that to Church Farm. Both institutions were minimum-security satellite prisons that doubled as farms. Our job at Renz Farm was to grow and harvest spinach, string beans, and peas, and then send it all off to other prisons around the country. I worked in the cannery on the assembly line, washing and canning vegetables. Even today most prison vegetables are grown at prison farms owned and run by the State. In 1985, Renz Farm became a co-ed prison, which back then was quite a concept for Missouri. In 1993, the big Missouri flood washed it all away.

Church Farm manufactured the milk and dairy products for the prisons, and at that prison I was a cowboy. In the mornings I'd put on my big boots, grab my stick, and walk up into the fields to round up the cows and bring them down for milking.

56

India had gotten busted and sent to prison again just after giving birth to her third baby. All three of her babies were by different men, and they were all living with India's mother while she served out her four-year sentence. We had been writing each other and making plans because we would both be getting out at the same time. India was also taking advantage of her time in prison and learning how to be a better criminal.

During those years, my education as a hustler got refined. I had only one desire at that time, one dream, and that was to get out and be the best damn player in Kansas City. I wanted what every other red-blooded American wanted: a house with a white picket fence and a nice car out front, a woman in the kitchen cooking for me, 2.2 kids, and a dog. I was just going about achieving the American dream by a different route, more or less down the back alley.

Church Farm is where I met Fat Charlie, an old player out of St. Louis Missouri who gave me the pimp game. Charlie was five feet, 300 pounds, and looked like a short, black Pillsbury Doughboy. He wore a little cap on his big head and always had a smile on his face. All the while he was the dirtiest, most scheming, lying son of a bitch you ever did see. You couldn't trust him as far as you could throw him, which wasn't too far. Not only was Charlie big and fat, he was a professional wrestler, con man, gorilla pimp, bank robber, dope fiend, snitch, and killer. You knew he'd have no problem killing you if he thought he needed to. At one time Charlie had also been India's lover and pimp, so we had that in common too.

An exceptionally pretty woman was coming in to visit Charlie on a regular basis. One day I asked him who she was.

"That's my wife, man."

"What does she do? She a ho?"

"No man, she was a jewelry thief. A good one too. She and her crew could really burn up a town. She's squared up now.

"You know, Kenny, if you get you some women and get them out there thieving, you'll get paid. Just don't get them out there flatbacking. There ain't no money in that game. It's too slow and you'll wear your women out."

My thoughts became focused on how to get some women and get them out there working for me. Every night I lay in bed having visions of women stealing for me and the money rolling in. I'd already told India my plan, and she was fully on board. Now I couldn't wait to get out there.

Pimping women was not restricted to sex. Pimping was about anything involving money. My plan was to be the best damn booster pimp in all of Kansas City.

Getting sent to Church Farm was both heaven and hell, heaven because the minimum level of security allowed us more freedom and more access to the outside world. It was almost like being on the streets. The prison was constructed in the usual layout, with the buildings arranged around a central yard, but there was no fence around Church Farm. If I wanted to, I could just open the door and walk out. Of course if I did that, I'd be re-arrested immediately, and I was so close to getting out that I wasn't going to do something that stupid.

Church Farm was also hell because some heavy shit came down, and I had to take up some violent measures in order to protect my prison reputation. I'm not particularly proud of this chapter in my life, and I don't see any real benefit in describing it here in detail, not for me or for you. Suffice it to say that on two different occasions I was reduced to the point of nearly killing a couple of men.

Before this time in my life, I hadn't been the perpetrator of all that much violence. I had mostly just defended myself whenever I'd been backed into a corner with no escape. Eventually a time came when I said to myself, *You know what? I ain't gonna take this shit anymore.* And I didn't. I did what I knew I had to do.

After the heavy shit went down and I'd gotten away with all of it, whenever I was harassed in prison or my limits were tested, my retaliation would be swift and often kind of crazy. A big part of prison education is learning when to fight and when not to. Whenever I had to fight in the joint, guerilla warfare was my tactic. This I learned from reading about Che Guevara and Niccolo Machiavelli, both revolutionaries in their own way.

In order to perform a monstrous act, I had to create a monster, and that mental preparation took a couple of weeks. It was a journey into a place of "no feeling." In order to get to that place, I first had to scroll through all my fears, all of the Bible teachings from my momma, all the rules and regulations of prison, and what the consequences might be for my actions. In the end I realized I was going to have to take some drastic action in order to survive in prison with dignity.

Prisons are jungles. The law of the jungle is that the strongest survive and the weakest get preyed upon. I knew that if I didn't save face, if I didn't let people know they couldn't fuck with me, guys were gonna keep coming at me and my life was going to get far worse. I'd seen what'd happened to other men. I didn't want to be washing other people's underwear. I didn't want my cigarettes taken from me. I didn't want to have to be paying protection fees. So I accessed a part of me that was non-feeling and non-caring, and then I went and did the work. Once you cross that line into violence and you get away with it, it gets easier to cross that line again.

The only other time I'd had to cross the line was during a jail stint in the Jackson County jail in Kansas City, where I had the title of "key man" for the G tank, which held thirty-six men.

In jail, we ran our own form of government, and as key man I was in charge of the tank. I was the Commander in Chief. I told everyone when they could line up to eat, when they could watch television, and when they had to turn it off, which was whenever I was ready to go to bed.

It was my job to resolve arguments and conflicts between the men. I was the one who matched men up for our Saturday night fights, a main source of entertainment that everybody looked forward to.

Each cell had six bunks, and Chevy, V.C., Low Baby, and I were all in the number one cell. Further down the floor were the cells for the "gandys," the people who weren't regulars. "Regulars" were the heavyweight hustlers, those who didn't snitch, and those whom everybody respected. Since we were regulars, we had the privilege of running the whole tank.

We kept our little commissary store on the two open bunks of our cell, from which we sold and controlled all the cigarettes, candy, cookies, and other incidentals available in the jail. If a man didn't have the cash to buy what he needed, he had to agree to the "two-for-one" policy of taxation and interest, which I had instigated. As soon as he was able to come up with the money, which had to be within a week or two, the goods were to be returned to me two times over, meaning two packs of cigarettes for the original pack, two candy bars for the original candy bar, and so on. It was how we kept our commissary stocked.

Being key man also meant I got the best food, the best cell, the best clothes, and first use of the shower. I'd gotten lucky and inherited the job from the last key man, but that also meant I'd never been tested for the rights to my position. The key man was key because he was also known as the toughest guy in the tank.

One day the heavyweight champion boxer of Kansas City, known as Kansas City Red, got placed into my tank. I knew him from the streets, and I was happy to see him.

"Hey Red," I said, "how you doin' man? Go ahead and take cell #2. Whatever you need, you just let me know, no problem."

A week or so later, me and V.C., my Number One Man, my vice president so to speak, were hanging out doing what people do in jail—writing letters, laughing, and joking around. Red comes walking up to me demanding that he wants my cell and he wants my bunk. Obviously it was a power move, and he was testing me. I knew I had no choice but to fight him.

Buying time to think, I said, "Sure, Red, no problem. You got it man."

He stood there a minute, obviously suspicious, sizing me up, and then he turned around and walked out, heading back to his cell to start packing his things up. I knew he imagined I was doing the same.

Immediately, I changed my flip-flops over for some hard-sole shoes. Then I whispered to V.C., "You see that mop bucket over in the back? Take and put the mop ringer up on the table in the chow hall, back by the door, and don't let nobody else into the tank."

The long tables of the chow hall had attached steel benches. I stepped up on top of the bench nearest the door where I could easily reach down and take hold of the handle of the mop wringer. When Red came around the corner, I grabbed him with one hand, reached for the mop wringer with the other, and brought it around, slamming him upside the head. He tried to catch the ringer, so I brought it around on top of his head a couple more times. Then I told V.C. to call the police.

"Stop, man! Stop hitting me!" Red screamed and begged, going totally coward.

The police came in, took Red out, and immediately my reputation went up. They thought anyone who would dare to take out the heavyweight champion of Kansas City had to be crazy and so I gained their respect.

I was relieved. I hadn't really wanted to do it, but I felt it was the only way out of my predicament. Obviously I couldn't have fought him face-to-face. He would've knocked me out in a minute.

After the violence had gone down at the Kansas City Jail and then again at Church Farm, whenever I was harassed in prison or my limits were tested, my retaliation would be swift and often kind of crazy. Once I had crossed that line of retaliation, people left me alone because they said I wasn't wrapped too tight, and that was just fine by me.

And Cookie Makes Three

By the time I left Church Farm it was October, 1972, and I was determined to rise to the top of my game. India was already out, and we were both living at our mothers' homes. Together we boosted some merchandize, sold it, and purchased a raggedy ole piece of shit car.

We were broke. Even though I'd sworn I'd never do it, I took India down to the 'ho stroll and put her down. She was making $10-20 dollars a trick. Before long it was clear that this was not gonna cut it. The money wasn't good enough, and India wasn't a good enough whore. But we both knew she was a great booster, so I took her off the track and we both started boosting in earnest.

We went after knit clothing and leather jackets. The money started rolling in. We had a great fence, Gino, whom we sold to for one-quarter the retail price. Gino turned it around and sold it to individual buyers, doubling his money. He could afford to sit on it and sell it piece by piece. Whenever I wanted to get my maximums, I'd sell it myself.

I had a route established where I would go from one beauty shop to the next along Prospect Avenue, displaying my wares. Women were happy to pay more than half-price as long as it was still a good deal. Everyone knew it was stolen goods, but it seemed like the entire African American culture along Prospect was in on the game. Looking for a thousand dollar suit for a couple hundred dollars was simply business. With the income most people were making there was a constant search going on for ways to cut corners. One of our specialties was stealing expensive wigs from department stores and selling them down at the beauty shops on Prospect. India was so good she would take orders from customers and deliver exactly what they wanted right down to the precise color and length.

Once I'd put together a little money, I talked my stepfather into cosigning a loan for me, and I bought my first legitimate car, a 1972 do-do brown Pontiac Grandville four-door, with a real title and monthly payment slips. I finally even had a driver's license. Car insurance wasn't such a huge money racket back then and so it wasn't mandatory.

With these new wheels, my name was once again ringing in the streets. That's when I caught Cookie, a booster who'd been out hustling in LA with Jimmy Campa and who had just gotten back to Kansas City.

Cookie was dark, smooth, and sweet like an Oreo pie. She was not skinny. She was not plump. She was just right. The beauty mark just below her right eye was her signature trait, along with soft curly hair and full luscious lips perpetually wet and shiny from the nervous play of her tongue. Cookie knew how to dress up classy, not like the young woman raised in the ghetto she really was. She prized her collection of fine leather coats with fur collars.

Cookie had been looking to hook up with the right pimp. She'd heard I'd just gotten out of the joint, and she approached me at a nightclub one night. She walked right up, looked me square in the eyes, and said, "I see you're in the game now, and I'm looking for a good man. I know how the game goes, and I'm coming correct." She didn't hesitate a second or wait for my acceptance. As always, Cookie was in total control. She was educating me now.

"I got me ten pieces in the car and I'm choosing."

When a woman came to a pimp, she had to come with something. More often than not she was broke, but if she wanted to choose a pimp, she'd have to find a way to come back with some money and prove she was serious about the game. If she didn't have choosing money, then at least it had to be some kind of choosing money.

Cookie came correctly. She came with ten silk dresses. We made love that night, and she became my third woman. I'd already picked up Mary, my second, while she was out working the streets one night. Now I had India, Mary, and Cookie. Mary worked the streets, and India and Cookie were boosters.

Cookie had tremendous self-confidence and knowledge far beyond her twenty-four years. That woman could take charge. She loved taking care of other people, and she was dedicated to all of us. I was lucky to have her.

Why would a woman who already knew how to make money on her own hook up with a pimp? I was always astonished when a square would ask me that question. Coming up in the life, it was just part of the play. We never questioned it. Hooking up with the right pimp gave a woman of the streets her identity, her status.

"A bitch have to be crazy to pay a motherfucker" was what my real pimpin' mentor, Minnesota Bob, would say when I was to hook up with him a few years down the road. One day, in the not-too-distant future, I'd be a fugitive from the law and running from the FBI. That's when Bob would teach me the real ins and outs of the pimpin' game.

Any way you sliced it, there had to be something about a pimp that appealed to a woman. She wanted to be with a man she thought was going somewhere, a man who had a good reputation as a money dog. If she was aligned with somebody successful, it meant that she was successful too. Not to mention that these women would usually be living well. They'd buy whatever clothes they wanted. They'd eat caviar all day, every day, if that's what they wanted.

It was my job to protect them from bad tricks, from other pimps, and from the law. If one of my women got busted, I would take care of her charges and make her bond. It was a business relationship. We were partners in crime, birds of a feather, water seeking its own level. In exchange for status and protection, I would get most of her money. She'd lift twenty to thirty pieces a day, keep five, and give me the rest. It was understood that I would have other women, and that wasn't a problem. Sometimes the women worked together, depending on the times, how bad our money situation was, or how tight my pimping. Sometimes we'd all even live together. I needed team players, people I could talk to and bounce ideas off of.

Cookie loved drugs, and drugs were definitely an element in our subculture, though my own love affair with cocaine would still be some years to come.

Alcohol had always been my drug of choice from way back. I had tried marijuana, cocaine, and heroin, otherwise known on the streets as "Mary Jane," "Girl," and "Boy," and I had experimented with every pill under the sun. I saw that both cocaine and heroin were taking men and women out of the game, so again I had to decide, to rightly divide, what it was I wanted. I chose Robitussin cough syrup. I loved the high that cough syrup gave me better than whisky or vodka. I could coast with Robitussin. I could be clean and cool, never sloppy. No hangover. No headache.

Down at the "syrup house," Simon's pharmacy on 27th and Prospect, I would order ten ounces of Robo at a time, at a cost of around $10. The high on one ounce would last six or seven hours.

I stayed away from heroin because I saw what it was doing to my friends. Later on I saw firsthand what it did to my brother. Every time I came out of prison I'd see some guy who used to be strong now homeless and on the streets, his clothes a wreck, his hair all matted up, his body wasted away.

Hangin' Paper

Cookie, Mary, and India were all rolling now, working the streets day and night. Our game was smooth, but it wasn't enough for me. My dream was to be sitting at the round table at the after-hours clubs with all the other pimps and players, an equally honored and respected member of that elite social order. Yet in order to realize that dream, I'd first have to bring something special to the table.

Take Radio, for instance. Radio was a killer for hire. When you saw Radio coming toward you, the first thing that came to most guys' minds was *Oh shit, am I gonna live, or am I gonna die?* He reminded me of one of those silent but deadly water moccasins in my grandma's pond back in Arkansas. You never knew what Radio was up to or who he was gonna be taking out of the game. I too needed to be known in the game as some kind of specialist.

Right around then was when Fat Reggie got out of the penitentiary and hit the bricks. Fat Reggie wasn't really fat. He just had a fat butt, round and heart-shaped like a woman's. You never could actually see into Reggie's eyes because they were more like slits. He looked shifty, like he was always scheming something, but you never knew what he was scheming about or who he was scheming on. He had this way of talking through his teeth with his lips barely moving, like his jaw was wired shut, and his voice came from deep down in his throat sort of sneaky like. Most guys didn't trust Reggie because of that, but he was my best friend, and we took advantage of his scheming looks and abilities for our hustles.

All the players were devious. You couldn't trust anybody. You couldn't take nothin' or nobody at face value. Everybody was constantly monitoring everybody else, constantly watching, constantly scanning. To this day people sense something about me that maybe they call "suspect." It's just that in all those years in the game I was trained not to let my left hand know what my right hand was doing. No player ever said what he meant or meant what he said. You couldn't afford to. Pimps especially couldn't be trusted because pimps pimped everybody.

The women couldn't be trusted either, even the ones you were sleeping with, because in the end they would be loyal to their own crew, and that crew could come and shoot you for sleeping with one of their women.

I found Reggie down on the strip his first night out and we went riding.

"Kenny, my man," Reggie whined through his teeth, "I want to introduce you to Lonnie. I met him in the penitentiary. He's got a slick game I think you'd really like."

A thrill shot up my spine. I knew in my bones that this was gonna be a good one. Grinning, I said, "All right, man, when?"

Reggie offered up his own rare flash of teeth. "Tomorrow," he said. "Come by and swoop me up." As Reggie was getting out of the car, I peeled off a couple of C-notes from out of my sock, slapping them in his mitt so he'd have some money to hold him.

The next day we went over to Lonnie's, whose house smelled permanently of cooked bacon. Again I was reminded of Grandma's house. He must've ate that shit every day. Whenever we'd ride together, I could almost taste the bacon grease wafting off his clothes.

Lonnie's eyes looked like eggs, huge white globes magnified behind tiny wire-rim glasses. Plus he had this stick-up-the-butt way of walking that matched his intellectual demeanor and proper way of pronouncing his words. For all intents and purposes, Lonnie was a square who just happened to be in the game. Yet for all his stiffness, he was a real friend's friend, and I thought I could trust him. Lonnie had discovered a check-cashing game in the federal penitentiary. "Let's ride tomorrow," Lonnie invited, "and I'll show you the game."

The next day when Lonnie showed us how easy cashing checks was and how large the return, I said, "Sign me up man.

Show me whatever I have to do to make that kind of money."

Lonnie turned out to be a real teacher, and I felt lucky to be on the receiving end of all that knowledge. The fact that I just happened to have a decent car at the time and Lonnie didn't was a stroke of luck. I had something he needed. Plus I had the connections to find us some great check cashers. "Go-ers" was what we called them, or "g-ers" for short. Each time one of them got back from a bank we'd immediately ask, "Did it gee?" Soon we could tell if the check cashed or not just from their body language.

"Reggie, man," I said one day, "it's time for us to create our own accounts. We'll get phony picture IDs, open accounts, and start cashing checks against them."

We put the word out on the streets that anybody who had any kind of checks or ID—blank checks, personal checks, business checks, cancelled checks, driver's licenses, social security cards, birth certificates, whatever—we would buy it all. Every day, cruising down Prospect Avenue, guys would call us over, flashing some kind of check or ID.

"Hey Kenny Dale, look at this here man; is it good?" they'd ask.

I'd inspect the goods then give them some money. We started stockpiling checks and IDs and gathering all the information we would need—names, addresses, phone numbers, account numbers, and signatures we could forge.

Eventually we got our hands on what was called a "check protector," a stamping machine used back in the day to prevent anyone from changing the dollar amount on a check or the recipient's name. The stamp machine would perforate those critical aspects of the check with a diagonal pattern of tiny holes. Stamping our checks like this made them look official.

Rather than complicating things with a whole crew of g-er's, we decided to handpick a couple of good-looking women. We came up with Big Janice and Sugar Cane because they were free of drugs, they looked classy enough, and we knew we could dress them up to look like women who might actually have a few thousand dollars in their lives. The g-er always had to look equal to the amount of paper we wrote.

We took a couple of stolen birth certificates that matched the approximate ages of Big Janice and Sugar Cane, had them memorize their birth dates and places of birth, then sent them off to the D.M.V to get picture IDs. Next we took them down to Saks Fifth Avenue and dressed them up in fine clothes and expensive wigs.

One day Lonnie said, "You know, Kenny, the best paper hanger is the guy who's had personal experience going into the banks and through the process of cashing a check. That way you learn what it takes and what to expect. Then you can teach your people how to do it."

This made sense, so finally one day I got up the courage to walk into a bank and get the feel for cashing a check. I walked in like any other customer, with my check in my pocket and my fake ID in hand. I looked for a teller I felt would be friendly to me. Lonnie's instructions had been to look for the young tellers and to stay away from the older ones.

I got in the line of a woman teller who looked to be about twenty-two. A real tug-of-war was going on inside. The check was burning in my pocket, but my eyes kept moving to the door and the bright sunshine on the other side.

As each person did their business and I got closer and closer to the point of no return, my heart was slamming away in my chest like a freight train. I kept nervously scanning the bank to see if any of the managers were looking at me. Paranoid thoughts filled my head that they might somehow know what I was up to. My hands were so sweaty they were getting the check wet. Finally, I got up to her window.

"Hi, how you doing?" I smiled hugely, snapping down my bankbook, my check, and my ID, overly solicitous in every way. Meanwhile, I was poised to bolt for the door at any second.

"I'd like to cash this check," I said, "and deposit a hundred of it." I knew that not taking all of it would help throw any suspicion away from me. She asked me to sign it, which I did, and since she seemed relaxed, I began to relax too.

"How would you like this?" she asked, smiling up me. That's when I knew it was a done deal.

"Twenties would be fine," I grinned, like the proverbial cat with a canary in its mouth, feathers flying everywhere.

"Thank you Ma'am. Have a very nice day." I tilted my head in thanks and headed for the door. My heart was pounding with joy as I made my way out. *Man, that was easy!* I rejoiced. There was no better feeling than writing a phony check and getting the money for it.

After that, the floodgates opened. It was a dream come true, the ultimate money tree, just like hitting the lotto. I no longer cared what Cookie, India, and Mary were doing. They could do whatever they wanted. They could keep all the money for all I cared. Matter of fact, they *did* keep all the money, and they were surprised that I'd let them. They thought I'd lost my marbles, when in reality I'd finally found the right marbles to play with.

Monday and Tuesday mornings Big Janice and Sugar Cane went out to different banks with their phony ID's and opened accounts with some insignificant amount of money like $25 or so. Back then an account wasn't required to have sufficient funds to cover the check you were trying to cash. They'd open personal accounts and sometimes business accounts, then we'd confiscate the new bankbooks and all the ID back from them so that they couldn't use the ID's for their own little scams. Wednesdays and Thursdays, we'd lay low. When Friday noon rolled around, we'd run our route, with Janice and Sugar Cane cashing checks against the new accounts. We'd instruct them to meet us at a certain place after they'd cashed their checks. Sometimes we'd cold trail them to be certain they were doing their jobs.

We had to be careful about the kind of cut we gave them, which was around $25 a check and sometimes up to $100. It had to be just the right amount to keep them interested. We knew if we gave them too much we might never see them again.

Reggie and I started pulling in thousands of dollars a day. We'd begin each day asking each other, "Okay, man, how much do you want to make today? Three grand? Four grand? Ten grand?" Trying to put it all together that first month had been rough, but finally we had turned it into a system. We now had a viable, first-class paper game.

I never had been all that successful at pimping. Even when I'd hit the level of having two or three women at one time, it was always kind of sketchy. I'd never been that great at robbing either, because I didn't like the possibility that I might get cornered into killing someone or get myself killed. Same with drug dealing, because again that game often involved killing or being killed. Sneak thieving or boosting hadn't panned out either, because the money never really added up to much.

I was great, however, at fabricating birth certificates and all manner of ID. Plus I had a talent for creating alliances. I was able to use my pimpin' skills to go out and catch the right women, build them a dream, and then get them to cash the checks for us. So when Reggie and Lonnie turned me on to the check game, every skill from every hustle I had ever learned over the years came together to create Kenny the prizewinning forger and check casher.

After a while we moved our game out into the suburbs. Same banks, just different branches. It took the authorities about five months to catch on to our racket. They knew somebody was burning up their local banks, but they couldn't catch us. They hadn't been ready for this kind of hustle. Eventually, however, they began to figure out our MO, and they started setting up sting operations.

The first time Reggie and I realized it was on a Friday. We had just set the women up and sent them out. Sitting in our car up on 24th and Grand, we started noticing unmarked police cars cruising back and forth down the street.

"Shit Reggie, check this out, man. Do you see what I see? This can't be! I think they're trying to bust our people!"

Immediately we knew we had to call it off. We caught up with Sugar Cane just as she was about to go into the bank and told her to just keep walking. Big Janice got busted that day, and we had to go downtown and make her bond. We knew it was time to give Kansas City some air, so we expanded our area out to smaller cities like Topeka and Lawrence.

During that period in 1973, Reggie and I were just as big and famous as the guys making the big drug deals or robbing the banks. Reggie was my brother. I could trust him with my life. The same guy who'd stolen the money out of my hat that first night in jail turned out to be one of the few real brothers of my life, and he was just about to get himself killed.

Some months later, as I was driving away from my house, a cop car suddenly appeared behind me, looming large in the rearview mirror. Seconds later, another headed me off. I was surrounded. I didn't even attempt to run. Within minutes I was handcuffed and taken off to jail.

One by one my old check cashers had been crossing me out, making deals with their attorneys and copping lesser pleas. The authorities weren't certain they could make the check charges stick, so they conjured up a phony bank robbery to sentence me on.

India had been busted again for boosting and was doing sixty days. Cookie and I had broken up. Mary was in jail on prostitution charges. Reggie took off for Atlanta where he had some women working the stroll. A few days later, he and Fast Black were pimping on another cat's woman, trying to add one more to their stable. The woman was ready to leave the chump, but he got so pissed he came after Reggie with a gun. Fast Black got to his own gat first and squeezed off a few shots, one of them accidently hitting Reggie and killing him on the spot. My best buddy, one of the only brothers I had ever trusted, was gone.

The news sent me reeling. Now my best friend was dead and the entire world I'd worked so hard to build had once again fallen completely apart.

Consequences of Conscience

Little did I know that things were about to go from bad to worse. They threw me in the Jackson County jail on the top floor of the Kansas City courthouse to await my sentencing, a place that I was already quite familiar with.

Vicks Vapor Rub was a big thing in the jails back then. Guys would take a glop of the stuff, stick it in a wad of gum, chew on it, and be high for a long, long time. Years it seemed. I hated that high because once you were up, there was no way you were gonna get back down anytime soon. One of the ingredients in Vicks Vapor Rub was a precursor of today's methamphetamine. One night a bunch of guys got high out of their minds on that stuff and came up with what they thought in their altered state was a brilliant plan to escape.

"You're nuts!" I told these guys right off the bat. "You're never gonna pull this off. Don't you include me in this."

They were determined to do it anyway.

At ten o'clock the guard came to rack us in for the night. As soon as he opened the door, the men rushed him, beating and stabbing him repeatedly with homemade ice picks. Some were made from toothbrushes filed down to lethally sharp points, others from broken off TV antennas. The guard had enough presence of mind to scream out for help and throw his keys back through the door before it slammed shut and locked.

Hearing his cries, other guards ran over and started locking down every gate and door until we were completely sealed in.

For some stupid reason, these guys hadn't been counting on there being more than one guard. When they realized their ridiculous plan had failed, they took the injured guard and threw him into a mop and broom closet. Bright red blood gushed down the guard's head and face, quickly spreading from the top of his uniform down to the other bloody mess of multiple stab wounds in his gut.

Looking at that poor guy, I experienced an uncustomary moment of real compassion.

Shit, this guy is gonna die! I thought. *Guard or no guard, this is a human being, and I've got to help him.* It seemed like the natural thing to do.

A group of policemen appeared on the other side of the door. I could see them through the little plate glass window. "Where's he at?" they screamed through the glass. "Where's the guard?!"

"He's here! In the closet!" I shouted back, then opened the door and pulled the guard's limp body out into the hallway.

Oh shit, he's dead! I cringed. *Those idiots! This is so fucked up. Now we're all gonna be indicted for murder.*

I laid him down on the floor where he remained unconscious.

"Get back!" the cops yelled. "Get away from the door!"

I stepped out of the way while they pulled the injured guard to safety. Then they tear-gassed the shit out of us.

I couldn't pull good air for what seemed like an eternity. We were all choking and hacking, and I thought for sure I'd suffocate. That gas was so thick in the tank that I'm lucky I have no permanent lung damage.

They rough-cuffed us, took us to another tank, and started interviewing us one by one.

"Kenneth," they said, "we thank you. That guard thanks you. He really appreciates you for pulling him out. He had a punctured lung, he was bleeding internally, and he could have died. So, we all thank you for what you did.

"We need your help," they went on to say. "We need to know who did this."

I refused to give them any information. If we stole from each other, it was not that big a deal. If we burned each other every once in a while, that was just part of the game. But if one brother ratted on another, then that brother was crossing a serious line. Just helping that guard put my life on the line. I knew that if I got sent to the penitentiary, one of those nut cases could easily hunt me down and kill me just for not going along with their crazy plan.

Part 2 —The Game

Luckily, the authorities agreed to ship me off to a tiny prison at Liberty, Missouri, a little old cracker-box jail where Jesse James had once been locked up.

Escape from Liberty

Four months later, a white van rolled up in front of the Liberty Jail. My personal limo had arrived to transport me back to Kansas City where I would stand trial and be sentenced to fifteen years' hard time. Fifteen years! Somehow the prosecutors had managed to "prove" the phony bank robbery. Back then it really wasn't hard to convict an innocent black man if that's what the court was intent on doing. I didn't think I could do fifteen years. I was only twenty-seven years old. I'd always heard about guys getting so much time they felt they couldn't do it and ended up killing themselves.

I was driven back to the Liberty Jail where my mind began working overtime. How was I going to deal with all that time? I paced the length of my cell, back and forth, all day long, day after day. I always paced in prison. What else was I going to do? My mind raced all day and all night in a state of high anxiety, grasping for ideas on how to get out of my predicament.

My cellie, Ken, had gotten a seventy-five year sentence for killing his wife. Ken was six-foot-three and two hundred and seventy pounds. His big white body filled up his whole bunk, spilling out over the sides. The rest of the inmates in that tiny jail were just a bunch of weed smokers and vagrants.

Ken had been watching me pace back and forth, day after day. Finally he asked, "What the hell's going on with you, man? You're like a crazed dog in a cage."

"I can't do all this time," I complained, continuing my pacing. "I'm too young. I could be out there making money. I just can't do it, man. It's impossible." On top of that, I was secretly terrified that one of the guys from back at the Kansas City jail was gonna find a way to get to me, or pay someone else to put a hit on me. I knew if they got their hands on me, I was dead meat.

Searching for a way to ease all the anxiety going on in my head, I began rereading *The Power of Positive Thinking*. I don't think

Norman Vincent Peale had my situation in mind when he wrote that book; but one morning at 3:00am, fully awake in the pitch black of my cell, I had a huge epiphany. I had found the solution.

"Ken, wake up man," I said, shaking him in his bed. "I got it, I got it, I got it! We're gonna escape!"

"Are you crazy man?" I know he thought I was losing it. "Just how in the hell do you think we're gonna do that?"

"My girl, India, I'll have her smuggle in some hacksaw blades. We'll cut the bars here, here, and over there," I said, pointing to each of the ¾-inch steel bars that fronted our cell. "Once we're in the hallway, we can cut the bars over the window to the outside, run down the ledge, jump into the alley, and be on our way down the tracks to Kansas City!" The whole plan had been downloaded into my mind in a flash of brilliance. "We're going to escape man!" I was absolutely confident about this.

I called India down the next day and told her my plan. "Go get some diamond-toothed hacksaw blades," I instructed. "Break them into pieces about four inches long, and put them in a Shower-to-Shower powder bottle. Next, get me some downers and marijuana, wrap them in aluminum foil, and tape it all up real tight in plastic bags. Stick those into a lotion bottle, and bring the two bottles in with a bunch of other bathroom products. I'll take care of the rest. Don't come back. I'll call you when I'm on the streets."

I'm going home! I rejoiced to myself. *I'm gonna be free!* There was no doubt in my mind. I had never felt so much power of certainty in all my life. I knew it in my bones. They couldn't take my freedom. I also knew where I was headed. I would be going to Minnesota.

Mail time came at the jail, and everybody got letters or a package except me. *What the hell?* I wondered.

"Kenny Johnson here," I said to the guard. "Where's my package?"

"Mr. Johnson, I'm sorry but there's nothing here for you," he replied. I ran down to the phone and called India.

"Kenny, I delivered the package for you in a Safeway sack," she insisted. I ran back and told the guard.

"Anybody get a package that wasn't yours?" he called out to the rest of the cells. Another black guy named Johnson stepped forward looking sheepish.

"Yeah, I got it here," he confessed. "I didn't know why I'd gotten it. I was just holding it." He'd been sitting on his bunk staring at my package!

The guard brought it down to me, and as soon as he left, I busted it open. The hacksaw blades, the money, and the pills were there. India had done exactly as I'd told her. My insides were doing somersaults.

"That's my girl!" I cheered to Ken. "That's my India."

I passed the marijuana and the pills out to all the guys, an assortment of yellows, reds, and blues, all downers. Now everybody was in on the scheme, and I knew that they would protect us and back us up. It felt like a script right out of Hogan's Heroes.

Ken and I had been using the bars of our cell as bookends for all our books. We had lined them up between the bars, tying a string from one bar to another to hold them in, which meant that the guard was already used to seeing the string.

We started on a Thursday night. I worked that blade with gusto, back and forth, back and forth, tiny little strokes. The bars were tempered steel, but slowly, surely, those little hacksaw blades sawed their way through. I sawed all night long, and even though I'd wrapped the ends with a rag, my fingers still blistered and bled. We worked in shifts; one of us sawing away while the other listened and watched for activity in the hallway.

The first night we made it through one bar, and then tied it back into place with the string. The next day we spent making sure that the bar we'd already cut stayed in place, and that everybody was cool. On the second night, we cut through a second bar. At the time I was so slender I could squeeze through the opening, so on the third night I was out in the hallway, sawing away on the big bars at the window. Those bars were made of iron, not tempered steel like the bars of our cell, and cutting through those was like cutting through butter. I zipped right on through and left the last little bit that would keep them standing in place. We were good to go.

"Brother," Ken said, "you know I can't get through there. I'm too big. I'll get stuck."

"But I can," I said ruefully, "and I've got to go. You can cover for me, and if by tomorrow night they haven't discovered my escape, cut another bar and follow me." I felt terrible for the guy, but I knew I had to go.

He sat there on his bunk, head hanging with the weight of his predicament. "I understand, man," he finally agreed. "I'll cover for you."

At ten o'clock, Saturday night, they shut the jail down and it was lights out. I put on my two shirts, tucked my money and my candy bars in my pockets, and slipped out through the opening in the bars of our cell. Across the hallway, I cut through the last bit of the bars and made it quickly out onto the ledge. I edged myself along toward the alleyway and then leaped over the fence, ran past the police station situated conveniently next to the jail, then headed south along the railroad tracks. A big dog started barking and making a racket. *Shit!* I thought, adrenalin pumping. *That damn dog's gonna wake up the whole town!*

I high tailed it down those train tracks as hard and as fast as I could for as long as I could, the full moon glistening on the rails, lighting my way to freedom. Eventually I walked along, eating my candy bars and singing a silent mantra of song—*I am free, I am free! Good God Almighty, I am free at last!*

I was on top of the world. I felt so powerful. I had screwed the system. I had screwed everybody.

I walked the tracks twenty-seven miles throughout that night and the next day on a direct route from Liberty to Kansas City. Nobody was looking for me yet because the guys back in the jail had covered for me. They had made my bed up like in the movies, stuffing pillows, clothes, whatever they could find to make it look like I was in my bed. Whenever the guard had come by, everybody had said I was sick. My cellie, Ken, never made it out. By Monday morning, my escape was in the newspapers with the headline:

ESCAPE FROM LIBERTY!

On Saturday night, a Mr. Kenneth Johnson escaped from the Liberty County Jail. His escape was discovered Sunday afternoon when authorities found a dummy under the covers of his cell bunk. A manhunt for Mr. Johnson is currently underway.

India picked me up and took me across the state line to Kansas. We booked a room at a little Bonnie and Clyde motel with tiny cabins around the back. The next day I was on a bus to Minneapolis. I knew I had to get away and start over again someplace fresh where the authorities didn't know me. I had finally learned the lesson that old Mr. Grant had tried to impart that day on his porch. Never again would I hustle in Kansas City.

PART 3

Muddy Waters

Say ho, are you looking at me?
I wonder if you know just what you see.
You know I pimp on 'hos, I slam Rolls Royce doors,
All I wear is tailor made clothes.
I got diamonds, dripping from everywhere,
I got the attitude that say, "I don't care."
I'm a real live pimp in every way,
You think you're pimpin'?
That's what your mouth say.

—Rosebudd Bitterdose, *The Gospel of the Game*

Minnesota Bob

Minnesota Bob, he changed my life. He taught me the pimpin' game, and for a while that kept me safe.

Arriving in Minneapolis with nothing but a ten-dollar bill in my pocket, the first thing I did was to hit the streets. Who did I run into but a couple of Kansas City hustlers I'd known in high school, Bob and his brother Coast-to-Coast. They had heard about my escape.

Bob starting giving me advice the moment we hooked up. "Listen man," he said, "now that you're on the run, you can't be cashing no checks, you can't be pulling no robberies, you got to be playing under the radar, man. You got be learning the pimp game. That rough hustling is over."

Ever since I'd known him, Bob had always been 100% comfortable in his skin. He stood tall but relaxed, confident and cool. He always had an easy smile on his face.

Bob was a turning point for me. I wanted to stay free, and I knew that in order to stay free, I had to expand my game. Pimpin' was a way not only to stay under the radar, free from the authorities, but also a way to stay powerful, to stay in control, to stay somebody in the game.

Nothing much about pimpin' had ever really stuck to me in the past. I didn't like the coldness of it. Yet at this stage, it was the hand I was dealt. I had to see it through.

Learning to be an excellent pimp was an education in human nature and human psychology. If I wanted to return to this part of the game and be a great pimp, I knew I had to catch great women. I had to understand women and to learn ways of communicating with women that kept them under my control.

The next four years would be about learning how to use women, how to manipulate women, and how to threaten physical violence against women to get them to do what I wanted.

The pimpin' game seemed like a natural part of the culture I lived in as a man, and being some man's ho was part of the culture our women lived in. Not until after my awakening many years later, when I was out of prison for good and successfully living the straight life, would I be able to look back on this time and ask for God's forgiveness, as well as forgiveness from myself, for all the pain I caused these women. Yet these realizations would not be for years to come. In the meantime, I became fully involved in the pimp game, and Minnesota Bob was the one who handed me the psychological keys to the kingdom.

"If a bitch grins, she's in," Bob instructed. I learned that if a woman smiled at me, she was catchable. If she didn't, I wouldn't waste any time; I'd already be moving on.

I learned that a pimp had to be a therapist at all times. He had to debrief his women every night after work to be sure they were okay emotionally and that they felt well cared for. If anything went wrong, he had to be a crime scene investigator. He also needed to be sure his women were always doing right by him and the game, and staying away from drugs, so he had to be a lie detector as well. Above all else, he had to be a motivational and inspirational speaker, handing out pep talks whenever his women were feeling down.

Bob and Coast-to-Coast insisted that I get a new name. "Bitches like skinny niggers," Bob maintained, "and you one skinny nigger, so we're gonna call you Slim. You need a new history too, so now you'll be from Cincinnati." For years to come, I would be known as Cincinnati Slim, if not that, then Kansas City Slim, Minnesota Slim, or Colorado Slim, depending.

For the guys I hung with, "nigger" was a term of affection. "You my nigger," or "Nigger, I'm gonna kill your motherfucking ass" was a common way of speaking. Communicating with each other from the perspective of violence was just the soup we lived in. To this day it's like that, and I wouldn't expect it any other way.

We didn't express love for each other with words. Expressing love and caring was through an exchange of something material, like "Here man, take this bag of weed," or "You need some bread, man? Here, here's five hundred dollars. Now you go take care of yourself."

The way that Minnesota Bob gave me the pimp game was by pimpin' on me. "Lacing up my boots" was what we called it. It was Bob's way of wanting the only best for me. "Motherfucka's in the game still have love for each other Slim, we just come at it from a different angle." He wanted to make sure I came into the game correct. If a player was laced right, he'd have no problems.

Riding in his Cadillac one day, Bob turned to me in the back seat and said, "Hey bitch, you got to get your shit together, or you're not gonna get any motherfuckin' work up here. Fool, you got to get you some fronts."

Every player had to have his "fronts," the three-piece suits, the lizard-skin shoes, the big tires on the Cadillacs, the diamonds, all the bling-bling. If your fronts were together, then your shit was tight. Women wanted to be with a guy who looked successful.

"You need to pimp up on some jewelry real quick," Bob went on. "That way you can make bond and get your ass out of jail anytime you need to.

"You got to get your motherfuckin' grill fixed too," he demanded with his usual bluntness. I had a front tooth missing at the time. In prison, if you had any kind of problem with a tooth, the only way they dealt with it was to pull it clean out.

Bob never let up on lacing me. Once when I was taking a piss in the bathroom of a strip joint, there'd come Bob. When I'd walked over to the basin to wash my hands, he'd started pimpin' on me.

"Man, what's you washing your hands for?" he'd demanded. "What's you been doing with that dick man? You gotta keep that motherfucking dick clean. A pimp's dick is never dirty."

Jesus Christ, I'd thought to myself, *I can't get away from this guy! He never stops pimpin'.*

Still, I kept on taking it because Bob was my mentor, and I knew he was taking me to the next level so that I could stay free. Staying free was what I wanted more than anything in the world, and that's why the universe had thrown me in bed with the pimps, the guys who never did much all day long but lie around and count their money.

Bob was 100% pimp. Wherever he is today, I can be sure he's still laying down the pimpin' game. He wouldn't be able to help it. Bob was no bank robber. He was no shoeshine salesman. He was a pimp. He had the Cadillac. He had the hos. He had the big ole twenty thousand dollar ring. He had the gold chains, yet he wasn't garish with the huge platform shoes. Bob wore skins and a three-piece suit with a flower in the lapel.

At the club, if Bob saw me talking to a dame, he'd of course feel compelled to comment on my style. "Man, you're too soft with that motherfucking bitch. Pimp that ho, man."

Saying something like, "Hi, sweetheart, how are you doing today, I'd really like to know your name," was not gonna cut it. It was more like, "Bitch get over here and get with this macaroni." Then she would respect you. Then she'd think you were strong enough to take care of her. The loudest guy, the most colorful guy, or the most silent guy in the game was the one who ended up with the most women.

We talked straight up about how we were qualified to be a pimp, how we were 100% pimp, not no 70/30. Woven throughout our language was an undercurrent of violence. Even when we complimented our women, they were affectionately referred to as "bitch."

In the nightclubs of Minneapolis, we pimps stood lined up against the walls, showcasing our wares for the highest bidder. It was an auction. We'd have on our best fronts, putting on the same kind of show our women working the streets did. I'd be standing there sweating like a pig in the hundred-degree heat, but at least I'd be looking good. The women looked us over, talked about us, each one wondering, *Which one is gonna be my man?*

There was a regular way of announcing yourself when entering a place where players were gathered. "There's a macaroni in the house," a cat would call out. "You motherfucking bitches better get with this pimpin'."

"Macaroni" has been in the pimp vernacular since time began. It's a verbal hustle. A mack man is someone who gets up in the morning to pimp whores and slam Cadillac doors. He's somebody who can con you, "mack you" out of something. Mackin' is all about how well you can present your case, how well you can paint a picture for someone, spin a dream.

Mack men are artists. They're dream weavers. They create a vision for a woman by telling her, "This is how we're gonna live our lives now. You're gonna have that house you want. You're gonna have that fur. What else did you say you wanted? Well, you're gonna get that too." Whatever she says she wants, he's gonna promise to get it for her. He'll promise her the world, promise her the moon, as long as she brings home the mean green.

What I see now is that while I treated women so badly, used and abused them, I was dependent on women even as I exploited them. That dependency angered and pissed me off, and so throughout my life I have continually been confronted by the feminine. I've learned to not only reconcile and make peace with the feminine, but to honor the presence of the divine feminine all around me. The feminine has been my salvation. My mother, my grandmother, Aunt Equator – they all gave me teaching and love in their own way. It seems no coincidence that it was the guru in the form of a woman who uttered the words that took me to awakening.

The Slum Game

There's no such thing as an honest person," Bob instructed. "There's only greedy people. So don't you feel bad when a person buys your jewelry for five or six thousand dollars, and you didn't pay a pretty cent for it. That person is a greedy motherfucker. He needs to get beat anyway cause he's trying to get somethin' for nothin'."

Wrapping it all up in our minds like that was how we did what we did. There had to be no conscience, no guilt, no shame. We had a good story going; not only were we conning others, we were conning ourselves.

Bob was teaching me the "slum game," otherwise known as the "brass-and-glass game." The slum game was a con a player could always fall back on no matter where he was. Bob taught me how to take phony jewelry, go anywhere in the world with it, and make money.

First I'd order jewelry from a wholesale warehouse in Los Angeles. When the package arrived Bob would say, "Let's go slumming brother!" Then we'd hop into his Cadillac and hit the nightclubs, the bars, and the car lots. A typical day went something like this:

Minnesota and I stop for coffee at a donut shop, and I spy a car lot across the street. Grabbing my jewelry case, I make a beeline for the front office. Sitting at a desk is a big fat guy, eatin' a baloney sandwich, brushing crumbs from his bulging belly, and slugging on a Budweiser. "How can I help you?" he asks, ending his query with a long belch.

"Brother," I say, "have I got a deal for you. It's your lucky day. Can I show you something?"

"Sure," he agrees, "but shut that door first." His voice is hushed, his head swiveling back and forth to scan the car lot through the big glass windows. I almost laugh because I know this guy is greedy, and I have me another vic. It's just a matter of how much I have him for.

I lay my case on the desk, pop the latches, and take out a newspaper clipping, which I then hand to him. The headlines read something like this: "Jewelry Store Burglarized—Thieves Get Away with Ten Thousand Dollars in Diamonds." He smiles slightly, and I know he believes I am the jewelry thief. The truth is I've purchased the jewelry from a catalog, and it's just come in the mail. Guys like this don't know a diamond from a zircon from a bit of polished glass. Plop goes his sandwich on the desk, and he wipes his hands on his pants, still scanning the lot for customers.

I open my case with a flourish and display my ten rings, four watches, and a couple of gold chains. As he eyes the price tags, the glistening jewelry is met by the greedy gleam in his eyes.

"My man," I say, "I'm trying to move them all at once. I'll give you a great deal. I'll sell you everything for just two g's." Then I carefully check his response to see if this is out of his league. Most of the time, a guy like this doesn't even flinch. Then he pretends to hesitate.

"Hmmm I don't know," he says.

"Listen brother, I can't give this away. The price is low enough for you to make a killing on each piece." By then I'm in full stride. I have all kinds of ways to hustle him. I pick up a diamond ring from the case and then quickly scratch the glass desktop with my own. "See how it cuts this glass?" I point out. Then I shove the phony diamond in his face.

"Tell you what," he offers, still ogling each piece, feeling them all, counting them again. "I'll take them all for a grand."

"Man that is too low," I counter. "Tell you what I can do. Give me sixteen hundred bucks."

"Can't do, thirteen is as high as I'll go." He's already walking over and reaching into the pocket of his shiny black suit coat, hanging on a hook by the door.

"Damn, man, you drive a hard bargain," I say. "Alright, let's do it."

His smile is smug. I eye the crisp c-notes he counts out on the desk, being careful not to reach for them until he slides them my way.

"Take it," he says.

I'm itching to get out of there as fast as I can, to find Minnesota and get as far away from this guy's fat ass as I can before he wakes up to realize that this skinny nigga' has beaten him out of his dough. I scoop up the bills, stuff them in my pocket, and bid him a good day. Grabbing my case, I damn near run out the door. As I fast-step it across the gravel lot, I'm spying for Minnesota and never looking back. It's just 11am, and I know it's going to be a good day.

Often I would buy me a whole bunch of slum, get in my car, and ride down the highway hitting the gas stations, the night-clubs, the car lots, and the strip joints. I liked going to a strip joint best because everyone in there was greedy. The slum game was always my backup hustle. Whenever things heated up in one city or I was broke, I'd get my woman and some slum and hit the road. That way I could make money right off anywhere I went.

Bob tried to give me the dope game too, but I didn't bite. In order to be a dope dealer, you had to also be a killer. Murder and dope went together.

Greed was king in the dope game. A junky would lie to you like crazy or do anything to get his fix. He'd promise you the world if only you'd give him that fix right now. If he burned you for ten dollars or a thousand, it didn't matter, you'd still have to prove that nobody could steal your merchandise and get away with it. If you didn't, you were gonna be out of business real quick, which meant that you had to maim or kill the guy. I didn't want to kill anybody. At yet another crossroads, rightly dividing showed me which path I didn't want to take.

Ollie

"Say baby, what's going on?" a guy called out from the bar. "You *sure* lookin' good!"

The woman shot him an annoyed glance, then turned her head and walked away. Like I said, if a guy's line was weak, she'd keep on walking every time.

Darrell and I were hanging together at the Moby Dick, a nightclub on Hennepin Avenue in downtown Minneapolis where a lot of pimps and players stood posing along the wall, trying to get chose.

"Hey man, what's up?" the dude to my right turned and asked.

"Ah man, I'm just a pimp trying to come up. Know what I'm sayin'?"

At that exact moment, Ollie walked into my life.

"Are you gonna stand there all night sugar, or are you gonna buy me a drink?" she asked coyly, turning to the side so that I could admire her legs in a red silk dress with the slits up the side. Umm, um, what a combination that was.

She wore no stockings because she didn't need to. Mother nature had blessed her skin with a creamy soft sheen that twinkled in the nightclub's dim lighting. I could already see what her assets were, and I was going to cash in tonight. As we made our way to her table, she looked down at the hem of her dress and then back at my smiling eyes, enjoying their caress.

Her wig that night was long and black. Ollie always wore wigs. Her real hair never grew out more than an inch. That wide mouth of hers and huge smile reeled me right in. Immediately I knew we were gonna be together.

Whatever brazenness Ollie had that night I later found out was totally out of character. Ollie's true nature was as meek and innocent as a lamb.

"Of course, darlin', I'll buy you a drink," I agreed. I assumed she was choosing me or was at least interested.

90

Ollie loved to laugh, especially with her sisters. Most of the time when she was with me she was quiet. Probably scared to death. We could drive for hours without talking, and I liked that. Ollie was the first woman I was ever comfortable being silent with.

But Ollie was never a good streetwalker because she was afraid of the game. She was too hesitant. Plus she didn't know how to lie. She knew how to lie to *me*, but not to a trick. Ollie was with me because she was crazy about me. Later I realized she never really was choosing me as a pimp. She hadn't come with a fee. She was always more my woman than she was my 'ho. Catching Ollie was the best thing that could've happened for me. It meant that in Minnesota I would always have a place to stay without worrying about paying rent. Being on the run was a whole new way of living and thinking.

In the wee hours of the morning we drove over to her house in the piece of shit that was my car. Those days I was back to buying illegal, hundred dollar cars so that if the car broke, no problem, I'd just walk away. No more driving the year I was living in. That kind of money was a thing of the past.

When we got to Ollie's, I walked back into the bedroom, and there in the center of the bed was this incredibly beautiful little baby. From the moment I laid eyes on Damon, that little boy totally captivated my attention.

"Ohhh, my goodness," I said, "look at that," and I walked over to examine the tiny caramel-colored bundle on the bed, asleep with his mouth half open, head lying to one side. I caught a whiff of his scent, just like milk and honey, and right then and there I fell in love. Immediately I wanted to kiss him. So I did.

Damon was just six weeks old, fresh out of the package, and oh so sweet. I stood there staring, completely entranced. Up until I met Damon, I had never really appreciated the essence of a baby. I hadn't been around when my own daughter Chanette had been born; so gazing down at Damon that night was like seeing a baby for the first time. We bonded to each other instantly, like a newborn imprinting on its mother.

After Ollie and I made love and showered, we went to sleep with the baby right there in the bed with us. Being with a baby like that totally shifted my universe. I woke up the next morning an instant Dad. Damon became the focus of everything. Did he have enough milk? Were his diapers dry? I did everything for that little dude. I *wanted* to take care of him.

Damon was a total gift out of nowhere. He became my boy. If it hadn't been for Damon, I don't think I would've stuck around so long. He was the determining factor that solidified my relationship with Ollie.

Ollie had three children by Damon's father, but the guy was never around. She had come from a large family with eight siblings. Her mother was a tyrant from hell, and she hardly knew her daddy.

I was with Damon off and on from the time he was six weeks old until he was around six years old, big enough for us to go out riding together.

I loved that boy with all my heart.

Chili Pimp

Minnesota Bob had warned me to play it safe and stick with the pimpin' game, but it wasn't long before I'd managed to get popped on suspicion of robbery. Maurice, Westbrook, and I had been robbing Burger Kings and McDonalds at night. We'd wait until just after ten o'clock when the restaurant closed and one of the workers, usually a young teenaged kid, would come out to dump the trash. Then we'd put a gun to his or her head, walk 'em right back inside the restaurant, stick everybody in the refrigerator, and rob the tills. As soon as we'd leave, we'd make an anonymous phone call to the police and tell them about the kids locked in the refrigerator. Each restaurant gave us an easy three-to-four grand. Sometimes we'd do a couple a night.

One day the cops pulled our car over for no reason and took us down to the police station. They put up a pretense that it had to do with some unrelated crime, but in reality they were investigating the Burger King robberies.

No one could have identified us. We had done the robberies at night with stocking caps over our faces. They didn't have enough on us to hold us. Remember, too, this was back in the day before computers. They never could put it together fast enough who I was and what they already had me on me before they had to let me go. By the time they figured out I'd given them a phony ID and address, I'd be gone.

One evening a couple of days later, a bunch of us players congregated in Bob's living room chopping it up, kicking it, snorting coke as usual. A blazing fire burned in the fireplace. Men lounged on soft Louis Philippe leather sofas. Plush velvet paintings of Coltrane, Parker, Billie Holiday, and Miles Davis covered the walls. It was the time of lava lamps and shag carpet. Marvin Gaye and Grover Washington Jr. played softly in the background. Whenever our noses got too ravished from snorting coke, we'd add it to our cigarettes and smoke it. The sweet aroma of cocaine-laced tobacco filled the room.

From time to time the women came in to see if we needed any weed, drinks, or food. Then they'd drift back into their own world in the kitchen or a back bedroom.

We talked in low tones, quiet like, not really wanting the women to hear what we were saying. Usually around 4:00 or so in the morning was when Bob started dropping his wisdom.

"Slim," he began one night, trying to warn me for the hundredth time, "you can't be hanging out with Westbrook, pulling robberies and shit. You're on the run man. You want to stay free, then you got to stay with pimpin'."

Of course what he was saying made perfect sense, yet somehow I'd gone and managed to fuck everything up again. The heat was on, and I knew I had to leave. Bob was in agreement, so I took off for Louisville, Kentucky and rented yet another totally forgettable studio apartment where I could lay low for a while. Those crappy little apartments and the piece-of-shit cars I drove around in symbolized my life on the run over the next four years. Yet I would always from time to time go back to Minnesota. Back to Ollie and Damon.

Life on the run meant devising certain strategies. I had to figure out how to conduct myself and run my life like any other businessman. I learned that if I changed my name and location every six months, the chances of having a run-in with the police were a lot less. Everywhere I went I bought a different cheap car that I could discard at a moment's notice. I had to lie to *everybody*. Telling anyone the truth about who I was or where I'd come from put me at risk. That being the case, how could I have any real friends or meaningful connections? I couldn't. I knew that if I got caught again I could be facing so much time I might never get out. Since living free could be over at any moment, I was determined to live life to the fullest.

Throughout those years, I was drinking every day. Cocaine, too, was just about to finally catch me, and I would become hooked on it. I enjoyed getting high. I enjoyed getting drunk.

Now I see that the pull to get stoned and drunk was mostly a way of covering my emotions, a way of not feeling the pain of never being able to connect with anyone. But, conversely, connecting with the cocaine and alcohol meant that I didn't have to connect with my own feelings in any kind of conscious way, let alone enjoy a truly intimate, honest, and vulnerable connection with another person.

Today I still find it challenging to shoot straight from the heart. I often find myself making unnecessary detours in delivering a thought or an idea. Through sheer grace I am surrounded by people who tell the truth and who support me in telling the truth, and I have a daily practice of meditation and looking inward. Back then I was mostly focused on how to shave up the truth and formulate a better lie.

It was a different story whenever India was with me, because India knew who I was. I never had to lie to her. I'd call for her to come be with me whenever I could. This time, when I got down to Louisville, I called her and she came down from Cincinnati where she'd been living and working the track. As soon as she arrived, I had her right back out on the streets making money for us. This was November 1974, only a few months after my escape from Liberty.

In Louisville, I was what was known as a chili pimp, otherwise referred to as a "truck stop" pimp. A lot of days a bowl of chili and some crackers were all I could afford to eat. On a good day, maybe some sardines. That would be my meal until India got another trick. That was all the money my woman was making, and the price I had to pay for staying free. I was determined to let my woman go out there and make the money so I could stay safe at home. Living this way was not comfortable for me. I didn't enjoy being home all day walking around in my robe, smoking cigarettes, drinking cognac, and watching TV. I saw myself as a hustling thoroughbred. I wanted to be out on the track. Allowing India to go out there and work every night was difficult for me, though she had no problem with it,

I was free from prison but I wasn't enjoying my freedom. I wasn't happy being this type of player, not only a pimp, but a chili pimp at that.

Seven-Dollar Trick

"Kenny! Come get me!" India screamed into the phone. "Some motherfucker just ran over my foot!"

"Who India?" A bolt of electricity shot through me.

"Some motherfucking trick!"

"What motherfucking trick?"

"*Just some motherfucking trick!* I can't believe this shit! Get down here now!"

She was yelling and talking so fast I could barely understand her. She seemed more enraged at the dude who'd run her over than she was in a panic about her foot. India was one tough 'ho.

"Where are you now?" I shouted into the phone, the handset already slick from my nervous sweat. I was feeling panicky even if India wasn't. It was a sultry summer night in Louisville, and beads of sweat had spontaneously started popping out of my scalp the minute I'd heard her voice. Now they were trickling down my face and neck. I wiped them off with the bottom of my T-shirt.

"I'm at a phone booth near the river on 1st and Washington," India shrieked into the phone. "Come get me *now!*"

"I'm coming baby. Don't you go anywhere."

"Go anywhere? How can I go anywhere with my mother-fucking foot like this?"

I dropped the phone, raced outside, and threw myself behind the wheel of my crappy car. As I peeled out, swerving down the block, my mind raced a million miles an hour.

How the fuck did this happen? I am ALWAYS telling her to be careful. Her foot's run over? What the hell does that look like? Squashed flat like in a cartoon? I didn't know what to expect.

I had grabbed my gun off the dresser on my way out. I always carried a Derringer in my pocket, so I could knock somebody up-side the head with it if I had to, or even shoot them. I definitely did not want to kill anybody, but I never knew when I might need that gun to save India's life or my own.

I parked on Washington, around the corner from the phone booth, and approached it cautiously. Would the police be there? The trick? I didn't really know what I was walking into.

As I came around the corner onto 1st, I saw the phone booth with India still inside. She was crying now. The jumpsuit she was wearing, once white and beautiful, was smeared with her bright red blood. The sight drew people's attention from blocks away. People walked by, drove by, but everybody just stared. Nobody was offering to help. What the fuck was wrong with people? When I got to her, I couldn't see her foot for all the blood pooling up in the bottom of the phone booth.

In seeing her foot like that, I had an immediate and powerful revelation: *I can't have her working the streets no more. This is my fault, my fault, MY FAULT! I have to get her to a hospital, get her home, get her back to Kansas City. She was only doing this because of me, to keep my black ass out on the streets. It's not worth it. She's the mother of my daughter for Christ's sake. I don't want her getting hurt no more all because of my selfishness.*

When you first get lured into the game, no one tells you just how painful it can get, how drastically things can go wrong, how people you love can get hurt or killed. I had promised her that life in the streets would be glamorous, that we'd eat steak and caviar every day and laugh our heads off for no reason at all. She had been certain she'd have fine clothes, a nice house, great friends, no pain, and now there she was bathed in blood. This is what our lives had come to.

Suddenly, my mother's words broke through the frenzy of thoughts: "Kenny Dale, the Lord don't like an ugly boy. Stay away from those hoodlums; they ain't nothin' but trouble." In a million different ways she had tried to warn me of this day, the day I would be faced with the consequences of my ways. In a flash I remembered all the times I had blown through town like a whirlwind in my fine clothes and slick cars, women dressed up like princesses hanging off my arm. My attitude was implicit:

"Momma, don't you say a word about my life cause I got it all together. Can't you see that?"

I picked India up gently, cradling her in my arms. She clung to my neck, tears running down her cheeks onto my T-shirt, blood dripping to the asphalt. People continued to gawk as I ran to the car and maneuvered her into the back seat, careful not to rake her foot over the edge of the door. I pulled off my T-shirt and wrapped it around her foot. Immediately the blood soaked through. Bare-chested, I headed for the emergency room at University Hospital on Goodman Street. The sounds of India's pained breath and whimpers filled the car.

"What happened, India?" I asked again.

"This trick from the Ramada pulled over and said he wanted to have sex with me for seven dollars. I said no and walked away. He got pissed off. When I walked away and started to cross the street behind his car, he threw it in reverse and tried to hit me. Kenny, I barely got out of the way!"

The emergency room staff called the police. When they arrived they kept questioning India, trying to get her to say that I was the one who'd done it. She had to tell them repeatedly, "No, he brought me here. He saved my life." She stuck to her guns. That was my India; the same woman who'd brought me hacksaw blades in jail. I never had to worry about her crossing me out. She was my first love and the most loyal woman I'd ever had in the game.

I carried her home and put her to bed. The next day when I was changing the bandages on her foot, again the truth struck me with the force of a locomotive: *I can't do this. She's out of the game. She's the mother of my daughter. She has three kids at home.*

"You know what's gotta happen, India," I said gently. "I got to send you back."

"No, no, honey. You don't have to do that. I'll get better." She started to raise up off the bed to show me she could walk.

I was determined. "No, India, you got to go home. You can come again after you heal up, but right now I want you to go back home and be with our kids." In my mind, I knew I would never send for her again. She knew it too.

"No, I'll be alright, Kenny Dale. Just give me some time, alright? Please baby?" She was determined to stay.

"No India!" I shouted. "I am telling you, you got to go back, *now!*" I had so many conflicting emotions going on. Seeing some-one I loved almost lose her foot over a few lousy dollars was not my idea of being a man. It was clear that not only could she have lost her foot, she could've lost her life. Even so, sending her back was the hardest thing I had ever had to do. I was scared shitless. How was I going to survive out there without her? There'd be no lying back in the cut, waiting for Momma to bring the food home. Up until that day I hadn't seen how protected I'd been by India all those years, and not just by her. Others had also stood on the front lines taking the heat for me.

I went out and hustled some money together, then put her on a bus. This was just as big a break from my dependence on a woman as the day I first left my mother's house. It was time for me to take the key from under India's pillow, just as I had once done with my mother. It was a critical moment. In sending her back I was being forced to take that key up again, go out there in the world and make a living for myself.

As it turned out, sending India back to Kansas City was prob-ably the worst thing that could have happened to her because that's when she got strung out. After all those years in the game, India would finally become a junkie.

I'm happy to say that today, however, India is doing just fine. She's living a married life and taking care of her mom. She and her husband now serve the community is so many small and lov-ing ways.

After India left, I felt frightened and alone. I had not a single friend. For the first time in my life I was on my own, depending on no one, not even a woman. Kenny Johnson had to feed himself, look after himself, and love himself. I hadn't a clue how to live life on my own, but I knew I had to prove to myself that I could.

I hit the road, hustling and slumming up and down the Cincinnati-Louisville corridor. I sold catnip as marijuana, vitamin pills as mescaline, phony rings and watches at elevated prices. The slum game fed me. I was able to keep a small studio or a cheap motel room and live like that for months at a time. Mostly I was okay with living like a gypsy with no place to call home because I was taking care of myself.

Turning myself in and going straight never felt like a viable option. I had escape charges hanging over my head. The check charges themselves, at the very least, would be an eight-year stint.

I was simply grateful to be free. Even if I could've had a normal life, I didn't know what a normal life was. I had never lived one. All I could envision at this point was a life of hiding. My focus was only to make my hustles more low key so that I could stay free. If the cops saw a guy selling catnip, they weren't going to send him to jail. Robbing banks and cashing checks was another story.

I wasn't in Cincinnati but six months before I got busted on a minor charge, taken down to the jail, and fingerprinted. I knew I had to run again before they figured out who I was.

I'd met a young woman in Cincinnati, Valerie, whom I'd been falling in love with. I could have put her down on the stroll, but I just couldn't do that. After what had happened to India, I could see myself getting soft, and feeling shit that was making me contemplate others people's pain. Or was it my own? At the time, I certainly did not have the consciousness to sort that one out.

Valerie could've been successful as a nurse, or she could have been a great mother, anything but just another 'ho on the track. We had a nice thing going and we were starting to make plans.

"Listen darlin'," I had to tell her after I'd gotten fingerprinted at the jail, "I've got to go. In fact, I've got to go right now. I was in jail yesterday. My name is not Kevin O'Neil. My name is Kenneth Johnson. I escaped from the Liberty Missouri jail. The FBI is looking for me for bank robbery, and if they catch me, I'll do a lot of time."

She stared at me in shock and disbelief. "But what about me?" she asked, her lip quivering.

"I can't take you with me now," I had to tell her, and right then and there, I broke her heart.

Seemed like every time I started building something up, just as it was getting good my whole life would come crashing down again. Nothing ever felt solid. Every situation was only temporary. One moment I'd be hustling on the streets, making money and putting together a nice life. The next moment I'd either be on the run again or going back to jail. Everything I'd managed to build up would be gone. House gone. Car gone. Money gone. Girl gone. Clothes gone. Everything gone. Eventually I got so used to everything going that I could walk away at a moment's notice.

My life was like one of those Tibetan Buddhist sand paintings, where once complete, all of those hundreds of hours of patience and devotion are wiped away in a single sweep of the broom. Nothing left but a pile of colored sand. Life in its wisdom was teaching me the meaning of non-attachment. Cling to nothing; all is not real.

Nowhere to Hide

You know how life sometimes gets so rough you just want to go somewhere and hide? Well, the pull was so strong, that's exactly what I tried to do. Just when I thought I was headed back to Minnesota and Ollie, a bone-deep weariness washed through me. A force inside longed desperately to restore some sense of sanity in my life, some sense of solid ground. *Go to Arkansas*, it whispered. *Go to Grandma. She loves you.* And so I did.

I wanted to return to those days of being "Lil' Kenny Dale," the innocent child whose life had no troubles, no complications. That boy could wake up in the morning and go out into the woods, lie in the grass looking up at the sky, and let all his thoughts drift by like big puffy clouds. No need to hold on to a single thought, just witnessing all things and not needing to be any specific thing.

I did not want to be Slim, an escaped con on the run with no money, no real friends, and no place to call home. I wished I could call the Feds and say, "I'm through. Can we just forget all this stuff now?"

When I knocked on the door at Grandma Oley's, all I said was, "Grandma, here I am." I hadn't seen her in years. She let me stay with her in what can only be called another little bitsy shotgun house, but this time it wasn't quite so far out in the country. This new place was on the edge of town. She had a small cot for me to sleep on.

Grandma still had her Bible right next to her, along with her coffee and a spittoon for the juice of her chewing tobacco. I didn't tell her anything about my life. Every morning I walked way out into the woods and just sat. I didn't want to think about the game. All I wanted to do was watch the leaves dancing in the sunlight and listen to the water dribbling in the creek.

The lyrics to an old Martha and the Vandellas tune drifted through my mind: *Nowhere to run, nowhere to hide from you.* The night I'd escaped from jail I'd been the happiest guy in the world. Now there I was in the woods, bemoaning life on the run and seeking solace from an insane world built by my own hands.

Finally after about a month or so Grandma came and found me in the woods early one morning.

"Kenny Dale?" she said.

"Yeah Grandma?"

"You got to go boy." Grandma, too, looked like she'd rather be enjoying the fresh morning woods than having this conversation.

I was completely taken off guard. *What? Again?* I thought to myself, but to her I said, "What are you talkin' about Grandma?"

"You got to go."

"I got to go?"

"Yes, son, you've got to leave here today." There was no mistaking her meaning and no sense trying to pretend I didn't. I felt like I was seven years old again, and this time as well, I never even asked her why.

"Alright Grandma, if that's what you want," I replied.

I felt confused, disoriented, like she had just pulled the planet out from under my feet. I walked back to the house, packed up my stuff, got in the car, and drove away. Four dollars was all the money I had, which I spent on filling up on gas. I still had some phony diamond rings and a watch or two, but all I really wanted was to be back out in the woods and left alone.

The next day I made some money hustling in Little Rock, slept in my car, and then headed up North.

Later I found out that Grandma knew the local Sheriff in town. He had heard the FBI was on its way down to Arkansas looking for me. He wanted to help Grandma out, to protect her, so he'd come and told her.

Back on the road I found myself siphoning gas out of cars. That was the lowest of the lows, and I will never forget it. I had to park my car next to someone else's and suck the gas out it. I hated doing that, but I had no choice until I got my hustles going again.

I was still bone weary, depressed, and burnt out from life on the run. Now I understand how it feels to play football, tennis, or basketball while injured, and still the show must go on. I had one other choice and that was to simply stop, but "be still; don't move" was not yet in my toolbox. That type of move requires heart, guts, and the willingness to die.

Back then, all I wanted was to hide, but the game wasn't gonna let me hide. It was forcing me to get right back out there and start playing.

Gorilla Pimps at My Door

Back in Minnesota, I moved in with Ollie and started pimping on her like never before. My car died and I got the first cheap raggedy old thing I could find, a cream-colored 1964 Chevy Impala. The whole ass end was rusted out of that car, and I ain't lying. There was nothing back there. No bumper and you could see clean through to the back of the trunk. Not only that but fumes were coming right up inside the car through a huge hole in the floorboards around the center console. I drove the car home to Ollie.

"Look at my new car!" I announced excitedly. I thought maybe she'd be happy cause it was better than no car at all, plus it only cost $99. She took one look at that car, and all she said was, "Shit."

What I didn't know was that Ollie had been hanging out with another pimp from North Minneapolis, and she'd told him all about me and my shitty car.

Early one Sunday morning I was sitting around in my favorite terrycloth robe, a garish mixture of bright colors in stripes and checks, talking on the phone to India in Kansas City. Suddenly someone was knocking on the door. With the phone still in my hand, I took three big strides across the living room and yanked the door open.

There stood this tall, skinny dude, wearing a green knick-knick shirt, green silk mohair slacks, green lizards, and a pimp perm. Dark ringlets framed a soft, round, baby gorilla face.

"You Slim?" he asked.

"Yeah, what d'ya want?" I barked. I was irritated at having my morning interrupted.

That's when dude number one pulled a shotgun on me, which didn't at all line up in my mind with the baby face. I immediately wished I had looked through the peephole instead of opening the door. Next thing I knew, three other guys appeared with

106

shotguns and pistols drawn.

What the fuck?

"India, baby, I got to call you back," I said evenly, abruptly hanging up on her. As I put the phone in the pocket of my robe of many colors, I never took my eyes off those dudes.

"What the hell's going on here?" I demanded.

Dude number two stepped to the front and announced, "Your woman Ollie has chose."

What the hell is he talking about? I wondered. I had just dropped Ollie off for her shift at the massage parlor. Suddenly it dawned on me that I was dealing with other pimps, so I went into full pimpin' mode. All my instincts went into high gear. I knew there was no room for any slipups or miscues. I had been there before.

Pulling myself up straight, glaring at them, I said, "What the fuck do you mean, she's chose? If this is about the pimpin', you can just put those guns down. We just need to get this here shit straight. If the bitch done chose, she done chose, no problem. But you can put those guns down, man. It ain't that serious."

The dude must've realized the truth in what I was saying cause he lowered his gun.

Suddenly gracious, I opened the door wide and stepped aside. "Come on in," I offered. We walked down into Ollie's upstairs apartment. The whole time I was thinking, *Holy shit, what have I gotten myself into now?* Yet there was somehow a sense of complete confidence that all would be okay.

"Shit man," I said, "I ain't got no cognac or cocaine to offer you, but I've got some water if you want that. Just let me put on some clothes first." I was already heading back to the bedroom where I had a 410 shotgun in the corner.

I calculated my options. They were all sitting there on the couch, guns on laps. I could easily get a drop on them. For a moment I was actually entertaining that thought, but then I realized I'd have to kill them all and I'd be up for multiple homicide. Instead, I threw on some clothes and went back into the living room without the gun.

"Alright, man," I said, "I don't know what's happening here, but give me the rundown."

Ollie's younger sister, Candy, had been talking about Ollie to pimp number one, whose name, coincidentally, was also Slim, Chicago Slim. He'd been asking her that age-old question, "Do you have a sister?"

"Yeah," Candy had replied, "she's got this pimp out of Kansas City, but he don't know what the fuck he's doing."

So the next day when he'd met Ollie, he'd put his game down and started mackin' on her. Ollie went along with it.

"Yes," she'd admitted, "this guy, he calls himself a pimp, but he's got this ratty old car with gas fumes coming up through the floor."

"Sugar," he'd told her, "I'm your man. Now, you go home and let him know you chose. Get rid of him. I'll come over tomorrow and make sure it's all taken care of."

"You be careful now," she warned. "He's crazy you know. That guy's dangerous."

In Ollie's mind, I wasn't wrapped too tight, cause crazy dangerous was the way I'd been treating her. I *wanted* her to feel like that. I *wanted* her to be thinking, *He's gonna kill me if I don't bring the money home.*

"Okay, man, let's let Ollie solve this," I suggested. "Let's go up to the massage parlor right now, call Ollie out, and let her choose."

I knew that there was no way she was gonna choose him right in front of me, simply because he had the game ass backwards. If he were a real mack, he would've come and shown me her choosing money to begin with. There wouldn't have been any gunplay.

We walked out into the perfectly sunny Minnesota morning and got into his Cadillac. Obviously there was no way we were gonna get into my car. I didn't even want them to *see* that piece of junk. We arrived at the massage parlor just as Ollie was coming out.

108

"Hey Ollie," I said calmly. "What's up? Let me see you for a minute." When she saw Chicago Slim standing there right beside me, her eyes just about popped out of her black face like she was being squeezed in half.

"Everything's cool baby," I reassured her. "We're just trying to get something straight here." I wanted to calm her down before she did something stupid. Chicago Slim's eyes shifted back and forth between us, catching every nuance.

"How much money you make today?" I asked her.

"Oh, I got hundred dollars or so." She reached down into her bra and brought it out.

I held my hand out and she gave me the money. I put it in my pocket.

"Everything straight now, man?" I asked Chicago Slim.

"Yeah, Slim, everything's straight man," he agreed, trying to save face.

"Alright, you can go back to work now," I told Ollie. Case closed.

As soon as Ollie got home that night, I went to work setting her straight. I won't go into details here. I'll only say that there were no broken bones or emergency room visits that night. I had read a book called *The Pimp*, by Iceberg Slim, which had taught me a few techniques for maintaining control over a woman both physically and psychologically. With Ollie that night, it wasn't easy. I didn't take any pleasure in punishing her. But at the time I felt it was my only option. It's what I had been taught. A pimp's got to keep his woman in line. The way I figured it, when she'd stepped across that line, she'd taken me with her. Not only me, but she'd put her children in jeopardy as well. We couldn't have no gorilla pimps coming to our door with shotguns. What if the children had been home?

I thought I had to make Ollie believe that I would kill her if she pushed things too far. I had to put the fear of God into her because she wasn't realizing the seriousness of this business we were all in. You had to watch what you did in this game, and you had to watch what you said. These men were gorilla pimps, the kind of pimps known to kidnap a woman on the stroll, throw her in the trunk of their car, and take her to another city. Once there, they'd put her on the track and work her as long as they were able or until she ran away. If Ollie was to be in this game, she had to realize the seriousness of the game, so I had to teach her a lesson. It was all business.

Back then I had very little awareness about what I was really feeling or the forces that drove me. I did not self-reflect. I did not inquire inside myself as to what was really going on. Only looking back from the present can I see the two main forces driving my actions, forces that I have since come to terms with in healing ways.

First of all, I was afraid for my life. Fear and self-preservation were the roots that most all my violent actions sprang from. Fear for my own life, fear for Ollie's life, and fear for her children's lives.

Secondly, I was reacting from a place of pure ego. I felt that my manhood was being challenged. I knew what she'd been thinking, *I'm out here selling pussy for you every day, and this is the best you can do? This is the kind of man you are that only has this piece of shit to drive around in?* I secretly felt like a failure as a man, and the way I reacted to those feelings of failure, fear, and anger was with violence.

From where I'm sitting now, I have come to a place where I can take responsibility for my emotions and my actions. I am finally reaping some benefit from all the work I had to do, and continue to do, to learn more compassionate ways of communicating. Back in those days, however, I mostly communicated with my fists. Violence was such a basic part of the fabric of my conditioning that it was a normal way of living. If a woman made me mad, I threatened her with violence.

A couple of years earlier, Minnesota Bob and I had each had women out on the track. We had been living out of motel rooms, and every night had found us hanging together in either his room or mine.

One night, India came out of the bathroom and casually declared, "I don't think I'm going to work tonight." I didn't ask her why. I didn't ask her if she felt ill. In my mind all I heard was an uppity woman telling me in front of another pimp that she wasn't gonna work the track that night. I had a cigarette lighter in my hand, so I threw it at her. It hit her in the eye so hard that blood shot out all over the place. India cried out and fell back on the floor.

"Bitch!" I yelled. "You're going to go out there and work tonight or you're out of this motherfucking house!"

Grabbing her face to stop the bleeding, terrified and half in shock, India ran out of the room and down the hill. I went back to eating my sardines with Bob. It was no big deal. I had no conscience about my ruthlessness. This was just the way a pimp acted. Every woman I was with, if we were together for any length of time, I ended up hitting.

How had I come to be so disconnected from my heart? I can remember at a very young age approaching people with a wide-open innocence. I wanted to believe that people really cared about me. Over time, the beatings I received as a child caused me to stop feeling myself, to shut down and go numb. Many times as a child, when I'd get hit, I'd either run off or be paralyzed on the spot, no reaction whatsoever. There had been times I'd gone to adults, asking for their support, and then gotten conned in different ways or just plain ignored.

Eventually the inner venom began to emerge. Those who hurt me I began to wish dead. As life progressed—the courts, the attorneys, the jails, the insane guards and inmates—all of it contributed to my disconnectedness. I became unmoved by the pain of others and numb to my own. I could watch other inmates being beaten and then look away, not feeling much of anything either way. What I mostly thought was *better him than me*.

Not feeling things came in handy in the game. How else could I send a woman out to the streets each night, possibly even to her death? I couldn't afford to feel for all the tellers who might lose their jobs cashing my many thousands in bad checks. In my fantasies of walking into a bank to rob it, with armed guards standing around and a possible unknown hero or two in the mix, I knew there was no way could I entertain fearful thoughts. Was I ever concerned about the damage cocaine, alcohol, and cigarettes were doing to my body? No. I was totally disconnected from that. The way I saw it, they were the only things keeping me half sane.

I was mummified, wrapped tight in a bundle of repressed pain. If I wanted to stay in the game, I knew I had to keep it wrapped. I was dead to myself, and the crazy thing is that I thought I was totally alive. I acted like I was alive. I looked as if I were having a great time. I thought it was pretty cool the way I could just roll with the punches, not sweat the small stuff. Every once in a while a pocket of pain would come to the surface, but mostly that showed up as feeling sorry for myself because I was in jail again.

Above the Radar

Having gorilla pimps arrive at my door with shotguns had been a pivotal event. I realized I had to come out from under the radar. I was tired of living like a chili pimp, tired of nickel and diming. It would be just fine by me if I never ate another sardine, and I sure didn't want people talking about the state of my car. I couldn't keep living the way I had been, hoping that my woman would bring back a hundred or two and then try to parlay that into a fortune. That just wasn't gonna happen.

Besides, as far as I was concerned, I never made 100% bona fide pimp anyway. Plus I already had a good money hustle. The game was where I flourished. I decided to take my pimping skills and incorporate them into my check game and my sneak thieving. It was time to go out there and start making some real money again. I was well aware of the risk, but I just couldn't live at that level anymore. As soon as I made the decision, everything shifted. Women came to me, fame came back to me, and eventually, of course, the police came for me.

Whenever I'd catch a woman I'd say, "Listen, I ain't gonna put you on the track. You don't have to sell your pussy. You give your pussy only to me." Then I'd paint an entirely different picture, an elaborate lie about how we were gonna get ourselves a nice house, a nice car, a whole different life.

"How we gonna do that?" she'd ask.

"Well, we're gonna do it real fast. I just want you to cash these checks for me. It's real easy. I'll show you how." This was a cleaner and more attractive hustle for her because most women didn't want to be on the track. They would much rather dress up in nice clothes, go into a bank and get thousands of dollars, and then go to the best hotels, eat the best meals, and get their hair and nails done. The promise of having a nice house, and the possibility of that happening in a matter of days? Well shit yes.

What she didn't know was that I was gonna "airplane" her.

By the time a woman had been working with me for a whole week, and she had made me thousands and thousands of dollars cashing checks, I would already be scheming on how I was gonna separate myself from her. I'd be telling her how much I loved her, how we were gonna stay to stay together from then on, but I'd be mackin' her the whole time.

This was just the business. I knew that eventually she was gonna get busted and tell everything. So when Saturday would roll around, and we'd done cashing checks for the week, I'd pull up in front of a hotel and say, "Okay darlin', you go on up and get us a nice room. I'm just gonna go park the car and I'll be up in a minute." I'd separate her luggage out, give her enough money to eat and live in the hotel for a week, or to catch a plane or a bus, and then I'd take off.

To me it felt like a way of compassion. The only way to protect either of us from getting popped was to work her for a week and then never see her again.

Within a matter of weeks I was able to get a new car, a black, Oldsmobile Regency with a black interior and a sunroof. No longer did I have a raggedy old car! I was flying high above the radar again.

Late one night, as Ollie and I were driving across the Minneapolis bridge spanning the Northern Mississippi, suddenly Coast-to-Coast's Cadillac came zooming up in the rearview mirror within inches of my tail. Honking at me to pull over, he passed us and then cut sharply in front, forcing us to the side of the bridge. We met in front of my car, two dark silhouettes on a misty October night, diamond rings flickering in the car's headlamps.

I knew trouble was in the air 'cause my mind and body were already tripping with the adrenalin. "What's up, baby?" I asked.

"Slim, you can't go back to your hotel, man. The FBI are all over the place."

"Shit, for real?" Yet when I looked into Coast's bloodshot eyes, I knew it was true.

114

"Yeah, man, Tony and I were just driving over to your place to cop some money orders from you. The FBI's got the place staked out and they're flashing your picture around!"

I felt the weight of another prison sentence begin its crushing descent through my belly.

"I'll be seeing you man," I said. "I love you."

He knew I meant that we might never see each other again. Back in the car, I sped away. We had to leave Minnesota immediately, yet I was already running out of money.

"We can't go home," I told Ollie, "not even to get our clothes or to see your kids," who were at her mother's. "We got to go just as we are with nothing on our backs. You ready?"

"Yes, baby, I'll go with you," Ollie agreed, her eyes steady on mine. "I always do." Ollie's eyes were filled with the usual innocence, but also a sparkle of excitement for that edge of danger and the unknown my life always seemed to be wrapped around. Since the day that the gorilla pimps had come to our door, Ollie had been completely loyal in every way.

The FBI caught up with us that very night at a motel in Des Moines, and I was arrested for multiple counts of forgery, robbery, and escape. They hauled me down to the Des Moines county jail. After four long years as a fugitive from the law, there I was again, sitting in a county jail. I'd left Ollie with the car, as well as my diamond rings and all the money I could give her.

Each time I knew without a doubt that I'd been caught, I would plead with the cops, plead with the detectives, plead with the judges, to let me off or to reduce my time. Each time I'd have to figure out how I was going to come up with the bond, begging my friends and family to help me out of my troubles once again. I'd do everything I could to make a deal with whomever was involved, whether it was the arresting cop or the detective doing the interviewing. There was always the possibility I might have information they wanted. That's where snitching came into the game, which was the only real leverage you ever had with the cops. If I'd been a junkie I would've had no problem making a

115

deal right then and there, promising that if they let me out, I'd give them the bigger fish. My problem was that I never really had any bargaining power. As far as they were concerned, I *was* the big fish. I was the one they wanted. It didn't matter anyway. I never felt desperate enough to want to rat anyone out, because back in the day I knew I could be selling my life away.

After a lot of finagling, I managed to get most of the check charges dropped. The escape charge also got dropped because by an unbelievable stroke of luck, I'd come across a newspaper article about a case in Atlanta, Georgia. The caption had read, "Young Man Escapes Jail in Fear of Losing His Life. High Court Upholds Escape." The court had deemed that if someone escaped from jail in fear for his or her life, then the escape was justifiable, and the person could not be charged for it.

I had given the article to my attorney who had managed to convince the judge that I'd been certain someone was gonna kill me there. In the end my time was reduced to two years, which I served at the penitentiary in Sioux Falls South Dakota, population barely five hundred men.

During that time, I knew this one little white guy who was doing everything he possibly could to get out and be with his wife. Seemed like every time I walked by his cell it was full of guys helping him plot how he could get out sooner. He'd heard his wife was with another man, and he wanted out as quick as possible to try and get her back.

He succeeded in getting out and getting his wife back, but within months he'd messed up and was right back in. This time she wrote him a Dear John letter. He was completely undone.

One night, in the middle of the night, I was walking down the hall to the communal restroom, when I noticed the door to his cell open and blood pooled up all over the floor. He'd cut his wrists, or as they say, "gone out sideways."

Damn, I thought to myself, *it ain't that serious. What made him go and kill himself like that?* I couldn't understand it. Over the years in prison I had heard stories of suicide on a regular basis.

Men hung themselves. Men maimed themselves. Men overdosed on drugs. They couldn't hold up under the pressures of prison life. If a man focused too much on the opposing realities of his prison life and his family's life on the outside, it would drive him to madness. Little did I know that in just a few short years, I'd be attempting the very same thing.

Losing It

Released again in 1980, I made my way back to Minneapolis and began driving the familiar neighborhoods, looking for my old crew. Right off the bat there was Ollie, walking down the street. It was good to see her.

"Where you staying?" I asked. "Who you with?"

"Nobody," she said, flashing me that big smile that said it all. Immediately we were hooked up again.

I'd been gone only two years, and it was already a whole new game on the streets. Coast-to-Coast and Minnesota Bob invited me over to their house to smoke some cocaine and get high. When I'd last left for prison, cocaine was being snorted, shot up, or smoked in cigarettes. When I'd gotten out, freebase cocaine was all the rage. The high, which was extreme, hit the brain within five seconds and lasted five to ten minutes. By the end of those few minutes, all you wanted was another hit.

"Here, Kenny, smoke some more," Coast-to-Coast offered, shoving a glass pipe in my face. I sucked on the bong, took a big hit, and then announced, "I'm going down to the store to get some cigarettes."

I overheard Coast-to-Coast whispering to Bob, "Don't let him out of the house."

"What do you mean don't let me out of the house?" I demanded. "I'm all right man. I'm cool." But they still got me to stay.

I hadn't realized it yet, but they were intentionally hooking me on the drug in order to get me on their crew again. These cats had gotten hooked on the shit out in Frisco and then brought it back to St Paul. They had become straight-up canines, and getting a money dog like me hooked was right out of the pimpin' handbook. Freebasing burns up money so fast you've got to have your own money tree, and here it was in the form of Slim, straight out of the joint and dumber than shit to this technology of freebase cocaine. It hadn't crossed my mind that I might get hooked. I was just enjoying the high. This was 1980, the same year that Richard Prior caught himself on fire freebasing cocaine.

Hanging out smoking cocaine every day was the beginning of my new life back in Minneapolis. Coast-to-Coast and I went over some scenarios on how to steal money orders, find women to cash them, then put them to work. For the next eighteen months I traveled around the Midwest from North Dakota to Arkansas to Kentucky to Colorado, cashing phony checks or money orders and making 5,000-10,000 dollars a day. We didn't even know how much money we were making. Nobody was counting it. Day after day, we just made more money and smoked more cocaine. I bought myself a new Cadillac.

After a day of raking it in, I'd go down and buy a pair of hundred-dollar boots, a brand new suit, a hat, and some gloves. Then I'd go straight to the dope house, and lay me down a thousand dollars. "Let me know when that runs out," I'd say. I wouldn't leave that kitchen until the cocaine was gone, even if it took two days. I had the capacity to drink Cognac for days, smoke cocaine for hours on end, and never pass out. I was already on violation. I knew I would eventually be going back to the penitentiary, so I just did whatever I felt like doing. I was making so much money and having so much fun, I didn't care. I was back on the run.

I had been living so long with something hanging over my head that I'd finally gotten comfortable with my life being like that. Somewhere inside I knew I was deeply *un*comfortable, but that awareness didn't have a chance of making its way up through all the drugs and alcohol and into my consciousness.

One night, I suddenly got this suspicion that Ollie was lovers with another woman. In a rage, I picked the whole bed up, Ollie in it, and tossed her in a tumbling heap onto the floor.

"What the hell's wrong with you?" she screamed, wide-eyed with surprise and fear.

"You're sleeping with that bitch!" I accused, jabbing my finger at her.

"You're a crazy man! I don't know what you're talking about!"

"That bitch, that dancer who brought you home last night! You're fucking her!"

"I just needed a ride home, and you weren't around!"

Shit, I thought, *I'm losing it. I am totally flipping out.*

I knew I was losing it. I was smoked out, hearing things that weren't there and imagining things that weren't real. Besides the cocaine, I'd also been drinking Cognac all day, every day.

I'd heard stories about this kind of thing. Our longtime friend Bowlegs had been out of the joint for a few months and was selling his weight in coke on a regular basis. He was also his own best customer. One day while smoking he'd thought he'd seen the police pull up outside his house, and he'd taken off running. Problem was he'd run straight through a plate glass door. He'd cut himself so bad that while he was running down the street away from his home he'd bled to death. Bowlegs had been making money hand over fist and his getting taken out of the game like that was a real shock to everybody. I always imagined shit like that happening to somebody else, never to me. Now I was wondering if I could trust my own mind.

I left Ollie and hit the road again, this time with a woman named Julie, cashing money orders in Pocatello, Boise, and all over Idaho. I was trying to outrun my addiction, but it just kept chasing me. A lot of addicts think that changing locations is the solution to their addiction, when really it's the inner landscape that needs to change.

Julie got pregnant, said she wanted to have our baby, and went back to Minnesota. After I'd left her, Ollie had cut her wrists and nearly died. I had gone back and put her on a bus to go be with her people in Minnesota.

How did I feel about Julie being pregnant or the fact that Ollie had tried to kill herself? Nothing at all. I was a desperate criminal on the run, hooked on cocaine and alcohol and disconnected from my heart. Eventually I landed in Denver in 1982, and that's when I met Clara.

120

Clara was a businesswoman. She had just opened Dahlia's, a seafood restaurant in the black section of Denver. Clara was a good woman, a square woman, and I respected her. I started pitching in and helping her manage the restaurant. Before long, I moved in with her.

Clara was beautiful, with long, softly curled dark hair and a wide welcoming smile. She had ample hips, small, perfect breasts, and a way of making me feel like I was the most important person in the world.

One night about eight, when I was in the alley behind the restaurant pouring grease into a trash container, I overheard Clara mention my name to Rasheed, our fry cook. Whatever she'd said had Rasheed laughing.

Why are they laughing at me? I wondered. At the time I had no awareness of the dark side of drug addiction and how past emotional demons can appear unbidden any time an addict takes a hit of something. In my own warped, alcoholic, cocaine-induced stupor, I thought they were making fun of me, demeaning me.

My mind raced back to when I was in school and this one kid, Emerson, drew a caricature of me. He'd made drawings of all us kids, but mine had this enormous oblong head, front to back, like a big watermelon stuck sideways on my neck. Huge African lips protruded out over a little bitty body. He had titled that picture "Head" and left it around the classroom for everyone to see. Of course they'd all started calling me Head, and ever since then I'd felt embarrassed by the shape of my head.

Plus I'd always believed I was too black, "African" black, which was not the color you wanted to be or the way you wanted to be labeled. African was not cool. You didn't want big African lips, and you didn't want a big African nose. The light-skinned men with the perfect hair were the ones who got the girls. Blue black was the worst, and I was on the darker end of the spectrum, more like dark chocolate.

Once while looking through a magazine I'd come across this bleaching cream. I secretly ordered it and applied it all over my face and hands at night so that no one would know. The next morning I'd woken up with light-colored blotches all over my face.

These memories only fueled my fury. I ran right over to Clara and punched her in the mouth. I hit her so hard her gums split and pulled away from her teeth. Then I turned around and walked out.

Rasheed rushed her to the hospital. When she finally came back around that night, she asked me, "What the fuck's wrong with you Slim? What did I do to make you so mad?"

"You were talking down about me to Rasheed," I said. I was completely convinced that they had been making fun of the way I ran the cash register. Clara's women friends were always telling her, "Man, you got to take him off that cash register. He don't know what the fuck he's doing." They were right, of course, I didn't. I had an altogether different kind of relationship with that cash register.

"I was complimenting you for how hard you were working!" she yelled. Somehow, in my own sick, drug-addicted mind, I had misunderstood. She was devastated that I had hit her for no real reason whatsoever.

I don't know how or why she did it, but Clara forgave me. She had already fallen deeply in love with me. Truth was I was too insecure at the time to receive the love of a woman like Clara.

After things with Clara and the restaurant eventually calmed down, I started hanging out at the nightclubs again and getting some hustles together on the side. That's when I met Dad, an old convict out of St. Louis.

Freebase Blues

"Hey, Dad, what's going on?" I asked.

"Nothin', man, I'm just sitting around the house."

"I'll come by, swoop you up, and we'll go shopping, alright?"

"Cool man, I'll be waiting."

It was a beautiful but chilly spring morning in 1983, and I'd just woken up in bed. First thing I'd done was to reach for the phone and call my buddy Dad. Outside my window, I could see the snow-covered Rocky Mountains backlit by a brilliant blue Colorado sky. Icicles hung from the eaves and the rainbow-colored drops forming along their tips glistened in the sunlight like prisms.

Clara was already up and moving around the house, getting ready to go to work at the restaurant. I didn't especially want to talk to her. I had some money, so I was thinking of not going to the restaurant that day. I felt like going shopping instead and getting me another pair of snakeskin shoes. I loved skins. First, however, I wanted a hit of cocaine and some cognac. I was drinking a lot those days, and Clara was always accusing me of being an alcoholic, so I had to wait until she left the house.

I went downstairs and told her I'd come by the restaurant later on. I could see on her face that she was worried about me. She was concerned about my drinking. She was concerned about my street life. She was concerned about the people I was hanging out with. She never really cared for any of them, Dad included. She didn't like Smokin' Bobby either. Whoever took up my time was bad for her business because it meant I wasn't around to help her.

When Clara finally left the house, I put on Ray Parker Jr's *A Woman Needs Love*, my favorite song at the time, and poured a nice glass of cognac, straight, no chase. Swirling it around in the glass, I took a big whiff and then let it fill my mouth. Warm sensations flooded my body. Next, I reached for the pipe, smoked a little cocaine, and started getting dressed. Now that I had me a nice buzz going, I was ready to coast through my day. Hitting the streets in my Cadillac, listening to The Dazz Band's *Let it Whip*, I was feeling just fine.

I picked Daddy up at his studio apartment down on 16th and Clarkson. He was already half drunk when he got in the car. Daddy loved his gin. We were drinking buddies, Dad and I, and we drank together just about every day.

That day, we went cruising downtown to my favorite shoe store where I bought some tan lizards. "Skins" we called them, and these looked great with the suit I was wearing that day, a three-piece, silver-grey, custom cut, silk and mohair blend. Now I was feeling even higher, hanging out with Daddy in my new skins.

We hit a hamburger joint for breakfast, and then headed down to the New Yorker on Colfax and York, a bar on the strip where all the players hung out in the daytime. We sat around the bar drinking, talking, and playing pool. Nighttime at the clubs was when we did all our business, and I don't mean playing tennis or racket ball. Our favorite club for partying at night was the Jet Set. That's where we talked about our women and hung out with other players.

I bought myself some cognac and kicked back. The drunker I got, the more I wanted a hit of coke. My main focus in life had become smoking as much cocaine and drinking as much cognac as possible.

Now Daddy, he didn't do cocaine, so if I wanted a hit I was gonna have to divorce myself from Dad and go find my man Brown, either him or Bobby and his woman Smokey. Besides, I'd already been hanging out with Dad all day long and I was getting tired of him.

I dropped Daddy off at his house, but then I realized I hadn't eaten since morning and it was already five o'clock. I headed over to Dahlia's Restaurant and Clara.

Barreling in through the back door, I ran smack into Clara who was sitting on a stool in the kitchen, talking with the new cook she'd just hired. I said hello to everybody. They were all wearing their hairnets. Clara told me to put mine on too because there were customers around. I had just gotten my hair straightened. It was about five inches long, and I looked like James Brown in a hairnet.

From the time I was a young boy, I would occasionally get my hair straightened and processed with Ultra Wave. Getting your hair to look as much as possible like a white man's was the goal. That's what was cool. All my sisters did it too. The greasy smell of burning hair was common in our house, usually on Saturday nights when my sisters were getting ready for Sunday church. That shit burnt the living daylights out of your scalp, but you had to leave it on 'til your head was on fire and your hair was limp. If your scalp wasn't burning, you knew your hair wasn't straightening.

At that time in Denver, Jheri Curls was the hairdo to have. First you'd straighten the hair, then perm it into soft, thick curls. You might think the players got their hair and dress style from the entertainers of the time, but it was actually the other way around.

I was hungry, but first on my agenda was to head to the refrigerator in the back where I'd hidden my little bottle of cognac. After taking a nice long pull, I realized the restaurant was not where I wanted to be. That square lifestyle was boring. Cooking fish and taking customer's orders was not what I wanted to be doing. Some days I enjoyed it, but on that day I wanted nothing to do with it. Clara was always happy to have me around, but it was never enough to keep me satisfied for long. I gave her a kiss on the cheek and told her I'd be back in a minute.

On my way out the back, I grabbed my cognac from the refrigerator. I was suddenly in such a hurry to get to Brown's house that I started pushing people out of my way. Brown was my supplier of cocaine. I was on a mission. I got in my car and sped the four blocks to his house. It was already dark when Brown opened the door.

"Give me a gram," I demanded without even saying hello. I wasn't interested in small talk. The tension inside was really building now. I'd been waiting all day to smoke.

Brown handed me a little waxed-paper package. I opened it and took in the nice "mellow yellow" color and the sweet smell. That little packet was like gold. I didn't want to keep it in my hand where the cocaine might get hot and melt, so I put it carefully into my coat pocket. Brown wouldn't allow you to smoke at his house; you had to leave right after you scored. I couldn't wait to get back out the door.

"You're my man, Brown. I love you like my brother," I told him. Then I took off like a heat-seeking missile headed for the pipe over at Bobby's house.

Back in the car I rushed over to Bobby and Smokey's. The three of us loved to smoke together and "freak," which was what we called having sex together. I was hooked on the atmosphere the three of us created. Bobby and I weren't into each other; we just liked watching each other with Smokey.

The door was always open at Bobby's. Taking the front steps three at a time, I rushed right in without knocking.

"What's up Bobby? How you doin' man?" He could tell from the big grin on my face that I had something for us. By then my body was so keyed up to take that first hit I was all over the room, pacing back and forth. Bobby, in contrast, was in his usual mode of relaxation. Bobby was small-bodied, short and caramel colored. His hair was long and wavy like Jesus Christ, except for the Afro Sheen massaged all through it.

"What's you got Slim?" Bobby drawled. He always talked nice and slow, like a philosopher, a wise man reflecting on the moment that was unfolding before him. He was always telling me, "Slim, man, you got to slow down, man. You're moving kind of fast, man. You want to stay out here as long as you can, man, and the way you're moving, you're not gonna be out here long."

"I just got some from our man Brown!" I cried triumphantly. That got a rise out him. I took the coke out of my pocket and we bent over our package like two kids at Christmas.

Bobby examined the coke and smelled it like the true cocaine connoisseur he was. I always let Bobby cook my dope. He knew how to cook it up and "bring it all back" so that nothing was wasted. First, he'd take a heat-tempered test tube and drop a few small rocks of cocaine into it along with a little water and some baking soda. Then he'd hold the mixture over the flame of the cook-stove, gently shaking until it was reduced to oil. The truly exciting part of the process, the part that lit a fire of craving in my blood, was watching the mixture begin to take on shape until it was just one big rock of pure cocaine. The point of this whole process was to cook off the cut without losing the cocaine. Bobby was like a professional chemist and he was never greedy. He'd always give you your lion's share.

Bobby, Smokey, and I did our thing, smoking and freaking together until around midnight. When the coke was finished, I ran back over to Brown's and got some more. By now we were just "tweaking," smoking for the sake of smoking. The more you smoked, the less each new hit got you high. At three in the morning, we were finished again. We sat at the table looking at each other. I wanted more, they wanted more, but it was gone.

"I'm going home," I said, and I meant it. I really thought I was on my way home. Driving down the street, I realized that I'd be passing by Brown's house again. The thought flashed through my mind that maybe he would give me some on credit. My addiction was totally in control of the moment. I knocked on Brown's door, waking him up.

"What's up, man?" he asked, letting me through the door. "What do you want? It's three o'clock in the fucking morning, man."

"I gotta have me one more hit man, and I've gotta have it on credit."

"Go get some cognac, man," he said.

"That ain't gonna do it Brown. I need me one more hit. I'm not finished yet, man."

127

"I can't do that, Slim." He was dead serious. "I love you man, but go home now. Go to bed. We'll talk about it tomorrow."

"Brown, buddy, what's goin' on?" I was shocked. Brown had never turned me away before.

"You gotta be through with that, man."

"Bro, I know what you're saying man, but right now I got to have me one more hit," I pleaded.

"I can't do it Slim."

"Tell you what, Brown, take my shoes. You can have these nice new skins," and I started taking off my shoes and handing them to Brown. He shoved the shoes back at me.

"Slim, man. Get the fuck out of here. I don't want your shoes."

"I don't give a fuck!" I was yelling now. "Just give me some blow! I'm good for it; you know I am. Come to my restaurant tomorrow and pick up the money." For some time I'd been dipping into the cash register to pay for my addiction.

"Slim, listen, I love you man. I respect you too much. Anybody else I'd give it to, but I don't like where you're going with this. Get out of here. Go home, man. This ain't the Slim I know. Go home."

He might as well have slammed me with a two-by-four. The reality of his refusal started to sink in. Embarrassment seared through my throat and chest. I was suddenly deeply ashamed for Brown to see me like this.

The moment he'd said, "This ain't you Slim," I'd known it was true. I'd suddenly woken up out of my drug-induced craze and realized, *He's right, Kenny, this ain't you. What's going on here?*

Without another word, I turned and headed home like a dog whipped for eating something rotten. For him to see me like that, someone I respected and admired, weighed on my soul. He knew that this crazed drug addict wasn't the real Kenny, and that's exactly why I had always loved and respected Brown. He had always seen me, the real me, in a higher light than I saw myself. He trusted me, but by that time in my life, I'd lost all trust in myself and all self-respect. I drove to the Seven Eleven, got me a beer, and then drove home.

What had started as a typical day in the life of Kenny, doing nothing but searching for one pleasurable experience after another, had ended in a soul-shattering moment of shame and embarrassment. I didn't really understand the ramifications, but I knew something big had happened.

Standing on Brown's doorstep in my socks in the middle of the night, begging for more drugs, had caused me to wake up to the price that drug addiction was having on my spirit.

I had never in my life stooped so low for anyone or anything. The force that had been driving me to get one more high, one more hit, was trying to fill some hole that hadn't been filled by all the other hits.

What was this hole that could not be filled? Day after day my life was adding up to nothing, an empty experience of always wanting more and never being satisfied. I felt hollow, alone in an empty canyon, as if someone could throw a coin into my heart and I'd never hear it hit a thing. What was it I was really looking for in this late night search for the ever-elusive "hit"? Whatever it was, I knew that it would not be found in a folded piece of golden paper.

Trapped

Police surrounded the entire apartment complex. Agents were everywhere, guns drawn. One was stationed right outside my door; the rest crouched behind their vehicles in the parking lot. Another cop was in a golf cart, eyeing our apartment, which stood adjacent to a golf course.

Christ, I'm trapped! I realized. *How in the hell am I gonna get out of this?* Within seconds I felt the panic start to overtake my mind.

With a jerk I woke up on the living room couch where I'd lain down for a nap. Cold sweat covered my body. The dream had been so real, so incredibly vivid. It had let know without a doubt that it was time to run again.

Immediately I thought of Little Sister, whom I'd met down at the Jet Set one night. She seemed like a potential candidate to take on the road. I called her up and asked if she wanted to go to Seattle with me. She agreed and right away I started setting everything up. It seemed only natural to take off and set up somewhere else with a new name and a new woman. My mind was on automatic; I was simply a player who had to do whatever it took to stay free and one step ahead of those who were chasing me. Throughout my life, the authorities had changed, but there had always been *something* chasing me.

I knew I had to be honest with Clara. It was hard, but I sat her down in a booth at Dahlia's and told her my plans. I described the dream and said that I knew the FBI was coming for me. I was sure of it.

"Clara," I said evenly, looking into her startled eyes. Already she could feel that something life-changing was about to happen, so I continued as gently as I could.

"Deep in my soul, I know I need to change my name again and take off."

Her beautiful brown eyes stared into mine. They were filled

with love, concern, and a million unanswered questions. "What makes you think you have to run, baby? Please don't go."

"Clara, if I stay and get caught, I could get a lot of time. I can't afford to stop now. I've got to go."

"Stay," she pleaded, "and we'll fight this together."

"You don't understand Clara. I've got a parole violation, and I'm facing a lot of check charges." No one knew better than me how limited my options were.

"Stay here," she begged. "I'll stand by you no matter what!" She looked so strong and fierce, so absolutely sincere. I knew Clara could see the real Kenny just like Brown could. She always had.

"Clara, honey, you don't understand. I can't do the time even if you do stand by me. I've been through this too many times. I can't go back to prison."

"Please don't run!" she begged. "When you get back out, I'll be there to support and help you."

Over the next few days Clara kept up her pleading, but I was determined. I had set it up with my new catch to pick her up on Monday morning, just two days away.

Everything was cool throughout the weekend. Clara left the apartment on Sunday to go take care of some business. I stayed, ironed my clothes, packed, and got ready to go.

A small, thin voice had started up inside me the day before. Dismayed, I had kept trying to pay it no mind. Yet damn it, there it was again! That voice was getting louder and louder. It was growing stronger. *Stay Kenny; don't run*, it kept saying.

I hadn't realized it at the time, but Clara's words had penetrated deep into my soul. I was so tired of running. I was tired of the game, and I was especially tired of the cocaine addiction I couldn't seem to shake. Somewhere inside I felt like I was truly ready to change my life.

I trusted Clara. For once, her promise that she'd stand by me meant more to me than taking off with another new young girl and starting life on the run all over again. Until Clara had pleaded with me, "don't run" was something I had never seriously considered. "Clean your life up baby. Do the right thing," she'd said. She had planted a seed of possibility inside me that maybe I really could change my life.

The whole situation reminded me of one my favorite cowboy movies where the outlaw knows he has to leave, yet he's finally met someone who touches that sacred space in his heart, and so he listens to her.

I *knew* the dream was real. I *knew* if I stayed, I was going to be surrounded and caught. Yet something inside me was saying, *Kenny, what if you don't run this time? What if you go ahead and face this, just finish it up?* I realized I really *did* want to change more deeply than I ever had before. I wanted out of the game. Maybe facing everything and getting it over with would be my ticket out.

Just as I was coming to the conclusion I wasn't going to run, the phone rang. When I answered it, a deep male voice said, "Go look out your window Johnson." As soon as he saw me peeking through the curtains, he went into full arrest mode. "Johnson, it's the FBI. We want to talk to you. Open your door, and walk out unarmed."

In a split second I resigned myself. I'd known for days it was coming, and now here it was. In some weird way I was even okay with it. "Alright, man," I agreed, "I'm coming out," and I opened the door and walked out.

Right there in the middle of the parking lot, watching this whole thing come down, was the uniformed security guard from our apartment complex, sitting in a golf cart. *Fuck,* I thought. *Here it is. Here's my dream.* They arrested me and took me down to the jail.

In the many years to come, whatever prison I was to be in, Clara would come to visit me. She stood by her word. She always made sure I had money on the prison books. I still have a whole suitcase of pictures of Clara and me taken while I was in prison. Later on, when I would fight my case and take it all the way to the Supreme Court, she would be right there beside me, helping in every way she could.

Forty Years

Transportation of stolen securities is what they had me on. Whenever a so-called "instrument" is transported across state lines, whether that instrument is stolen goods or a prostitute transported for the purpose of prostitution, it is a federal offense.

It was true, of course. I *had* taken prostitutes over state lines, but they couldn't prove that particular case. What they *could* prove was that I had sent women into banks cashing checks in one state, which drew funds from banks in other states. In this way instruments had crossed state lines through the mail or even electronically, which was still a federal offense. I was told I had fourteen counts against me at ten years apiece, plus five years for conspiracy, totaling one hundred forty-five years, plus eight more for the Missouri parole violation.

The plea bargain agreement my lawyer put together with the prosecuting attorney was that they would drop all the other charges if I would plead guilty to four counts, so I went before the judge and pleaded guilty to those four. I was guessing I'd be looking at maybe seven years. My public defender led me to believe that he had it all wrapped up, even though all along the prosecuting attorney had said he couldn't make any promises as to how much time I would get. In the end it was up to the judge.

That night I had a very dark and heavy dream in which the prosecuting attorney told me that I'd be getting an indefinite amount of time. I woke up feeling like I was dragging an extra two hundred pounds around. I have always paid attention to the energy of my dreams. I've come to realize that it's the *energy* of the dream that holds the real information. The energy of this dream was not good at all, no way, no how.

Over the years I've done my best to write my dreams down, feeling that "dreams unopened are like letters never read." All dreams, both positive and negative, are precious gems to be honored, respected, and interpreted correctly. They are messages from the true teacher and master, creation itself. Since all things are one, there can be only one dreamer; and all characters in the dream, both human and animal, are different aspects of myself, trying to get my attention.

Two days later, I was back before the judge pleading guilty to what I had been led to believe was only four counts.

"Your honor," I said, "I know what I am pleading guilty to. No one has made me any promises, but I would like you to take into consideration that I am a servant of Allah, and all I want is to serve my God." (In the short time I'd been back in jail, I had adopted Islam, mostly because Clara had sent me a Qur'an.)

"Well, young man," the judge said, "I'm going to give you plenty of time to find your God. I'm sentencing you to ten years on count one, ten years on count three, and ten years on count seven, to be run consecutively with a total of ten years for counts two, four, eight, and ten.

"You are dismissed," he said solemnly. Then he banged his mallet three times on the judge's bench, got up, and walked out.

My mind exploded. *What the hell just happened? Did he just say forty years?* A firestorm of confusion burst inside me. My lawyer, the prosecuting attorney, and the stenographer were all looking at each other stunned. Even the marshals were shaking their heads. Now the judge had vaporized, the bench was empty, and I'd just gotten sentenced to forty years! No way could I comprehend that much time.

PART 4

Belly of the Beast

Just as Jonah was in the belly of the huge fish...
so would the Son of Man be in the heart of the earth...

—Matthew 12:40

Death Dream

"Guard, guard, guard!" I screamed. It was three in the morning at the Denver jail, and I'd just awakened from a terrifying dream.

"Guard! Let me out! Now!" I panicked, kicking and shaking the bars of my cell. I had to get out.

The guard ran up from the level below, the beam of his flashlight dancing crazily over the walls until eventually it landed straight in my face.

"What the hell's going on, Johnson?" he demanded, lines of concern etched across his forehead. Sometimes you have the good fortune of getting assigned to a guard who is truly in your corner. When it happened, it was nothing short of amazing grace. This guy was one of them, and it couldn't have been a better moment to have that kind of luck.

"Get me out of here!" I yelled repeatedly. "I've got to call my mother! I've got to talk to my mother, *now"!* I was freaking out and waking the whole jail up in the process.

"Alright, Johnson. Alright, son. We'll get you to the phone. Relax, son. Just calm down now," he tried to soothe.

Finally he got the door open to my cell and escorted me downstairs to the phone. The second Momma answered, I started in pleading with her. I didn't even say hello.

"Momma, I want out of this jail. I can't do this. I've got to get out of here. Momma, you've got to help me now."

"What's wrong, boy?"

"They just gave me forty years, Momma. Forty years! I can't do that much time. I'm only thirty-two years old. I'll be seventy-two when I get out!"

My mother, true to her usual ways, simply said, "Son, there's nothing I can do to help. You know I don't have the money to get you out of jail. Even if I had the money, there's nothing I could do about it. You done messed up again, son. You're gonna be okay. The Lord's gonna take care of you. Just keep praying on it."

"But Momma, I need you," I continued to beg. "I can't do this much time."

Tears ran down my face, mixing with the snot from my nose. I had never, ever, cried in front of a guard or even in front of another inmate. I had never broken down like this before, but facing that much time felt unbearable. A chilling dread gripped my heart. I was certain I was gonna die in prison. The dream I'd just woken up from had clearly shown me that.

"Momma," I pleaded, "I swear before you and God that I'll change my ways. I'll turn it all around. Please just help me get out of here!"

"I'll pray for you, son," was all she finally said. Once again I felt like she wasn't gonna be there for me. Her words, "Nothing I can do . . ." echoed in the empty chambers of my heart. She hadn't even offered to call an attorney.

"All right, Momma," I finally said. I hung up the phone feeling utterly abandoned, helpless, and filled with regret. I trudged back to my cell where I lay on my bunk the rest of the morning.

How did I get into this mess? I kept thinking. *Why did I get so much time? How can I get out of it?* The same useless thoughts kept recycling through my mind. I hadn't really thought my mother could help. I just needed to talk to her. I hadn't even planned on calling her. It had just been a spontaneous reaction to waking up from a nightmare.

In the dream I had been hovering over my body and looking down at it. It had looked so lifeless, my face and lips all slack. I believed I was looking at my dead body.

Years later, when I was to be incarcerated at Talladega, Alabama, I would come to learn that we all possess a second, more subtle form of the physical body called the astral body. The astral body is purely energetic, and it can be projected away from the physical body. I would become obsessed with this phenomenon called astral projection, and eventually I'd get pretty good at it. Not until then, however, would I come to understand that my "dream" that night had been a classic case of astral projection. Of course my body had looked dead because my spirit had momentarily vacated the premises. The dream had been not only terrifying; it had seemed a prophetic prediction of my certain, imminent death.

Two of Me

During every prison sentence I ever endured, at some point I'd get "reformed," even if just for a short while. I'd start reaching for my Bible or any other spiritual text I could get my hands on in the hopes of finding some way to escape my situation. All of that activity was driven by a despair so strong and so hopeless it would well up inside me until I felt trapped like an animal in a cage.

"Lord, please just get me out of this!" I'd pray. "Lord, I swear, if you get me out of this one, I won't do it again." I'd use my Bible, my books, whatever religion I could find to wash myself clean of my sins, then as soon as I was out, I'd get busy getting dirty again. I'd immediately forget the pain I had experienced and leave my religion at the gate. Once back in prison, it would start all over again. "Lord, I know you know my heart. I know I messed up again, but will you get me out just *one more time?*"

That was the cycle. That was the madness. That was the self-sabotage. I was always finding these little pieces of truth in prison, and then throwing it all away as soon as I got out. Somehow I had always been praying myself into a prison sentence that would eventually make or break me, and that time had finally arrived.

If ever I cried in prison, my tears were internal, and I assumed most of the guys on the inside were doing the same. A man could never afford to be seen crying real tears because that signified weakness, and any sign of weakness left him open to physical danger, rape, or plunder. A male prison is a human jungle. I knew that if anybody sensed *any* vulnerability in me, I would be labeled weak and I would suffer the consequences. No matter how high up on the totem pole a guy was, once he started weeping, other men would either move in to take advantage of him or move far away to be disassociated from him.

Waking up at three or four in the morning was a regular occurrence. I'd lie there knowing there was no way I was gonna be able to get back to sleep. In those dark hours I'd be forced to start looking at my life, contemplating all the ways I had messed up, and to start thinking about what I really wanted for myself.

Each time I was newly incarcerated I would swear to myself, *When I get out of here, I'm gonna be a reformed man. I'm gonna have a whole new life. I'll go home, get a job, and do the right thing.* Yet as soon as they'd open those gates and let my butt out of jail, I would be thrown back onto the streets with nothing on my mind but survival.

I can see now that since I did not have the influence of a father while growing up, there was a way that the prison system became a father to me. All of my male indoctrination came from the prison system. My advisors were always older men, and I got all my education from older convicts. Prison offered a father's sense of discipline and structure. There was a comfort in that. I knew that in many ways I'd be taken care of in prison.

Many people, when they screw up in life, will go back to live with their parents for a while to get straight again. Whenever I screwed up, I went back to prison to do the same. After awhile, prison became my home base.

Someone once asked me if I ever got institutionalized in prison the way some men do. After being incarcerated for so many years, a lot of guys become afraid of living outside prison walls. I would say that yes, I did get institutionalized, but with a different kind of twist that went something like this:

I'd be sitting out in front of the Celebrity Lounge or some such place in my brand new car and my fancy clothes. There might be a ton of money in my pockets and my reputation as a top player known throughout the streets. Out of nowhere a voice would rise up inside and whisper in my ear, *Kenny, it's time to go to jail. You've had your freedom long enough now. You don't deserve all this success. You need to be in jail for this.*

The crazy part was that on some subterranean level of my consciousness I believed that voice, and I was okay with the thought of going back to jail. As much as I thought I loved my freedom, and as much as my conscious mind believed more than anything else that I wanted to live my life a free man, some part of me was actually uncomfortable being free. I could never stay on the outside long enough to get genuinely comfortable, or even better yet, to find my way clear to a life free of crime.

I accepted that voice and never challenged it, and believe it or not, this occurred more than once. Each time that voice would come, sure enough, not long afterward, everything would start falling apart before my eyes. Before I knew it, I'd be back in prison.

That Light Inside

The day after my nightmare they came and plucked my ass out of jail, threw me in a van, and transferred me to the Metropolitan Correctional Center in Chicago. I had no idea why I was being sent to MCC, where I'd be transferred to after that, or when. I was still in shock, deeply depressed, and I couldn't sleep. I went to a psychiatrist and asked for some sleeping pills, which, thankfully, he had no problem giving me.

Now that I had a supply of sleeping pills, thoughts of suicide started creeping into my head, thoughts like, *Okay, now I've got my ticket out of this mess. Rather than die in here alone, I'll take my own life. I'll show them. I'll teach them all a lesson. Once that judge who gave me all this time sees that he caused me to die, he'll regret his decision.*

I was blind to myself in every possible way. I had no sense of my soul, and no sense of responsibility that it was me, my own actions, that had gotten me into this predicament. I was enraged with everything and everyone, blaming everybody else for my misery, including Clara and my mother, which made no sense whatsoever. Crazy as it seems now, never once did my mind turn toward the obvious reason for my troubles—myself. *I* was the one who had cashed those checks. *I* was the one who'd done all those drugs. *I* was the one who'd used people, hit people, robbed people, and stolen from businesses. I had never been able to see that it was my own choices, not the failing of others, that had led to my wanting to take my life.

Ever heard the saying, "Whenever you point one finger at somebody, three fingers are pointed back at you"?

Today I know the peace of mind that comes from owning up to my actions and admitting my mistakes. I have learned that when I take my own negative actions into my heart and own them, a transformative process occurs that brings a state of grace, of peace, not only to me but to everyone involved. I realize now that it's possible for me to live as a conscious, self-reflective human being. It took a very long time, but I finally came to realize that I was never a victim of the system, nor of the color of my skin, nor of poverty. I was only ever a victim of myself.

Back then at the Chicago jail, I had yet to taste any of these truths. I felt so angry and deeply let down by life. I believed I was utterly alone. All the pain and loneliness of my childhood rose up to crush in on me with an even greater weight than the walls of my tiny cell.

Little Kenny Dale, he had been so angry. Angry at everybody. Angry at everything. He had never shared his pain or his anger with anyone, because he had never thought anybody really wanted to hear about it. No one had ever talked to him or took an interest in him. He hadn't had a father to talk to, nor had anyone else ever asked him what he was feeling or what was on his mind. Since nobody seemed to care, he eventually quit caring too.

In my misery and my depression, I began hiding my sleeping pills under my tongue at every pill call. Once back in my cell, I'd spit them out into a bit of toilet paper, pop the castor wheel off the bottom of one of the bed legs, and hide them up inside the leg.

I began amassing the thirty pills I thought I would need for a successful suicide. I was saving two a day, so I figured it would take about two weeks. I wanted to be sure that I had enough. Yet all the while this nagging thought kept floating around in the back of my head: *Once you take these pills, Kenny, you know there's no turning back.* Though I was still convinced that I'd found the perfect solution to my situation, that sense of irreversibility wouldn't quite let me rest in peace.

On the thirteenth day of saving the pills, an old black guard named Officer Ricks came knocking at my cell door. I was in a one-man cell on the fourteenth floor. Rather than the open bars of most cells, mine had closed walls and a regular door. I opened the door and let him in.

Officer Ricks sat down on the bunk and looked me straight in the eye. "Kenny," he said, "that light you're trying to put out? It ain't gonna die. There ain't nowhere it can go."

Whoa! How does he know? I wondered. Nevertheless, I played dumb.

"What are you talking about man? I ain't trying to put nothin' out. I'm just doing my time."

"I know what you're trying to do," he pressed, "but it won't work. There's no way you can put that light out, so why try?"

I wasn't about to divulge any information about my plans, so I only said, "Okay, man, whatever you say," then opened the door for him to walk out.

That guard had been watching me every day as the physician's assistant came through with the medication cart. He must have seen me cuffing one of the pills or hiding it under my tongue. Now he was on a mission to save me.

A few days later when he passed by me in the hall, he said it again: "That light in you ain't gonna die, Kenny. You cannot put that out."

I kept thinking, *What the hell does he mean by that? This light inside me cannot die? What light? Where is it? What does it look like?* I didn't really quite understand what he was trying to tell me, but it did serve to turn my attention inward toward the light rather than outward toward the practice of blaming everything and everybody else for my misery. It was the very beginning of my coming out of a lifetime of darkness. Little did I know that the words of this caring guard, after observing a desperate convict cuffing his pills, had planted seeds in my consciousness that would one day grow into a strong, abiding practice of self-inquiry and looking within. On that day, however, all I said was "Okay, sure man. Whatever."

"You see those guys over there?" he asked, pointing into the TV room where a bunch of big black guys sat around looking at the television. "Those guys are pretty smart guys. Why don't you go hang with them? They can help you out."

143

I came to find out that these men called themselves Black Israelites, and were followers of Ben Ammi, the new prophet for their generation of Black Israelites.

Officer Ricks and I walked over and he introduced me to them. We hung out for a while, shared some small talk, and the next day when I ventured over again, they greeted me with open arms.

"Hey Kenny, what's up, bro? How you doing, man?" said Israel, the guy who looked to be the leader of the group.

"Shit, man, this racist mother fucker judge gave me too much time," I said. "All I did was write a few bad checks and I got forty years."

"Checks!" he bellowed, incredulous. "Forty years? Who'd you kill, man?"

"I ain't killed nobody, man."

"Man, we're going to take you to the law library. There's this Italian dude down there, Gino. He's sharp. He can help you out. I think you got something coming man."

The next day he took me to the law library and introduced me to Gino, who told me to bring my court transcript down, which he then read.

"Listen Kenny," he said, "I think you've got some action here, ineffective assistance of council and probably a whole bunch of other stuff. You got to take charge of your life. You got to learn the law. Learn what you're in here for, what it carries, what the ins and outs of your charges are. Learn as much as you can about interstate transportation of stolen securities, cruel and unusual punishment, etc. Let me study it for a while, okay? I'll see how I can get you started."

"Of course, man, thanks." Now I had some hope.

The Black Israelites started taking me up on top the roof where we walked, talked, and gazed at the skyline. They gave me a little book to read by Ben Ammi called *God, the Black Man, and Truth*. This man and his message were the fuel that began my exploration into further esoteric and exoteric works. Not only did he help to instill in me pride as a man and a black man, he also introduced my mind to the power of the spoken word.

This book was the perfect antidote to my suicidal thoughts. No longer did I want to destroy this beautiful body of God's creation. I began to walk upright and proud of myself as a child of something very powerful at a time when I desperately needed to feel empowered.

I was drawn to the peace these men seemed to embody. Their air of tranquility permeated the whole pod. They were always smiling and talking to the other guys. These were loving black men who cared for others, and because of the state I was in, I needed someone to care for me.

One day one of the brothers, Yahweh, approached me and asked, "Kenny, where are those pills you been saving?" I went and got him the pills, which he took over to a dope fiend who was thrilled to get them. The guy literally glowed with the anticipation of getting high. He was happy and I was happy, because I knew I didn't need them anymore.

Blood of Men

"Johnson, pack your stuff!" a guard suddenly yelled through the meal slot in the wall of my cell. His beady eyes peered in at me. I was getting transferred to the penitentiary at Terre Haute, Indiana.

Sometimes I would know that I had an approximate amount of time in one facility before I would be transferred to another, but usually there was no forewarning. An inmate was never informed about an impending transfer. The authorities said it weakened security. Someone could be waiting along the transfer route to help him escape. I might hear rumors that a group of prisoners was going to be traveling north, east, south, or west, but I never really knew if I'd be among them or where exactly they were headed.

An hour later they took me to an exit area where I was chained around the waist, legs, and arms. All I could do was shuffle. Then they loaded me into a van, which proceeded to drive all over the countryside for days.

These rides, referred to as "diesel therapy," were filled with a kind of bittersweet clinging. Looking out over the countryside, I would try to suck in all the nature through my eyes, suck in all the life, because I knew I wouldn't be seeing it for a good long time. For all I knew, forty more years. I needed something to remind me of the free world and to give me hope. I had to gather it all up and store it in my mind so that I'd have something to think about, meditate upon, and contemplate in the deep, sad, depressing moments I knew were coming. So I sat there on my seat in the van, sucking in the trees, sucking in the cows, sucking in the grass, the cars, the road, the heat.

When we arrived at the reception area at Terre Haute, the entire floor was covered in blood. *Oh, no, sweet Jesus,* I panicked, *I'm not staying here. I don't know what kind of penitentiary this is, but I am not staying here!* It was a grisly welcome, an ominous sign. If there is blood all over the floor at reception, what do you think you're gonna find out in the prison population? Blood!

"Officer," I said to the man at reception, "whenever we get finished here, just lock me down in solitary."

"What? You just walked in here!" he said, incredulous.

"Lock me down," I insisted. "Put me in solitary, I'm refusing to program."

They put me in a holding cell and sent a counselor to speak to me.

"Why you locking up?" he questioned.

"I'm not doing time in this prison. It's too dangerous."

"You can't do that."

"Like I said, I ain't doing time in the program here." I wasn't about to be intimidated by this scrawny little white counselor.

The authorities can't make you "program," meaning they can't make you live out in the general prison population and follow the regular work program. Any prisoner has the right to refuse the program, but then of course the prison authorities have a right to try to convince you otherwise.

Every prison has an SHU, a Segregated Housing Unit, which is a block of cells where particular inmates are housed separately from the main population. You might get put in a one-man cell, a two-man cell, or larger, depending on the prison.

Then there's what is called the "hole." If an inmate has been determined to pose a threat to the rest of the population, he can get locked up in a solitary cell, often somewhere in the bowels of the prison. Solitary confinement wreaks havoc on any man's mind.

When you're "programming," you're going to your job, going to the chow hall, going to recreation at the appointed times. The benefits of programming are that you're not locked up throughout the day, which means you have more contact with other inmates and more freedom to roam around the prison. You might live in a two-man cell, a six-man cell, or a dormitory, but you can come and go from your cell as you please from six in the morning until nine at night. You can work out in the gym, play tennis or basketball, go to the music room, the library, or the chapel area to practice your religion. The only time you absolutely have to be back in your cell, on your bunk and not moving, is count time.

Count, in most prisons, occurs six times a day at 10:30am, 4:00pm, 10:00pm, midnight, 3:00am, and 5:00am. In a federal prison, the 4:00pm count is considered the most important because that count is reported daily to the central office in Washington, DC. In any prison in the USA, whether federal or state, at four o'clock there's "no dick swinging."

Usually just after the 4:00pm count is mail call, something everyone looks forward to. It's the best time of day because you might get a letter, a package, or some money from a loved one.

After locking me up in segregation for ninety days, they finally convinced me to "try the population and see how it feels." As soon as they escorted me to my new bunk, this Black Muslim guy with a kufi on top his bald head came over and read me the Muslim riot act.

"Your name Kenny?" he demanded.

"Yeah," I said warily.

"Listen up, Kenny, I'm gonna tell you something right now. I'm a Muslim. I pray six times a day at 5:47, 7:20, 12:28, 3:13, 5:35, and 7:08. You can't be disturbing my prayer. You got to stay in bed and be quiet until 6:00." Clearly he thought I should be doing my time according to how he did his.

"Sure, brother," I said. "No problem." He didn't know his blatant aggressiveness was causing me major inner trembulation. I was thinking the whole while, *You stupid motherfucker, I'm not going into your cell and bothering your crazy ass. You think I'm nuts?*

Immediately, I called the guard over and demanded to be locked back up in segregation. I had seen enough of what the population was offering, and I wanted nothing to do with it. My mind quickly went back to that first day with the blood all over the reception floor and nobody seeming to care enough to mop it up.

When they realized I was serious about not going into the population, they transferred me again, this time to the federal penitentiary at Lewisburg, Pennsylvania, exactly where this story began.

There I was, on that bus for more than eighteen hours straight, meandering all over the countryside, stopping at various institutions, with everybody just sitting and waiting and waiting, never knowing where they're headed or when their ride was going to end.

Sure, on the one hand it's great because again we all get to feast our eyes on nature, the cars, the people, the world. But on the other hand it's excruciating being chained right next to somebody, always having to hold your piss until the bus stops. You're horrendously uncomfortable the entire time.

Little did I know that the people I would meet at Lewisburg, and the education I would acquire over the next ten years in prison, would set the stage and ripen my soul for the most pivotal moment of my life.

The Big House

The men were dead silent as the bus pulled in through the iron-jaws of Lewisburg. When you hear a full bus quiet like that, you know everybody is terrified. The inner gate opened and the guards stood waiting for us in front of the reception area door. As we awaited our orders to get off the bus, a ferocious buzz of chatter broke out.

"I'm not programming man; don't you do it. Don't you program. Don't go to population."

I didn't know why the hell they were talking like that, and I didn't have time to ask questions because the guards started marching us off the bus. One after another we began our slow, shackled shuffle down some steps and into a room filled with counselors, case vendors, guards, and other inmates. Some of the men were shackled with a black lockbox across their bellies from which chains traveled to the four points of their extremities. Both ankles and wrists were secured to their middles, restricting their movement so severely they could barely shuffle along.

Some of these guys I knew were in for life. They were desperate. Anything could happen at any moment, and I knew that no matter what, if any heavy shit were to come down, I'd be fending for myself. Nobody there was gonna be watching out after my ass but me.

The guards began to unshackle us. "Against the wall!" barked the head lieutenant.

Standing next to me in the long line was a short fat guy whose name I would later learn was Gene. He leaned over and whispered, "Man, don't you go there."

"What the hell are you *talking* about, man?" I hissed back. The lack of information was starting to piss me off. Dark feelings of foreboding continued their chilly march through my veins. It was urgent I learn more.

"Don't go there, man," he insisted again. "Refuse population."

"Why? What's going on in there?" I could hardly contain my impatience.

"Just don't go along with anything they say."

Fuck! I had just gotten out of segregation in Indiana, and I didn't want to be in that situation again. I trusted Gene, and I didn't trust him. As always in prison, I never knew whom or what I could trust. At least Gene was giving me *something* to hold on to, some kind of information to move forward with. Before he said that, all I had were my fears, and those hadn't been helping me one fucking bit. I needed to know what to *do*.

The guards filed us into another room and ordered us to strip. *Shit*, I thought, *here we go again*. Each time I'd had to go through this, I had sworn it would be the last.

First they dusted us with a powder for killing lice.

"Open your mouth," the guard ordered, checking out my teeth.

"Roll your tongue back.

"Run your fingers through your hair.

"Lift your nuts up.

"Right side." Flip.

"Left side." Flop.

Next came the snap of the rubber gloves.

"Bend over and spread your cheeks."

One by one, each man bent over while the guard squirted Vaseline jelly from a squeeze tube into the crack of his ass. With one hand on the prisoner's back, the guard took his other hand and rammed the middle finger up the man's butt, searching for drugs, weapons, or any kind of contraband. The whole process was painful and humiliating. No matter how much I tried to prepare for it psychologically, I'd gasp every time. My guts would cramp up with the effort to control the impulse to take a shit right there on the floor.

Jerking his finger back out, the guard snapped the gloves off inside out and threw them into the trash. They didn't always hit the trashcan, so bloody, goopy gloves hung off the rim of the can or lay scattered limply nearby.

"Next!" trumpeted the lead guard, and the next group of guys filed in and bent over while my group made its way in to the shower room. I was grateful because you didn't always get a shower in reception, it depended on the institution, and we all reeked after the long bus ride. On this occasion we were a group of forty men, 70% African American and the rest Caucasian. One by one we were handed a clean set of prison clothes. I put mine on.

My anxiety and paranoia were growing by the minute. I didn't want to go back into segregation. Lewisburg, however, was an East Coast prison, and I knew my chances of knowing any of the other inmates were slim. Known as "The Butcher Shop," Lewisburg was the last prison any convict wanted to find himself in. The message in my part of the country had always been, "Man, don't you ever, ever, ever get sent to Lewisburg!"

The Mafia ran Lewisburg from deep inside. All the Italians from New York City and Philadelphia, otherwise known as "the mob," supplied the drugs, controlled the money, and ran the day-to-day activities inside the prison. They had hit squads to enforce their will and their control. Guys got killed on a regular basis.

Gangs of blacks from Washington DC and Baltimore also held positions of power inside the population, mostly as hit men. Whoever had the drugs had the power, and many of the guys out of Baltimore were drug addicts who'd do anything for their drugs, including rob, rape, and kill.

Since I didn't know a soul, I didn't know how I was going to survive in the general population. I decided to follow Gene's advice and told my intake counselor that I wasn't going to program; they should just go ahead and lock me up in segregation.

The counselors were all about as honest as used car salesmen. "I've got the perfect cell for you," mine assured me. He made Lewisburg sound like a rest home. He was wearing a cheap suit with his hair all slicked back. The only thing missing was some mustard on the lapel.

"All you gotta do is program for a couple of months, and then I'll get you transferred somewhere closer to your home," he assured me. "I'll make sure you get put in a nice dorm away from drugs and violence, that you're given a nice job, and everything will be fine." Eventually he wooed me into it.

Back out in the main hall, another guy, Big Cuba, was now huddled up with Gene. Cuba was huge and black, dark blue-black. Every muscle on his six-foot-three, 270-pound body bulged like a big black boulder. In talking with them I found out that the counselors had told everybody the exact same thing.

"We've got to form a buddy system," Cuba insisted. "Don't let them separate us if we can help it."

I pushed right back in through the other inmates and informed my counselor I was refusing population. It was my final answer. The subject was no longer up for discussion.

They took our property, then classified and registered us, a process that assigned every inmate to a cell and gave him a registration number from the BOP (Bureau of Prisons).

Whether you get incarcerated into a federal prison or a state prison depends on whose jurisdiction the crime falls under. Federal crimes are considered treason against the people of the United States, such as drug trafficking, kidnapping, bank robbery, mail fraud, money laundering, interstate transportation of stolen securities, and various white collar crimes. This means that mob members and drug lords can be mixed in with doctors, lawyers, and CEOs. State prisons are for crimes against the people of the state, crimes such as murder, assault, rape, and child abuse, which means that the population of some state prisons tends to be even more violent. County jails are for misdemeanor crimes, short felony sentences up to a year or so, and for holding accused criminals while they await their trials.

Another big difference between state and federal prisons is that state prisons operate under a more limited budget. Consequently, the food is worse, the healthcare is worse, and the library is slim pickin's.

A penitentiary, whether a state or federal penitentiary, is "the last stop on the line," the "big house" where there might be five, six, or seven thousand inmates and a maximum level of security. The bigger the crime, the higher the security. Some prisons, like Pelican Bay in California or Florence in Colorado, are such high-security facilities that one man might be locked down alone in a cell with constant camera surveillance.

Lewisburg was and is a high-security federal penitentiary, and as far as I was concerned, I was not penitentiary material. I belonged in an FCI (Federal Correctional Institution), a medium to low-security prison. My crimes hadn't been violent and the robbery had occurred a long time ago. But by that time my record was so long and so complicated, I had somehow qualified for high security.

Fortunately for me the new "three strikes" state-by-state law for habitual felony offenders had yet to be enacted. This would not become popular until the early 1990's. Under that style of sentencing, a recurring felon could be convicted for life with no possibility of parole until a minimum twenty-five-year sentence had been served.

Other new laws would come into effect in the 90's as well, requiring convicted criminals to serve out 85% of their sentences, which to my way of thinking was completely draconian, too much, too severe, and totally senseless. Under the laws of my day, convicts usually served 35-45% of their sentences, maybe even 25%, so my forty years meant I could possibly make parole in ten if I were lucky, if I toed the line, and if I didn't get sucked into trouble while in prison.

Little Pockets of Air

Arriving at my cell in segregation, there was Gene! We were locking up together!

Gene, a heavyset black dude, had this gravelly southern slur that sounded like he'd smoked one cigarette too many. Looking into Gene's eyes there was no mistaking he'd killed a few people, and this fact made him a good ally for me, one who wasn't afraid and could watch my back. Later I would come to find out that he had indeed been incarcerated for a murder in Alabama, his home state. I was a little afraid of Gene, rightfully so, but I had to trust somebody in that prison. I decided to trust Gene and Big Cuba, who had ended up in the cell next to ours.

Our cell was at level four of a four-story building, and it looked out across a long chasm that ran between our segregated building and the building that housed the general population. Whenever we wanted we could call across to the other inmates doing their time in the next building. All day and half the night men were yelling to each other back and forth over the thirty-foot divide. Over time, Gene discovered a fellow Alabamian in the adjacent building, and they kept up a running conversation.

The top bunk was mine. Gene had the bottom because he was too old and too fat to climb. In his fifties, Gene wasn't able to move his bulk around all that easily. He spent most of his time sitting on his bunk. I spent most of my time in our cell pacing back and forth. Even when I would go out and play basketball during our one-hour a day of exercise, Gene would hang back in our cell. For the most part I looked forward to that hour of exercise and sweat, because I was still only thirty-two years old, and I needed a way to purge my energy.

I was playing basketball with a group of guys from Baltimore, and that put me at some risk. I never knew who was who at Lewisburg or what the fuck was going on. I knew that if I even

155

looked at somebody wrong, their buddies could be threatening me the very next day, telling me how they were going to burn me, stab me, rape me, or otherwise fuck me up. It was impossible to know what kind of deranged minds I was in contact with. Many guys in these big penitentiaries had so much pent-up hatred and rage, there was no way of knowing when those energies might spontaneously explode. Scars from old stab wounds were plainly visible on many a shirtless torso.

It seemed like everything in that prison was about drugs, drugs, drugs. Drugs ran everything. Drugs were the magic elixirs that helped to keep a lot of guys halfway sane. However, if a guy got some dope from somebody and used it all up knowing he couldn't pay up, then that was a definite dope fiend move. Acting that desperate and stupid usually meant getting a hit put on you by the mob, with orders to either injure or kill, depending on the severity of the move.

Only once in a blue moon did I do drugs or alcohol in prison. I wanted to stay sane, sober, and out of danger. Drugs were too expensive, and besides, I was more than happy to finally have that monkey off my back.

In the 80's, a common strategy for getting to an enemy was to set him on fire inside his cell. Usually the target was someone who hadn't paid off his dope debt. The reason he hadn't paid up never mattered, just the fact that he hadn't.

That system of retribution involved three men. One guy with a chain and a combination lock would walk by a cell and secure the cell door. The next guy would walk by with a can of lighter fluid and throw it on his target. The third guy would come by with the matches, or one of those old metal lighters that stayed lit until you closed the cover, and he'd throw some fire into the cell. Either the guy targeted would catch on fire or the cell itself would, which was usually the case. What actually cooked a person was the paint on the walls. That old paint was so flammable that within seconds the entire cell would be engulfed in a firestorm, flames belching out into the hallway.

Then, of course, there was always the prison sex trade. Here at Lewisburg, smaller, weaker men got "turned out" as punks, just as they had in Hutchinson. Whoever does the turning out owns them and from then on out, they can be sold to another inmate or pimped out for money or for drugs.

Every man has to confront his sexuality in prison. Most men in prison aren't gay, but after living for years without any type of touching or affection, men can suddenly start looking like women. When by necessity that need to love and be loved gets suppressed, those repressed energies can all too often come out in aggressive or even violent ways.

Relationships between women in prison are altogether different. Women bond instantly. It's easier for them to derive intimacy from their friendships. They can hug each other, touch each other on the yard, and walk arm-in-arm without any stigma attached to it.

Men, on the other hand, are shown little tolerance by society in general for walking arm-in-arm, but in a man's prison, forget it. It's a beacon for trouble.

The protection racket is another integral part of prison life. If I couldn't pay for protection, which I couldn't, I would hopefully be able to make the right alliances to help keep me safe. Both Lewisburg and Terre Haute had a large Aryan Brotherhood, a ruthless gang of white racist thugs and murderers who lynched and killed blacks. In order to be initiated and gain entry into this supposed "brotherhood," you had to go out and kill somebody, and this was another reason for many of the cell fires.

The prison staff also couldn't be trusted because the guards themselves were always in danger. They, too, were busy making sure they didn't get killed, which is why they overlooked a lot of stuff. If a guard made a lifer mad, a guy who knew he was never getting out of prison, he might kill that guard without thinking twice. What did he have to lose?

The tension at Lewisburg was so palpable you could smell it and taste it like a big ole stew. The drug racket and racism created a recipe for violence made of two parts fear and hopelessness, and two parts rage and insanity. Somehow, in the midst of all that hatred and rage, I managed to find a few little pockets of air. It was like swimming back and forth through an underwater cave, looking for the way out and finally discovering these little pockets of air at the top. If I could just bring my face up next to them, I could catch a breath.

One of those pockets was the way Gene loved country-western music. Day after day, he'd sit in our cell, listening to country radio.

"Kenny, check this out man," he'd turn to me and say. "Check out Hank Williams. He's singing the blues!"

I had never appreciated the beauty of country-western music until Gene started educating me. He turned me on to songs like Jerry Reed's, *She Got the Goldmine; I Got the Shaft*. I found it hilarious that a black man, a con man, a player and a killer out of Alabama not only loved country-western music, but was thoroughly knowledgeable about it.

The lyrics of those songs had the power to make me smile and laugh. My heart would sing along as some country guy crooned his version of the blues—how his woman was no good, how she'd run off with his best friend, but in the end it was okay cause he'd got the dog.

Good for you, man, I'd think. *You got the dog. Whatever floats your boat!* I loved the irony of a white man singing the blues.

Life Inside

Library cart!" The call came from down the hallway. I could hear the library cart's wheels clanking across the marble tile floor. In the old days prisons were works of art and built to last. Nowadays, prisons are mostly constructed of steel, glass, and concrete, plain and ugly, except of course for the big reception rotundas where all the VIPs, senators, congressmen, and big attorneys come to meet and greet. Those floors are still marble, all shiny and clean, so that a VIP's first taste of prison is a positive one. That way everyone can feel real good about the way their prisoners are housed. Whatever horrors might be going on inside the prison are out of sight and out of mind.

I could always tell the library cart from the meal cart. The meal cart not only went clickety-clank, it wobbled as well. As soon as the clank and wobble started up way down the hallway, my stomach would growl in response.

Usually we ate at six, at twelve noon, and at five. Men locked up in the segregation unit couldn't go to the chow hall, so our meals and our plastic tableware were pushed through a slot in the wall. Gene and I would take our meals and go sit down and eat together. This is what we looked forward to every day, the library cart, the meal cart, and the mail cart.

Typical meals were stuff like fish sticks, shit on a shingle (creamed chipped beef on toast), runny mashed potatoes, creamed corn, and syrupy fruit cocktail out of the can. The meals were rarely warm.

Occasionally they served breakfast food for dinner, and since breakfast was my favorite meal, I'd always get excited. Very simple things like this could bring a moment of joy.

Christmas was always an emotionally charged time. Every holiday was hard because the men wanted to be with their families and loved ones, and a lot of guys did drugs or drank some form of hooch on the holidays just to forget. Christmas was the hardest because it was filled with so many opposing emotions. On the one hand, I'd feel totally alone and cut off from my family, yet on the other hand I'd be looking forward to the little gift most prisons gave out on Christmas mornings. Everybody made sure they were in their cells waiting, and a big canvas laundry cart would get pushed from one cell to the next, the guard handing out the packages. Maybe it would be a sack of candy, maybe a toothbrush or some socks.

The other reason holidays were hard, or weekends for that matter, was because no mail got delivered on holidays and weekends. There'd be no chance of communication from the outside world.

The mail cart was an even bigger deal than the meal cart, if that were possible, and a letter with a picture inside it... *Oh... my... God*, that was Christmas right there.

Prison life, in general, was living from one meal to the next, so any kind of special meal made for a special kind of day and a break from the monotony. Fourth of July meant watermelon and hot dogs, games and races. Thanksgivings were cool because for once we got a real good meal, a traditional turkey dinner with dressing, candied yams, cranberry sauce, and green beans. Whenever the food was good and my appetite sated, I had a better chance of making a little peace with my situation. Just for a moment I could rest my mind and let go of the outside world and the stark reality of how miserable the condition of my life was.

Holidays were also the time when once again the desire would arise to do the right thing and straighten my life out for good. For a moment I'd come to my senses and realize that this was not the life I wanted to be living. I wanted to have a square job. I wanted to be home and going to church with my family.

At some point Gene and I got our hands on a little mirror from the commissary, and a mirror like this was always a hot commodity in prison. We could stick the mirror out through the meal slot or the bottom of the door and see two-to-three hundred feet down the hallway. As soon as I would hear the steel door open down the hall, I'd dive down to the floor with my mirror and stick it under the door to see who was coming. At other prisons we had bars on the front of our cells. I could use my mirror to play cards, chess, or checkers in the hallway with the guy in the adjoining cell. Sometimes I'd use it just to watch the action on the ward, guys passing notes to each other or playing cards from cell to cell.

The days were a constant buzz of activity, and I mean a real racket, all day long. There was always something going on. Radios blaring, televisions broadcasting, telephones ringing, doors slamming, toilets flushing, guys horse-playing, multiple conversations going on at the same time, and nearly constant shouting. There was never a moment of silence, not even throughout the night. I had to learn to sleep through anything. If two guys were killing each other next door, no problem, I was going to bed. I learned to fall asleep regardless of my environment, light or dark, quiet or loud.

"Library cart!" the call came again. Curt, the library guy, pulled up in front of our cell, stomping down hard on the wheel lock. "What books you want, man?" he asked.

That day I chose a book called *We're All Doing Time*, by Bo Lozoff. It was a moment of pure grace. That little book would come to be one the most influential books of my life and eventually bring me great mental and emotional stabilization. Even today, Bo's Human Kindness Foundation operates the Prison-Ashram Project across the US.

Most of my previous studies had been dealing with the Masons, with Islam, or with positive thinking. Bo's book was my initiation into Eastern philosophy and the practice of meditation. The book had these little cartoons of guys doing meditation with funny balloon captions that illustrated the crazy, restless thoughts a person can have while first learning to meditate.

I enjoyed reading about peace and calmness. Through Bo's guidance I began to teach myself how to meditate. I wasn't going anywhere for a long time, so why not?

I started with a simple meditation just before bedtime. I'd simply sit and watch my breath go in and out. Whenever thoughts started to come, I'd just bring my attention back to the breath. I couldn't sit cross-legged in the correct meditation posture like the book showed, and twenty minutes was all I could handle. Even then I'd be watching the clock and looking around.

Break with Reality

I'm a man! I'm a man! I'll always be a man!" somebody was screaming. *What the hell is all that noise?* I wondered. *Am I dreaming?*

The strange, droning roar had started in my sleep. As I climbed my way up to consciousness, I finally came around enough to realize that the sound was someone screaming.

"I'm a man! I'm a man! I'll always be a man!"

I was trying to wake up, get my bearings, and focus my eyes in the darkness of the cell. My head was next to the toilet seat in the back of the cell, and the sound was coming from the direction of the door. Finally my eyes landed on Gene, my buddy Gene, the man who loved country-western, the man I trusted as much as I could trust anyone there. He was standing by the ancient six-inch steam pipe that kept us warm at night, its grey surface dimpled and textured by a hundred layers of paint. Buck-naked, his backside to me, butt fat jiggling in the wind, Gene kept screaming at the top of his lungs, "I'm a man! I'm a real player! I've always been a player!" Suddenly he looked right at me, eyes wild and huge as saucers. *Shit!*

I jumped out of my bed and started pounding on the bars with my fists. *Bam, bam, bam!* "Guard, guard, guard!" I was waking up the whole tier. I could hear the guard running down, his keys jingling in his hand.

"Get me out of here! Now!" I shouted. I was scared and confused. I didn't know what the hell was going on with Gene, but it wasn't looking good. His state of mind was not shifting a bit.

"I'm a man! I'm a man! I'm a real player. You know I'm a player. I'm true to the game!" He was hanging on to that steam pipe for dear life, as if it was the only thing keeping him anchored in this world. His eyes were blank, empty, like they weren't connecting with anything. I was afraid that any second he was gonna grab on to me and squeeze me to death instead of that pipe.

The guard took one look at Gene and barked into his walkie-talkie, "Open 122! Open 122!" I couldn't get out of there fast enough. The guard pulled me out and slammed the door. Then he stuck me in a cell with two other guys where I was to stay until the next morning.

Forty minutes later four big burly guards showed up in full riot gear with batons and shields. One of them was dressed in white clothing like a medic. They all rushed Gene and got him down. Then the medic pulled out a long needle and shoved it into Gene's leg.

"Let me go! I'm a man!" Gene continued his screaming.

"Be still, motherfucker!" the guard yelled back, finally wrestling him down and chaining him to the bunk.

The goon squad came out of the cell all huffing and puffing, the medic carrying the empty needle. We went back to sleep until morning, me on the hard floor with images of Gene going berserk flashing through my head.

It had happened so suddenly. No warning. He'd been just fine all that day and the day before that. I couldn't make any sense of it. It happened pretty frequently with guys locked down in solitary, but this was the first I knew of it with a guy who wasn't.

Only once had I been locked down alone in a cell, and that was for ninety days. It's rough for anybody, no matter how tough you are. Sometimes it's the toughest guys who have the hardest time.

The first thing you do is fight against it with everything you've got. You start trying to file grievances, appeal your sentence, or get transferred quickly, anything you can to get out of that solitary environment. At some point you've thought all the same thoughts a thousand times over. You've masturbated all that you can masturbate. You've created all of the fantasies you can create. You've read all the books you can read. Eventually you just have to surrender and accept your situation or go insane. Hopefully, you surrender and come to some sort of terms with your situation, some sort of peace.

No matter what type of cell I was in, alone or with a cell-mate, I always paced. If my cell were five steps across, I'd pace five steps. If it were twenty, I'd pace twenty. If it were a hundred, I'd pace a hundred. I always felt so much energy pent up inside, and pacing helped to throw it off. If I were strategizing my legal case, I'd pace. If I were contemplating the books I was reading, I'd pace. Pacing was my meditation, my spiritual practice. Pacing kept me sane. Even today pacing has a calming influence on me.

I also did a lot of exercise in my cell. I had my daily routine—sit-ups, push-ups, jogging in place.

A lot of guys tried to sleep their time away, but I couldn't do that. If I slept too much, I got headaches.

Being in solitary confinement, or even in the segregation unit, was a luxury to a certain degree because I felt safer there, but it could also turn into a liability. If a man didn't have a strong mind, if he didn't have some kind of spiritual practice, it could nag on him, turn on him, until pretty soon he'd be losing it.

Gene didn't pace back and forth. He didn't have a spiritual practice. Maybe that's why he lost his mind.

Years later I told a psychologist about what had happened to Gene and he told me that most likely Gene had experienced a psychotic break. He said that shouting things like "I'm a man!" or even "I'm Jesus Christ" was a way of trying to hang on, of trying to prove to themselves that there is still somebody in there.

They left Gene locked to his bunk for two days before they determined it was safe to move him. He had pissed and shit himself. His whole body was shaking when they went to take him out, his legs so wobbly he could barely walk.

As the guards walked him out, I went up and said, "Gene, hey man, it's me, Kenny." I was hoping he'd recognize me and we'd make real contact.

"You got a cigarette?" he croaked, not really looking at me.

"Yeah, sure Gene, here you go." I lit a cigarette and handed it to him. I had to hold his hand to keep it still enough to take the cigarette from me. He didn't recognize me. He didn't know

THE LAST HUSTLE

who I was. All I could think was, *Oh man, I can't lose my mind. I can't let this happen to me. There's no way I could go through that. I've got to stay sane.*

Here we were in the depth of hell in one of the craziest prisons in America. I had to trust someone and the guy I trusted and loved had lost his mind.

Eighteen months later I met up with Gene in Talladega, Alabama, where he'd been sent because it was close to his home and his release was coming up. His friends came to me and said, "Kenny, Gene's in the yard, he wants to talk to you."

We walked the yard and he still wasn't all there. He said, "Man, the beauty of our friendship is that you saw me at my best. Now, you see me like this, and this is not me."

"I know, Gene, I know," I said.

It was so hard to see him crushed and broken. I prefer to keep the image of Gene, as he was, the guy who taught me how to be tough and to love country-western music. To this day I love country-western music because of him.

PART 5

Higher Ground

"There is no rest for the weary mind.
Then, comes the awakening!
The mind is slain. Awareness is revealed."

—K.J.

Pops

Pops was like the grandfather I never had. He sparked in me a new way of seeing this vast universe. Each day, all day, Pops kept on telling me, "You're listening to what you're thinking, Kenny, not to what I'm saying."

"What are you talking about, man?" I'd protest. "I'm listening to you."

"No," he'd insist, "you're listening to what you're thinking, not to what I'm saying."

I always did make an honest effort to listen to what he was saying. I just didn't know what I was listening for. I asked Pops every question under the sun, but he always refused to give me straight answers. He had his own way of teaching me, mostly in silence. Pops taught me by what he didn't say, what he didn't do.

Pops was my new cellie, and believe me I knew how lucky I was to be sharing that cell with him. He was a sixty-six-year-old drug dealer and Mason from New York. I still wanted to be

167

a Mason, but he told me the same thing that Buford had told me back at Hutchinson: "If you've been to prison, you can't get anybody to sponsor you."

Pops was short and clean-shaven, with kinky grey hair on top his round head. Plus he wore little round John Lennon glasses. The whole package looked just how you'd imagine a "Pops" would look. And Pops was loving. He was my Yoda from *Star Wars*, and I loved him back.

Ever since I'd been at Lewisburg, I'd kept on pursuing my studies. Clara's Godmother, Sister Khadijah, had Clara send me a Holy Qur'an, so then I had two versions, an Ali and a Pickthall. She thought it would help me. I was excited to be reading about the Prophet Mohammad, *peace be upon him*, and his journey to bring Islam to a people totally set against this new teaching and new way of being. Mohammed had gone through many wars and struggles, and I could relate because in my own way I had been struggling too.

My reading material was a real smorgasbord: I was also into reading *Player Magazine*, the African American version of *Playboy*.

I had been seeking some way to stay quiet and in peace, so I decided to observe the holy month of Ramadan. I told the guards I'd be fasting, plus I started abstaining from cigarettes, which wasn't easy. I wasn't even drinking water during the daytime. But it was when Pops arrived that things got truly exciting. I became his student.

"Never stop pursuing knowledge," he instructed me, "both of the sciences and of yourself. All the religious works are here for you to come to know creation from different angles. Do not be like the monkey who puts its hand in the nut but won't let go, then along comes the trapper and carts the monkey away. Be willing to not hold on to any viewpoint. Our viewpoint will change and does change, but the Creator does not."

I'd sit on the toilet that had become my schoolroom chair, not wanting to miss one single word. Elbows on knees, chin on fists, eyes wide open, and ears tracking every word that fell from his lips. Never a word fell that wasn't well thought out.

"Pops," I said to him one day from my top bunk, "when I get out of this time, I'm going to be a good father to my daughters. It's time I turned my life around, you know?"

Pops peered up at me, listening to me rant on about being a good father and all. He handed me his Bible, and said, "Read the twelfth chapter of Ecclesiastes."

"The whole thing?" I asked.

"Yes, the whole thing."

That chapter hit home and still does. Pops was pointing to something deeper than being a good father. It was all about serving Our Father first.

Pops had an easel and a drawing pad on which he worked mathematics and drew geometric shapes.

"What are you doing there, Pops?" I asked him one day.

"They say everything equals one, so I'm trying to work that out on paper." This was way too abstract for me to grasp.

Pops went on to predict my future, just as Aunt Equator had. "Soon son," Pops said, "if you stay on the path of knowledge, this abstraction will become a living truth for you. The birds, the geometrical shapes of buildings, all numbers, all humans, and everything you can or cannot see, will not only equal one, you will know them as oneness."

Pops didn't move around a lot because his legs couldn't hold him too well. He had false teeth, a knowing smile, and a knowing way about him. You just knew Pops knew stuff. He was a wise man, and somehow I knew I was being initiated onto some path, I just didn't know exactly what path it was. Pops really *saw* me. He saw the good in me. I fell so in love with that guy.

Some days his sixty-six-year-old joints would give him pain. I had seen the difficulty he had doing things with his fingers, all knotted up with arthritis the way they were. That's why one day I decided to wash Pops' sheets for him. They'd come and taken Pops off to court and he was to be gone all day. I was so grateful

169

for his presence in my life, I wanted to do something for him, so while he was away, I went and got his sheets and took them into the shower with me, washed them, then hung them up to dry. Pops came back that night and saw his sheets hanging. "Did you do that?" he asked me, his eyes wide with surprise.

"Yeah," I said, looking shyly at my feet.

"Why'd you do it?" he said, looking amused.

"Because I wanted to, man. I like you Pops."

I was just so glad to have somebody in my cell who was a teacher for me, who could educate me. Someone I could trust and be relaxed with. I didn't have to wonder whether he was going to get me killed. Plus Pops was keeping his mind straight, and that's what I wanted for myself.

Pops and I both got transferred about the same time, me to Talladega Alabama, and Pops to a lower security institution in New York. Transfers can happen for various reasons such as if you're dangerous to other prisoners. If you've been on good behavior, it's possible to request to be transferred somewhere closer to your family. Most often the transfers were for mysterious reasons. They don't want you to get too comfortable or to build up too much social power and control, so they break up any of those possibilities by moving you along somewhere else. A "stagnation transfer" it was called. The reason they moved me this time was because I had continued to refuse to enter the general population at Lewisburg.

Astral Espionage

Once situated in Talladega, my spiritual search began in earnest. I knew I had to find some kind of peace inside of me, not only to endure the long sentence stretching before me for a still unknown length of time, but also to get myself centered enough to study law so that I could try to appeal my case. I'd been studying ever since I'd met Gino, the Italian lawyer back at MCC. Eventually my appeal would make it all the way to the Supreme Court. The courts would finally acknowledge that my sentencing had been unusually severe, yet they would also argue that nothing about it had been illegal. They couldn't find any legal grounds upon which to grant my appeal, and so they didn't. Obviously, God had something else in store for me.

At Talladega it was only a matter of days before I found a meditation teacher named Cassell, and I began attending his meditation sessions near the prison chapel. It was in the chapel library that I came across a classic little book on astral projection by Sylvan Muldoon, *The Projection of the Astral Body*. Thus began my journey of learning the different processes involved for projecting my consciousness out of the body.

I was in a two-man cell. In the early morning my cellie was usually out doing something else, and that's when I'd lie down on my hard little mattress to meditate and attempt to astrally project. I'd get real still inside, watching and waiting, trying to allow my astral body to slip out of my physical body the way the book instructed.

My motive for learning astral projection was not exactly spiritual. I wanted to spy on Clara because I'd heard she had a new boyfriend and that they were lovers. I was pretty shook up about it.

I remember clearly that first successful projection. This time it was in the afternoon. I had been lying on my bunk for a couple of hours, watching and waiting, when all of a sudden I felt this falling sensation. *It's happening!* I realized. I was excited because I'd been at it for some months already, and I knew that this falling sensation signified the beginning of projecting out.

Okay, it's happening, you're projecting out, I coached myself. *Now get away from the body. Project at least ten feet!* I could feel the sensations at the base of my head near the occipital region, the medulla oblongata, where the astral body is connected to the physical body like a baby in the womb is connected to its mother by the umbilical cord.

All at once I was out, and I saw my body lying there on the bed. I wanted to get as far away as I consciously could. I wasn't afraid. I felt myself move through the wall of my cell, and right away I was on the outside of the prison, hovering above it.

Colorado! I thought, and immediately I was in an apartment in Colorado. There was Clara, sitting on a couch in a blue silk dress. Next to her was this guy, running his hand up and down her leg. After a moment of watching this scene, the emotions started coming, the jealousy and the rage. If you get emotional, you get pulled right back into your body, and I was definitely getting emotional. Next thing I knew my consciousness was being sucked back into my body like a reverse canon ball.

As soon as they opened my cell at six o'clock the next morning I was running to the phone to call Clara collect.

"What's up, Clara? How you doing?" I said, my tone sweet and mellow. I wanted to sneak up on her with my accusations, catch her off guard.

"What're you calling me for?" she stammered. "It's early. Is everything okay?"

"Everything's fine baby. What'd you do last night?"

"Oh, nothing much."

"Were you at a party, wearing a blue silk dress? Was a guy rubbing your leg?"

"How do you know that, Kenny? Where are you? What's going on?" She was starting to freak out.

I couldn't believe it. *Oh my God, it really happened!* I realized.

Her reaction confirmed that I had really been there. Yet I kept control of my excitement and responded with a smooth, "Nothin's going on darlin'."

"Yeah," she said, "me and Tim, we went to this party. It was nice. But how'd you know what I was wearing? Who you got watching me, Kenny?"

"Nobody, Clara," I replied. I didn't want her to know about the astral projection because I didn't want her to know I was spying on her. "I just had a real strong dream. It was so real. It's amazing that you were wearing the same dress I saw in my dream."

That was all the confirmation I needed. I had been working it and working it, and now I had finally managed to successfully project out of my body. Eventually, I would become proficient at it, familiar with the different sensations involved—the pressures on the head, the different vibrations along the "umbilical cord," and the return to the body. I never actually saw the silver cord talked about by the experts, but I sensed it. Flying through walls was like, *Wow! To the bat cave, Robin!* It was a magic carpet ride right out of a fairy tale.

After hanging up the phone with Clara, however, I started stewing. The rage and the jealousy hit like a blast of hot air. I remembered Tim. He used to come around the restaurant, and he'd always been sweet on Clara. Now she was dating him.

The most popular song at the time was Marvin Gaye's *Sexual Healing*. The last letter Clara had written to me was about how she'd been hanging out with Tim and how she loved that song. I started putting two and two together, and I felt certain that Clara and Tim had become lovers. How I hated that song! Seemed like every time I turned on the radio, there it was reminding me that my woman was with another man. Most of all, I hated that Clara was getting sexual healing and I wasn't.

Clara was scheduled to come for a visit a few days later. Before she arrived I wrote her a long, rambling letter about how she'd promised she'd stand by me, yet here she was messing around with this other man. I told her how much I hated her for it. Then I stuck a razorblade in the letter, folded it up, and took it into the visiting room with me. My plan was to cut her throat without a single thought about the consequences.

Was I crazy? Yes. I was crazy with pain and crazy with self-pity. Truth was I'd been calling Clara so often, pestering and interrogating her about where she was and what she was doing, that she'd had to get two phones so she'd know when it was me calling.

A man in prison doesn't normally put himself in his woman's shoes. He doesn't feel her suffering. He doesn't realize that now she has to support the kids on her own. Now she has to make the money to pay for his cigarettes and incidentals in prison. Now she no longer has a man to talk to at three in the morning because that's been taken from her. Now she has to find the time for prison visits. All of it is an extra pressure that wasn't there before. In the meantime, he's getting three meals a day, and he doesn't have to worry about the rent, the gas, or the grocery bills.

If a man could turn all that self-pity around to where he was asking his woman, "How can I support your life out there; how can I make life easier for you?" he would be able to more easily find peace in prison. Instead, so many men end up going crazy, killing themselves, or inflicting violence on their women when they get out.

When I saw Clara coming in to the visiting room, I realized I wasn't going to cut her. I cared for her more than I hated her. By coming to see me I knew she was standing by me the same as she always had. I threw the letter in the trashcan, and the razorblade went with it.

"I know you've been with another man," I accused. "You said I was your man, and now you're in love with this guy. Are you living with him?"

"Can I read this letter you just threw away? Was this for me?" Before I could stop her, she reached for the letter in the trashcan. She opened it up, and the razorblade fell out. She didn't say a word about it. She read the letter, her eyes growing moist with tears, and then she said, "Listen, honey, Tim's a good friend. He comes by and helps me out. He gives me business advice. He's married, and he has another girlfriend on the side. We're just companions, just friends. He's a smart businessman, and I'm trying to get a loan for the business."

I still had absolutely no communication skills at the time. Until that moment I hadn't realized it was possible to simply ask her about her feelings and her motives. The way I dealt with the situation was to accuse her of lying to me, betraying me, and abandoning me. Yet she had shared so freely what was going on.

It was at this point in my life that I began to realize my mind was nothing but a projection machine. More often than not, what I was thinking had no basis in reality.

Gently, she continued. "I'm trying to recuperate, you know? You took a lot of money from the restaurant and bought cocaine and cognac with it. I'm just trying to make my business work. I'm still coming down here to see you. I'm here with you now. I've been helping with your legal case. Kenny, I'm not going anywhere."

All of my anger and rage, all of my insecurity, melted in that moment. We started kissing and hugging. It's the most wonderful thing when your woman comes into prison because you get to touch her and feel her all over her body. You don't really want to hear what's happening on the outside. You just want to rub on her like a magic lamp. When you come back to your cell, guys will sometimes ask if they can smell your fingers.

Birth of Compassion

Back in my day-to-day routine, I was still marveling about this phenomenon of astral projection. Having discovered this power, I became obsessed with it. I kept practicing daily. My one objective was to escape prison, at least at night. By projecting I had found a way out of the federal industrial complex, and from my legal woes. It actually kept me sane and focused on something other than my forty-year sentence.

My intentions were not pure or selfless, and I was practicing from a dark place, but I learned from this practice that the more my feelings were neutral, the longer I could stay in the astral plane. I was often fearful or angry, and these feelings would snap me right out of the next world and back to the prison cell. This was the beginning of my understanding that resting in emptiness has its rewards and benefits in staying free—even astrally.

Finally one day I was blessed with my first taste of awakening.

I had been meditating and practicing astral projection for over a year. I had been learning what the Buddhists called "one-pointed concentration," which was to get myself perfectly still and empty my mind of any thought.

I'd also read a Bible passage that told about "the morning dew that flows from the back of the head," so I made a practice of lying in my bunk for hours at a time with my attention focused up inside my skull.

One night I woke up in the middle of the night with a heavy sensation on the top of my head as if I were wearing a *yarmulke* or a Muslim *kufi*. Every time I closed my eyes and put my attention there I'd get to feeling high. The more I was able to direct my attention to the center of that spot, the happier and more blissful I'd become.

I had this buddy, Freddy, a light-skinned brother out of Mobile, Alabama, who was just so darned likeable, so friendly, that he was like a light in a dark place. He liked to smoke weed and do drugs, so he always had some kind of hustle going on for his next fix. Eventually he'd gotten himself into trouble with some guys, and now they were threatening to hurt him. I started feeling so upset about all the threats coming at him that I wanted to cry. I realize now that what I was feeling for Freddy was compassion, but I couldn't identify it at the time because I actually had never before felt that for another person. A desire started filling up inside me to protect Freddy. All the love I was feeling, I started focusing on him. *Leave him alone,* I kept praying; *Freddy is a good guy.*

After that, whenever I felt confused or upset, all I had to do was turn my attention up into the crown of my head, like looking to heaven, and immediately I would go straight into bliss. All my concerns would simply vanish. I had never experienced anything like it. I was definitely starting to master one-pointed concentration, but I was doing it for selfish reasons, all because it felt so damn good.

This experience of bliss lasted three days. Sitting out on the yard, I'd close my eyes and put my attention on the dew sensation on the top of my head, and all this warmth would envelop me, this nectar, like honey dripping down inside. Amazingly, my thoughts would be of nothing but love. *I'm in love,* I kept marveling to myself. *I am so much in love.*

A clear, thick, gooey substance started dripping from my eyes, so much so that I had to wipe it out of my eyes and shake it off my hand. The more I kept my mind on the "dew" sensation, which by now had traveled down into my belly as a warm presence, the more I'd experience this state of extreme love and feel like this love was all that mattered.

Much later I learned that there is a Tibetan Buddhist meditation practice called *phowa,* otherwise known as the "practice of conscious dying." It is a preparation for the time of one's death and the transfer of consciousness from the dying body into what the Buddhists call the "pure realm." This all happens through the crown of the head. It is said that if the practitioner is successful, he or she can bypass some of the typical experiences of confusion the Tibetan Buddhists believe occur after death. The sign that the practitioner has successfully completed their initiation into the lifelong practice of phowa is that a drop of viscous fluid or "dew" appears on the crown of the head.

On the fourth day I woke up and the dew sensation was gone. Zippo. Nothing. Completely vanished. I was just Kenny, and I was no longer in love. I tried to get it all back, but nothing I tried worked. I was just a regular guy again, but I was still feeling a lot of compassion for Freddy.

"Freddy, man," I pleaded, "why don't you just quit all this? You could get yourself hurt playing with these guys like this. I don't want anything to happen to you, man."

He heard me, and he let up on some of the crazy stuff he'd been doing. He knew that I loved him, that I cared for him, and it really touched him.

Nothing bad ever did happen to Freddy, but the whole experience was of great import for me because I'd never experienced that kind of compassion for another human being, least of all another guy in prison. We were the best of friends until I got transferred to El Reno, Oklahoma, in 1985, where I was to serve the remaining seven years of my sentence.

Those seven years gave me further opportunity to reflect on myself in ways that I may never have otherwise, from studying the Bible and the Koran, to learning meditation, yoga, and astral projection. Every prison sentence I ever endured turned out to be the best of opportunities to develop my inner self.

One of the other benefits of being locked up in a federal prison rather than a state prison is the chance to meet people from all over the world and every walk of life. Take Harry, for instance. Harry was a brilliant commodities trader. He taught me how to read commodities charts. He taught me all about trading pork bellies, wheat, rice, corn, gold, oil, shorting the market, going long, bidding, options, tops, bottoms, and trend formations. He taught me about the stock market, the basics of supply and demand, and about stochastics, the science of probabilities and random behaviors. I never did get the chance to trade anything, but it wasn't because I was at a loss in the brains department. I just never could hold on to my money long enough to invest it.

I continued to seek out the guys in prison who had some intelligence, the guys who didn't get involved in the bullshit of prison life. I didn't hang out with the ones who played cards and dominos every day. I wanted to spend my time with the guys using their minds.

If a guy was reading Karl Marx, I'd ask him why he was reading Karl Marx, what it was he liked about him. Same thing if a guy was listening to Brahms or Beethoven.

If somebody was reading the New York Times or the Washington Post, I wanted to know what was so special about those papers out of all the papers in the world.

Prison is a unique opportunity for self-study and contemplation. I'm not the only man who claims that his prison sentence turned out to be a gift from God. Prison was where I discovered my soul and so much more. For this, I will always be eternally grateful.

Reverend Chicken Foot

Iwas paroled in February 1992 after having served ten of my forty-year sentence. I stayed the first couple of months in a halfway house in Cedar Rapids, Iowa, where I had first been sentenced. Clara came up to Cedar Rapids after that, and we got an apartment together. She had finally closed Dahlia's Restaurant.

I got a job doing landscape maintenance for the City, and I was starting to make some decent money. I was able to put down the first and last month's rent on our apartment, as well as a cleaning deposit. I was saving my money, and I was confident I was free of crime.

After Clara got a job as a telemarketer, she got me a job working there too because it was better money than the landscaping job. The only drawback was that the company was hiring a lot of ex-cons, so there I was again hanging around a bunch of criminals. It wasn't long before I was chasing other women, drinking again, and fighting with Clara. I was still meditating, and those two conflicting parts of my personality were vying for my attention, trying to find a way to live with each other on opposing but parallel tracks. I didn't have a clue which was gonna win, my past conditioning or my longing for something true.

Back at Talladega, Cassell, my meditation teacher, had been a follower of an Indian female guru. Though I had never met her, I followed suit and adopted her as my guru as well. Now that I was out, I wanted to go see both her and another spiritual teacher whose books I'd read in prison. That one was scheduled to speak in Des Moines, closer to home, so Clara and I drove up to hear him.

The first glitch happened as soon as Clara and I walked into the room. Men and women had been separated on opposite sides of the room, which meant that Clara and I couldn't sit together. The next thing that happened was a fundraiser came out on the stage and blatantly started hitting us all up for donations.

"The Minister's coming out in one minute," he announced, "but there is a brother over there in the back, and he's got a hundred dollar bill. Who can match that hundred dollar donation?"

It was like a bad hustle, pushy and unclean. I felt manipulated, like God was being auctioned off to the highest bidder, and if I wanted a piece of God's grace, I'd better pay up. The hustle went on and on, and I started wanting out, out, out.

"The Minister's coming out soon now," he kept promising, "and I know you all want to see him. The Minister's come all the way from Chicago to see you; I know you brothers can do more." Squirming in my seat, I was feeling like a prisoner held captive by a master manipulator.

Finally the spiritual leader came out, but by then I was so agitated I couldn't take in a word he said. Here I had painted this picture in my mind of a beautiful man who cared only for the people, and it had never occurred to me it was a moneymaking business. I thought he would be about teaching us, not fleecing us. I was hungry for the teaching part, yet this felt like just another street hustle. I had had so many expectations—*Here comes Papa, he's gonna make everything alright. The Good Man, the Big Daddy, the Daddy I never had, he's gonna take care of my soul's needs.* If the man had a spiritual message, I wasn't able to hear it. He gave a short speech, and before I knew it, he was gone. Feeling betrayed and abandoned, I couldn't get out of that meeting fast enough.

After Bob had broken me in to pimpin' back in Minnesota, he had started letting me in on some of the finer secrets of the game. He had reversed his earlier instruction, and starting teaching me how to pimp women with "sweet macaroni."

"Buy a woman flowers," he had instructed. "Walk down the street holding her hand. Talk sweet to her. None of that gorilla pimpin'. None of that screaming and cussing, grabbing women by the hair and dragging them around. The sweeter you are, the faster and the easier they'll come to you. A smart pimp uses his mouth to get paid, same as the preachers, same as the politicians."

"The greatest pimp is the pimp who can pimp men," Minnesota Bob had gone on to say, "and the highest pimpin' game of all is the 'Bless Your Heart' game.

"Reverend Chicken Foot (Bob's pet name for all preachers) is the highest form of pimp. Preachers like that know what they're doin', Kenny. They's pimpin'."

I remembered other times when I'd seen preachers wearing diamonds and three-piece suits, their bottom ho sitting in the front pew. Every pimp had a bottom ho, the one who wasn't gonna run away, the one who was his rock, his First Lady, same as with the politicians.

My mind went back to Hutchinson Reformatory when Buford had told me about the Freemasons and other secret organizations controlling things behind the scenes. Minnesota Bob had been giving me the same game from a pimp's perspective.

"Kenny, the preachers, the politicians, are controlling the masses. They's pimpin' us."

By my estimation, anyone using their mouth to get paid was pimpin'. Most ministers preaching from the pulpit were manipulating people's minds to get paid. Their macaroni was to promise you a place in heaven. The politicians, on the other hand, were promising you a great job, a great education for your kids, that pie-in-the-sky American dream. All you need do for it was whatever they told you to do, and then bring them back the money.

Powerful white pimps, the ones pimpin' the shit out of everybody, had always been glorified, but the poor black pimp who had to figure out a way to make money and survive in the free world was a lowdown rotten scoundrel. White boy pimps, those who owned huge churches, Mustang Ranches in Las Vegas and the like, were considered cool. But the one little black guy who had himself a ho out on the track was a no good "*pimp*."

The highest pimp was the one pimping everybody, so to my way of thinking, the highest pimp of all was God. His basic message was this: "If you love me, if you obey me, I'll answer your prayers. If you don't, I'm gonna kick your ass."

I don't mind being pimped if the mack is strong and powerful and true. But if I feel like I'm being manipulated for money and the mack's not coming from a true place, I'll walk right out. As Malcolm X had said, "Brother, God is not a hustle." Deep down inside I was having to wade through all of my stuff to find the real and true God. Like the teachings say, the kingdom is within, and I knew it was not out in the marketplace.

Now, twenty-seven years later, as I speak to groups and do my work in the prisons, I find myself in the position of the Bless Your Heart Game. Now I am regarded as a spiritual counselor and teacher. I speak to people, both in prison and out, about waking up to the truth of themselves as peace and love. Am I going to cross that line of manipulating people for money? I don't think so. My heart won't let me. My conscience won't let me. God is not for sale. I was never that good at pimping anyway. It was never my true game.

I have a choice. I can ask for a small payment for this work I do, or I can take no payment and let this universe reward me accordingly. I don't follow anyone else's model in this; I follow the model of my heart. My heart says this: "Stay true to me, and I will take care of you." I don't want to be lying on my death bed gasping for air, knowing that I have lied to thousands of human beings and those lies are gonna follow me into eternity. All I want following me into eternity is peoples' love and prayers and to let that be the magic carpet ride.

Back in Iowa, I was still hoping to put together a trip to see the Indian guru at her ashram in New York State. Before I went, however, I wanted to hear more of her teachings. I sent for a catalog of her books and tapes, but all of those materials were too expensive for me. Again I was disillusioned because of the money issue.

Money was becoming a big problem again, and the lure of the game once again began tugging at the edges of my mind. It wasn't long before I was hustling, stealing, and violating my parole. Clara and I separated, and I started staying with different hustling buddies or different women, or at some two-bit ratty motel. During that period I got into a domestic abuse situation with Clara again, only this time she filed charges. When it came to Clara, I had finally blown it for good.

It felt like some kind of malevolent force was chasing me. I had wanted to wipe the slate clean and start over again. I had wanted to treat Clara right. I had wanted to get a job and live respectably. I knew that it was possible for me to be a responsible person, not this good-hearted yet mean man who created more trouble for himself every time he turned around. Sometimes I felt like a wild animal run amuck, so it made sense that I be hunted down, trapped, and caged.

Birth of Conscience

Something's not right here, man," I complained to my old buddy Wes. He was the guy I'd done the tire heist with all those years back, and whom I was hustling with again. "Every time I try to make some money, I catch a case. I've got to stop, man. This shit's only getting worse." I had already caught three robbery cases since my last release. Now I was paying attorney fees, and I was broke.

I had gotten out of prison with the full intention of finding a teacher and continuing with my spiritual program. Even though I was back out on the streets hustling, I had kept doing my yoga and meditation. My spiritual practice was shaky, I'll admit. How could it not be? Running alongside it in equal measure were my practices of thieving and alcoholism. Still, there were at least *some* moments of lucidity and consciousness. Every once in a while this little window would open up for a moment, and I would have a flicker of clarity about myself and my life's situation.

"You know what, man," I confided to Wes, "I'm done. I'm going to turn myself in."

"What?" Wes shouted into the phone. "Are you nuts, man?" He couldn't even begin to understand where I was coming from. Wes was a dope fiend, and that kept him busy doing whatever he could to stay free so he could keep doing his dope. Never before had I considered stopping, and I had no idea how much time I might have to face.

Back in my last five years at the El Reno prison, when I had been meditating daily, I had begun to realize that what I wanted more than anything was freedom, real freedom, true and lasting self-realization. But how was I going to find it? All the books I'd read about Muktananda had said that if you wanted to awaken, if you wanted lasting freedom, you needed a teacher, a living master. So I began praying for a teacher, a guru, a sign that would tell me the direction I needed to go. I didn't realize at the time that in order to stay free I'd have to have a *shift in consciousness*. I didn't really know what that was. But I had read about it in books, so I knew it existed, and for my remaining years at El Reno, every night before I went to sleep, I had prayed for the right teacher or a sign that would lead me to one. Soon thereafter, I'd had a powerfully prophetic dream.

In the dream I saw myself getting out of prison, getting back with Clara, and the two of us moving to another city. I saw myself drinking and going in and out of all kinds of drug houses, and I actually experienced the alcohol and the drugs in my body. I saw myself with women whom I'd never before met. Then I saw myself getting locked back up in prison and sitting in a room with this white-haired person who was talking about God, about consciousness, about awakening. The main message the dream had seemed to impart was this: "You're going to get out of prison, you'll be back on the streets, but in order to meet your teacher, you're going to have to go back to prison again."

I had awakened the next morning, thinking, *This is a nightmare! The last thing I want is to get out of prison and then have to go back in order to meet my teacher! After all this work I've done, all the yoga, all the books, all the praying, I'm gonna have to come back to prison?* But in my very bones, I knew it was true. I hadn't even gotten out yet, and I knew I'd be coming back. I had already failed.

That day I'd walked the long, hot track at El Reno totally devastated, my head hanging down like a beaten prizefighter. I had been so completely overwhelmed that I had stuffed it. I'd purposefully forgotten that dream.

Four years later, there I was in Iowa, and the first part of the dream had come true, yet I still wasn't consciously remembering the dream. I wasn't thinking about it. That remembrance would still be a couple years away. For the time being, I was just soberly assessing my situation.

Why do I keep putting myself through this? I pondered. *Clara's left me. I'm wanted by the police. Is this shit ever going to end?*

I didn't realize at the time that my destiny was squeezing in on me, that my yearning for self-realization was finally starting to run the show, even though, for the most part, it was still part hiding subterraneously in my consciousness. Something wanted me back in prison, but for the life of me I didn't know who or what. All I knew was that my hustles were ragged, I couldn't seem to get on top of them, and I was forty-five years old. *If I keep doing this,* I thought, *I'm gonna catch thirty cases. I can't do that much time. I've got to stop now.* I could hardly believe what I was about to do.

I called my parole officer and said, "Listen man, I've got a jewelry case, I've got a tire theft, and now I've got a domestic abuse charge. I'm tired, man. I'm done. I'm cooked. I want to come in." I was so happy when I hung up the phone. On my own, I had made the declaration, "I want the madness to stop." Relief flooded my whole being. I knew I was finished, that all the running and craziness were over. I was getting arrested again, yet this time I was filled with peace rather than the usual hopelessness, regret, and scheming.

I had no idea that I was on a collision course with my mom and aunt's prayers, and all of the hundreds of people who are praying for peoples' souls—the old church ladies, the Buddhist monks, the pious men and women at the Wailing Wall, the millions of Muslims making *salat* daily, and myself.

I knew it wasn't going to be easy. The prisons had been changing. Gangs of Bloods and Crips had begun flooding into the prison population. The crackdown on drugs was in motion, laws were changing, sentencing was becoming more stringent, and there was frequent rioting. But I also knew how to do time and I was confident that if I could face it now, I'd get through it. I knew I'd be going back to a federal prison because I had purposely called my federal parole officer as opposed to turning myself in to the state. I didn't want to do state time because I knew I wouldn't get the same opportunities for rehabilitation. By then I already had so many charges going on, I could actually choose which prison system to turn myself in to. It was all about jurisdiction. I wanted the feds to have control of my life.

"Have a seat," my parole officer said, pulling a chair out from the table. I knew what that meant. He was going to call the marshals who would soon arrive to take me away. Even though I knew what was coming down, I was still scared because I didn't know how long this stretch was going to be.

The marshals arrived a few minutes later. I knew the drill. For once they handcuffed me in the front, not behind like a dangerous criminal. Even that small difference felt good.

I called my mother and told her I had turned myself in, and I was going back to jail the next day. She was happy because she had suspected I'd gotten back into the life. She had seen the way I was dripping in bling-bling again.

That night, Clara came down to the jail. "I've turned myself in," I told her. "I'm going back to prison. Are you going to stick with me?"

"I don't know, Kenny. I'm gonna have to think about that."

I knew it was over between her and me. She had stuck by me in prison for ten years. Why would she want to see me through another prison term given the way I'd treated her? I had done everything I'd promised her I was done doing.

So many of my fellow ex-cons say the same thing. "When I got out man, things were not the way I thought they would be, and I just violated." For so many of us, the challenges are so great and seem so insurmountable until prison once again becomes an option. I had thought I was ready, but I'd proven once again that I wasn't.

"You just go on in and get yourself together," she said. "Then we'll see." When Clara left that day, she promised to write me, but I knew it was over. I saw it in her eyes. It hurt, but I was ready to let everything go, including Clara. I just wanted to clean up my life.

I pled guilty to all my charges and got sentenced to five years in a federal prison. I had orchestrated everything to do my federal time first and to deal with the state time later on. They wanted me to give up Wes for the tires and the jewelry. Since I wouldn't implicate him, I had no real leverage for reducing my sentence. I was shipped off to a prison outside of Springfield, Missouri.

Beginning of the End

It was June 1993 and hot and humid as hell. I had fallen into one of the worst depressions I had ever experienced. I had already spent so much of my life in prison, I was getting older, and now there I was right back in the joint again. I had let Clara down. I had no money to show for my hustles. After doing some law research, it was looking like I'd be doing about twenty-eight months, and with the added domestic violence charge, about six more on top of that. Plus my mother had gotten wind of the abuse charge and didn't want to hear a thing I had to say. When I'd called her on the phone and told her "Momma I am in jail again," she'd said, "Kenny Dale, I am done boy. You are on your own. Don't ask me for anything." That was the last button on Gabriel's coat, as the saying goes. I had let down everyone I had ever cared about. I was totally, completely alone.

I started attending a Buddhist meditation group led by another inmate, Fleet Maull, who was in for drug smuggling. Slowly I began to get back into my practice.

Springfield was the US medical center for federal prisoners in need of medical care, which could be either physical or mental. I wasn't sick. I'd simply gotten sent there because it was the closest prison to my hometown of Kansas City.

This was a totally different prison setting than I'd ever experienced. A lot of very strange guys were in there, many of them extremely mentally ill, and I mean right out of *Silence of the Lambs*. Stories flourished about the crazy Vietnam vet down in the basement. It was said that he was so dangerous, if a guard were kind to him, he'd find a way to lure him into his cell and kill him. His cell was rigged with ways to feed him and communicate with him without getting close to the cell. Cameras were on him every second of the day and night.

Springfield was a maximum-security prison, but since it was also a hospital, the population was small, only five or six hundred guys as opposed to five or six thousand. Even though it was a high-security prison, I didn't feel in any danger because there were plenty of good men in the prison caring for the not so fortunate. It seemed like almost every guy I met started telling me about his illness—kidney failure, leukemia, liver damage, colostomy—you name it. There was an entire ward just for tuberculosis patients. Since TB is airborne, the whole ward was quarantined off from the rest of the hospital.

Every few days I'd have to get a shot for some new disease that had just entered the grounds. We had to get shots to inoculate us against every malady known to man. Stories abounded about crazy diseases or the criminally insane coming through.

There were transsexuals at Springfield who'd gotten arrested in the middle of the surgical aspect of his or her sex change. Because they'd been incarcerated they were now the property of the government, so they'd gotten sent to Springfield to finish up with their gender operations. There were guys walking around the yard with breasts. A guy with breasts was accepted as long as he still had a penis, but it also put him in danger of being raped. Once he'd completed the change and possessed a vagina, "she" wouldn't necessarily be transferred to a women's prison where she could live as a woman. Often times the Bureau of Prisons decided that she should be put in isolation.

Then there were the horror stories about the doctors at the hospital, renowned for their incompetence. I had heard about guys going in to get one leg amputated and coming out with the other one cut off by mistake. People put in requests like crazy to be sent to a street hospital for their surgeries.

Springfield had hospice care for the terminally ill, and it was Fleet who introduced me to the hospice program. Providing hospice counseling was part of his spiritual practice. Cultivating greater compassion for all beings was what Buddhism was all about. In the Hindu tradition, it is said that *seva*, service, is the overflowing of *sadhana*, spiritual practice. Fleet simply said, "Kenny, when your own spiritual practice gets full, then you go out and you start serving."

I know it sounds crazy, but I had actually become excited about doing my time at this prison hospital. It didn't matter that winter was cold as a witch's tit and the summers were hot enough to fry an egg on my bald head. They hadn't given me a job yet, I was still floating, but I was hoping they'd give me some type of job caring for people. All my life, all I had ever done was take things. I had never been concerned about giving back. Now there I was, so curious about the practice of *seva* and serving others.

One day, with no warning whatsoever, I got a request to go see my counselor, Mr. Jacobson. He was a professorial kind of guy, with wire-rim glasses and gray hair. Neither warm nor cold, Jacobson was a real Mr. Vanilla.

Straight out he informed me, "Mr. Johnson, we're transferring you to FCI Englewood at Littleton Colorado."

"Why?" I demanded. "My family's only a few miles away from here! I can't believe this shit!" The rug was once again being pulled out from under my feet.

"Mr. Johnson, I don't make the decision. The order just came down from Regional."

I had just gotten comfortable at Springfield and had settled into my routine. "Jailing" we called it. When an inmate lets go of the streets and turns his or her attention to the world of guards, rules, and how to survive in prison, he's jailing. I had finally begun to see little glimmers of light rather than the bleak darkness of what had felt like a terminal depression. I had gotten anxious to see my daughter and my grandkids. Losing the possibility of seeing my family, as well as having to leave my new meditation group, was more than I thought I could bear.

"What can I do to change this?" I asked.

"Once you get to FCI Englewood, you can take it up there."

"Yeah, right, man, I just saw on TV that they're rioting down there!"

I don't know why I was feeling so surprised that they were doing it to me again. You'd think I'd have been used to it by then, but I was devastated. I was in shock. I wanted to stay at Springfield. My daughter and my whole family were only 150 miles away, and they had started coming out to visit me. I was gonna get a job helping to care for people. Yet there I was listening to this baldheaded, freckled-faced asshole, with his two gigantic teeth hanging over his bottom lip, telling me with a fake smile that they were transferring me in a few days. It was so fucked up!

None of my concerns mattered to the prison system. When they say they're gonna transfer you, you can fight against it, or you can get depressed about it. Either way, you're gonna be going. I'd had enough experience with the federal government to know that once the ink hit the paper, you had nothing coming. Saying a silent *fuck you* to those long teeth and that square-as-American-flag tie, I pushed myself out of the green leather chair, grabbed the papers he was handing me, and stormed out of his office, slamming the door behind me.

Immediately I started asking everyone I saw if they knew what type of place Englewood was. I found out it was a good place to do time, and that relieved my depression a bit. Fleet was one hundred percent behind it. He knew some of the men in the Buddhist community there, and he gave me some names of people to hook up with.

I went back to my bunk and hurled myself into it, feeling totally helpless, staring at the ceiling. Fans that sounded like jet engines blew hot air around my cell. As I drifted off to sleep, leaving the hot, sticky, noisy world of men, I was hoping for a good dream.

PART 6

Freedom Behind Bars

You are what you are searching for.
Freedom is WHO YOU ARE.

                                    —Gangaji

The Dream Comes True

Once again I was back on the bus, riding all over the countryside for days. At least this time was a more comfortable ride. I could actually stretch my arms and legs out a tiny bit.

At Englewood, depression struck again full force. I felt like I was being buried alive, darkness squeezing in on all sides. I found myself sitting on my bunk for hours, elbows on knees, hands holding up the weight of my two-ton skull. My jaw rhythmically clenched and unclenched. I wanted to die, to vanish, to be no more. What was the sense in staying alive anyway? I felt hopelessly trapped in my circumstances, devoid of any value or worth. Frantically, I searched in my mind for something, someone, anyone, who could lift this burden from me. I couldn't come up with a single person that I could really confide in. While I was at Springfield Clara had sent me all the pictures she had of us together with our families, further proof that she was done with me.

I had gotten attached to my life in Springfield. I had gotten into the rhythm of jailing and counting the days 'til I got out.

194

Now I was at a new prison where I didn't know anybody, and my mind was spinning with the same old futile thoughts: *How did I get here? How did this happen? How can I get out of this?* As usual everything had shifted unexpectedly at the whims of the prison system.

I didn't have the awareness at that time to see how this was all working towards awakening, but now I see that this is how it worked: I would go to jail so constantly and be immediately forced to surrender in order to deal with the situation I faced. What I was being pointed towards was more than just jailing. I was actually being prepared for the spiritual path. Since my path wasn't directing me to Buddhist caves or monasteries in the mountains, I had to go to prison to be taught how to surrender—over and over again. Now, when I'm faced with a difficult situation, I'm able to say to myself, *Kenny, you've got to let this go now, you've got to surrender to what is.*

However, back in that first month at Englewood FCI I was so depressed I had trouble keeping up with my meditation practice. This one night, however, after meditating for many hours, I finally got very still inside. Suddenly this huge fear welled up in my mind, and an inner voiced whispered, *If you meditate any longer, you're gonna die.* I didn't know what it meant exactly, but it scared me stupid. Immediately I flashed back on Gene going crazy in our cell at Lewisburg. I didn't want to die, and I didn't want to lose my mind, so I stopped meditating. It would be weeks before I'd even go near it again. Without the support of a spiritual practice, I quickly spiraled down into an even deeper depression. Once again I was being pointed towards awakening. I wasn't destined to die like a dog in prison. It was everything else I'd built up over the years, my whole idea of Kenny/Slim, that was going to die... and to be reborn. That glorious fate was closer than I could have imagined.

By the end of the first month at Englewood, I'd met a band of Buddhists and other meditators doing time. A couple of them were dope smugglers who had traveled the world over. One man,

Michael, told me stories about hanging out in India in his sail-boat, and about the different spiritual teachers he'd met there, and so my prayers for a teacher became more fervent than ever.

One night I walked into the prison chapel and found the guys watching a video of a woman with white hair.

"Who is that woman?" I asked.

"That's Gangaji," they replied in unison. "She was just in here last month."

"What?!" I shouted, incredulous. "She was here when I was here? Are you sure, man? Just last month? When's she coming again?"

"Sorry, man. She ain't coming back until April."

I calculated quickly. It was August, and she wasn't gonna be back for another eight months! I had been so depressed and fucked up in the head that I'd missed her. I attributed a large part of that to the alcoholic stupor I was still in. Even though I'd been sober for months, my brain and body were still saturated with the stuff. I hadn't gotten into cocaine the last time out, but I'd been drinking like a fish, and I was still going through some kind of withdrawal period.

Now I had a new mantra of misery. *I missed her. I can't believe I missed her,* my mind kept repeating, *and I was right here!* The guys were all talking about her. Something inside me knew I'd missed something important.

As it turned out, missing Gangaji's first visit had been for the best. It was a kind of wake-up call that kicked me off my little pity pot. I got really pissed off with myself for being in a depressed stupor. After that, the pity party was over. I had been in that funk for weeks, and now I was ready to get back to making the most of my time in prison. I got fully engaged in life again.

I was excited about Gangaji, and I wasn't even sure why. When I watched her videos, I didn't understand what she was saying, yet I was drawn to her anyway. She had this brilliant, silver-white hair, soft and curly, like a big halo around her head. That first moment I'd seen her on video, all I could think was,

She looks so familiar. Where have I seen her before? I still wasn't putting it together that the person in my prophetic dream back in El Reno had had that same white hair.

Tuesday nights were the Buddhist meetings; Wednesdays were Gangaji videos. I looked forward to those meetings all week. Volunteers were coming in and sharing all kinds of things. One volunteer, Crystal, was sharing about rebirthing and about the chakras, the seven energy centers that radiate out from the physical body with the colors of the rainbow.

Dayanand, another volunteer, was himself an ex-con. He was the one who first brought the Gangaji videos into the prison. His wife, Maitri, was the director of Gangaji's nonprofit organization, The Gangaji Foundation, at that time headquartered in Boulder, Colorado, just a couple hours' drive from the prison. Susan Carabello and a man named Satchitananda were also coming from The Gangaji Foundation regularly.

The Buddhists from the Naropa Institute that Fleet Maull had turned me on to were coming in to teach Tibetan Buddhism and its three paths, *Hinayana*, *Mahayana*, and *Vajrayana*. They brought in copies of different Buddhist texts, and we all talked about the teachings of the Buddha, which they called the *dharma*.

Eight or so of us were attending both of these meetings. Even though Gangaji's teachings and the teachings of Tibetan Buddhism were different from each other, they were both Eastern philosophies, and that's what our group was into. It wasn't exactly a clique, at least not for me, because I was also hanging out with some of the Muslims and the Christians, and still spending time with the drug dealers and the pimps. We'd walk the yard together, talking about the pimp game. Stuntman, my best buddy in that group, was a pimp and drug dealer out of Twin Cities, Minnesota, so we had a lot in common.

Finally the day arrived for Gangaji's next visit. It was April 1994. By then I had remembered my dream about the white-haired person, the one I thought was gonna give me my get-out-of-jail-free card. Now I felt certain that she was the one who had shown up in that dream. I floated through my morning routine, from bunk to bathroom to chow hall, with only one thing in mind, the gift I was gonna receive that evening. Everything else was a blur.

In the months prior to that day, I had slowly been coming back to life. Our group had been talking a lot about spiritual awakening, and more than anything I wanted something like that to happen for me.

I'd been spending time doing different arts and crafts, and I'd made Gangaji a little ceramic incense burner shaped like a teepee. This was because Dayanand had told me, "If you want something from the guru, you have to bring the guru a gift," so I'd been scheming on how to manipulate the guru to give me what I wanted. The hustler was still in charge to a large degree.

The ceramic teepee, 2 ½ inches in diameter, sat on a little platform with a white stripe spiraling up to the top and a hole at the apex to put a stick of incense in. If you wanted to burn cone-shaped incense, you could stick it inside the little door at the bottom of the teepee.

That evening after Gangaji arrived, I introduced myself.

"Hi, my name is Kenny," I blurted out, "and I brought this for you." Then I held out my little incense burner for her to take.

"Oh," she said happily, "just the other day somebody gave me some wonderful incense, and I didn't know what I was going to do with it. Now I've got this. Thank you, Kenny. That is so sweet."

Happiness flooded my whole being. For a moment it felt like the sun was shining on me alone. I had given the teacher an apple in the hopes of getting a good grade.

We sat in silent meditation for about fifteen minutes, and then this one guy, John Sherman, started talking to her about Buddhism and the different Eastern philosophies. She talked with a few other guys as well. When our meeting was over, about an hour later, we went into the hall and shared some snacks together. At the time she called her meetings *satsang*, which in

Sanskrit translates closely into "association with truth."

Except when I had given her the gift, I hadn't really spoken to Gangaji. John Sherman was so excited about their conversation that he was lit up like the proverbial Christmas tree. I didn't really get why he was so thrilled. Nothing big had happened to me. My understanding had been that when you gave the teacher a gift, she'd give you something back, like *darshan*, a transmission of blessing from a holy person. The words she'd spoken that day had had no real meaning for me. Mostly I thought, *Here I am the one who gave her the gift, and John Sherman got the blessing. This is so fucked up!*

The next day in the commissary where we worked together filling orders, John was like a different person. He was in the last few years of an eighteen-year prison sentence for being a bomber and a bank robber. John had been a revolutionary and loved to pontificate his revolutionary zeal for hours on end, talking endlessly about "fighting the system." He was on such a conspiracy theory kick at the time that even today you might find me looking under my bed for the boogieman called "One World Order" or "The Illuminati."

"Kenny, they are out to get us and keep us all enslaved," he preached. "Republicans, democrats, independents, they are all the same. Don't trust any of them."

John was stocky, serious, imposing, with thinning gray hair and a pair of keen blue eyes that left you feeling exposed like they could see straight through you. He walked the same way he spoke, slow, deliberate, and measured like a metronome. What had always struck me about John was his extreme confidence. He seemed unshakable, untouchable.

The morning after Gangaji's visit he was more like a revolutionary meditator. He had slowed down even more, like he wasn't totally there. I wondered if he'd been smoking dope or something. Curious, I watched him closely, sensing that something had changed.

"What's going on, man?" I finally asked. "Are you all right?"

"I'm in love," he answered softly. He was dead serious.

"You are? With who?" You never knew who a guy was in love with in prison. It could be a guard, another staff person, or even another inmate.

"*Her*," he said.

"John, you're not making sense, man. Who's 'her'?"

"Gangaji."

"Well you can't be in love with her, man, because she's married and she's a guru, and you can't love her like that, you know."

"I love her. She's all that there is."

"She's got a husband, John. His name is Eli."

"I don't care. I love her."

Oh man, this guy is gone! I decided, and we went back to work.

It was a little unnerving. John had never been so peaceful, so "other-worldly." To this day John still speaks like that, except that same slow, deliberate, measured delivery of words is now filled with peace. Now when I see John, what comes to mind is the Hindu elephant God, Ganesh, remover of all obstacles to the truth. Some years after his release from prison, John began talking with people about his spiritual experience, and to this day he continues to help many others remove the obstacles to truth within their minds and hearts.

The following Wednesday at our Gangaji video night, Dayanand could tell that something had happened to John. He tried to explain to us that John had experienced a shift, an awakening, but it still didn't mean much to the rest of us. Nevertheless, the pump was primed. All those years I had wanted something that I had no name for, no form for, but when I saw it in John, I knew that what he had was it, and *I wanted it.*

Later I would come to understand that John had, for all intents and purposes and in reality, stopped his whole story, his mindset, and the lifestyle of the old John. He had been born again as an empty vessel filled with a new wine called peace. His nervous system was being reset to allow the power of universal creative energy to consciously flow through him. The constant letting go of all his old stories was plunging John deeper and deeper into a natural state of meditation. He was a new man being recreated right before our eyes.

Awakening

Over the ensuing days, John became increasingly quiet and withdrawn. All he wanted to do was write these long, long letters to Gangaji. I loved reading his letters because of all the love that was in them. And I loved reading Gangaji's letters back to him, because I could catch the tiniest bit of that love for myself. I wanted it so badly, and I continued to pray for a bigger glimpse.

Whenever I read Gangaji's letters, everything in my mind, body, soul, and spirit would relax. For a moment there would be peace, a slight foretelling of what was to come.

The love coming from her was totally impersonal. It wasn't the usual love between a woman and a man, or for that matter any kind of love I'd ever experienced.

"John, I am your own heart," she wrote. "Rest in the awareness of your Heart."

Somehow I felt it was my duty to keep reminding John, "She's not talking about sex here, man. You know you can't have sex with her. She's married. She's got a husband. His name is Eli Jaxon-Bear. It's not gonna happen, you know. She's a guru. You're supposed to bow to her."

"It doesn't matter," he always responded. "I love nothing but her."

All the other members of our little group were pissed off at John as well because all he ever talked about anymore were those two things: He was in love with her, and nothing else mattered.

"John, it *does* matter," we all told him. "You *do* have to try to change yourself and be as clear as you possibly can. It *does* matter that you pay your bills. It *does* matter that you don't buy hooch."

"None of those things matter," he'd say. "There is nothing but this Love, nothing but this Truth, and everything rests in That."

We were pulling our hair out with the guy, imagining that he had gone off the deep end. I didn't even have hair; I was pulling at my bald head! The whole thing was crazy. What the hell had happened to John? I decided to start writing Gangaji myself.

"Gangaji," I wrote, "John Sherman is starting to sound hysterical. All he talks about is that nothing matters, and he's causing an upset in our little spiritual community, especially with the Buddhists, who believe that it does matter, that actions cause karma, and that we still have to be concerned with the way we conduct ourselves."

"Kenny," she wrote back, "John is your brother, your ally, support him."

Okay, I thought. *She's not even my teacher yet, but she's right, so I will support him.*

After that, I became John's protector, his bodyguard, his greatest supporter. I also became John's first student. I started going to his cell and listening to him speak about the truth he was witnessing inside himself, drinking in the knowledge and the wisdom that he shared.

Mostly John would say, "Just being here fully, just resting in this love, is all that really matters."

He was speaking the truth, and we all knew it, including the Buddhists. We were happy because we were having our own *satsang* meetings, and we had John right there walking the yard with us. It was so cool. It felt like we were lighting up the whole prison.

We started sneaking over to John's cell every chance we got, even risking being written up just so we could sit there with him. It reminded me of all the stories of men and women living under the threat of death if they were caught practicing an outlawed religion. It was also like sitting around a campfire, getting warmed, and the campfire was our love of inner freedom.

Michael, Pete, Dane, and I would pack into John's cell, on the floor, on the bed, and listen to him talk. Sometimes I could "catch" that truth he was talking about. I could get just a taste of that love.

John was priming me, and so was Gangaji. She'd been writing me, and I was preparing myself for her next visit in September.

We continued to have group meetings with John. It was the most beautiful summer of my life.

The Buddhists teachers, Gary and Bill, were upset with John because now he was going in and totally disrupting their services. He was challenging them.

"I don't see how all of this has any relevance to the truth," he told them one day. "There is only *this* moment." The rest of us just sat back to watch the fireworks.

"John, everyone needs a container," they protested. "Everyone needs a practice."

"There's no need for a practice," John countered. "There is only *This*. When there is only *One*, what need is there for practice?"

This conversation kept up all summer long. It was incredibly cool how he challenged them all, how he made them put up or shut up.

As I see it now, it made perfectly good sense for Gary and Bill to stick to their guns. They surely recognized what had happened to John but did not want the rest of us to get lost.

In September, Dayanand came in and counseled us, "Listen guys, when Gangaji comes in, have your best question available. You've got to put together your very best question."

Reading the Bible, looking through all my spiritual texts, I tried to formulate my best question. I prayed. I crossed my fingers. I felt that unless I found my best question, I wasn't going to get my best answer, the answer that would give me what John had.

The day of the meeting finally arrived. Gangaji came in to the big chapel room with her other volunteers, Susan, Shanti, and Dayanand. We gathered around, sitting on little meditation pillows in front of Gangaji, who sat in a chair. We went into meditation together, our eyes closed, sitting silently and letting our thoughts quiet down.

I hadn't brought Gangaji a gift this time. The last one I'd brought she'd given to John Sherman, and I wasn't too happy about that. Later I found out that she usually gave her gifts away. She didn't take personal ownership; she just kept passing along the gift of giving.

Finally Gangaji opened her eyes, turned, and looked directly at me. "I've been thinking about you Kenny," she said. Her voice was so soft I had to strain to hear her.

I had my question together. I was prepared, but for some reason I didn't ask it. Instead, I blurted out, "Gangaji, it's my understanding that we have to die before we can receive God's Grace, at least that's what the preachers tell us."

Looking into my eyes, she said, simply, "Kenny, God's Grace is here now."

Her whole demeanor was so peaceful. Her voice. Her eyes. When she looked at me and said that, whatever tension there was inside me just let go. I relaxed completely.

"You think you are a black man, but you are not that.

"You think you are the son of your mother, but you are not that.

"You think you are a criminal; you are not that.

"You are none of these things."

I wasn't able to take in that last part, because as soon as she'd said, "God's Grace is here now," my mind had gone totally blank. She looked into my eyes, and I looked directly back into hers. It was like she sensed I wasn't getting something.

"Come here, Kenny," she said softly, her eyes sparkling. "Lean your head over here," and she gestured for me to come closer. She picked up this little mallet on the table next to her that was used to ring the bell that signified the end of the meditation period. Then she tapped it on the crown of my bald head three times. *Ding, ding, ding.*

It was the confirmation that I needed. I had had this concept in my mind that in order to receive the guru's power, knowledge, and blessing, something definitive was supposed to happen. I had read stories about other gurus using some kind of symbolic action to transmit their wisdom to the student, like blessing them by touching the top of their head with a peacock feather. Later I found out that this wasn't in fact true. A guru doesn't *give* you anything. A real guru, a true guru, simply, mysteriously, reveals inside your own mind and heart that you already *have*, and you already *are*, everything that you've been looking for from a guru.

Gangaji must have sensed that I needed a ritual in order to receive what she was offering. She didn't do that with anyone else that day, and I've never seen her do it since.

After she tapped me on the head, my consciousness dropped down so deep inside that I lost all awareness of my surroundings. Whatever she was saying, whomever she was talking to, all of it just vanished, and I was enveloped in this vast warmth. Everything relaxed. Into what, I didn't know. I just relaxed like I had never relaxed before. There were no thoughts in my mind. I was at peace.

Next thing I knew, the meeting was over, and we stacked our cushions up along the wall. The chapel was closing, and our group walked outside. As I walked down the corridor, I saw one of the volunteers, Susan Carabello, looking back at me. Her lovely olive-skinned face was completely open, and her huge, welcoming smile seemed just for me.

As I walked toward her, looking into her twinkling eyes, I started to recognize something I had never seen before. It was like this vast, peaceful emptiness, free of any sense of separation. For the first time I experienced oneness, absolute sameness, with another person. Joy and appreciation filled me to the brim. Still looking into her eyes, I saw that the recognition was mutual.

"Are you like this always?" I asked her.

"Yes," she said simply. Her gaze went right through my heart.

My whole body, my whole being, fell completely in love with her right there on the spot. I felt love well up inside my heart like I had never experienced with anyone before. It felt like I had never truly *seen* another human being before, like I had never truly *honored* another human being, or even seen this basic goodness in another human being. In that moment I felt so much compassion and love. I fell totally head-over-heels in love with another human being for the sake of nothing but love itself.

I turned, looked up into the sky at all the stars strewn out across the galaxy, and I felt even more love, if that were possible. It was like I was seeing the stars for the first time.

"Look at all those stars," I whispered, as I fell up into the sky.

"Aren't they beautiful?" she whispered back.

Again, it felt like I had never seen nature before, never seen the night sky. Definitely it was the first time I'd ever recognized love in nature. I saw no difference between nature and love. At that exact moment, for the first time, I saw that same loving goodness inside myself, and I fell in love with it. It would be the very beginning of my starting to honor myself and treat myself in a loving fashion. That was the moment I finally stopped putting myself in prison and started honoring my own goodness.

We stood there holding hands, reveling in the night sky, glorifying ourselves in this feeling of oneness with the stars. It was a perfect feeling. Right there on the spot, in the middle of a prison yard, I had my first experience, ever, of pure love.

Oh my God, I gasped inside myself, *I never knew there could be this much love.*

Free at Last

I didn't understand what had happened in that conversation with Gangaji, or even afterwards with Susan as we gazed at the stars. I had no reference point for this kind of love, a love that was quickly stealing possession of my mind and heart.

I hung out with the guys for a while, smoked a cigarette, and took off for my cell. I talked with my roommate, Mack, for a few minutes, then lay down on my bunk and closed my eyes.

All night long this humming sensation kept up inside my head. *Hmmmmmmmm* it went throughout the night, and that was ALL. I could not grab on to a single thought. I kept trying to reach into the stream of thoughts moving by like a rushing river, to grab a twig and hold onto it, but I couldn't catch a single one of them. All I could do was lay there, listening to the humming and witnessing the growing emptiness of my mind. It was like my mind was being erased, like everything I had ever known was simply draining out of my head.

I have since learned that the sound *OM* is the primordial sound of the universe, and I believe that's what I was hearing. I was being thrown back into the primordial truth of myself beyond and before all thoughts.

The next morning I got up and did my usual routine. I ate breakfast in the chow hall, I waited for the bell to ring, and then I went to work. I had a new job as a computer clerk, researching machine parts in the records room for FCI Industries at two hundred dollars a month. It was an upgrade from my job in the commissary where I'd only made sixty dollars a month.

The federal government runs FCI Industries, a company that employs inmates within the federal correctional system. It serves a dual purpose, providing services for other government agencies such as the U.S. Army, Navy, Air Force, Marine Corps, and Postal Service, and it also provides a way to manage, train, and rehabilitate inmates in the federal prison system through employment in one of its industries.

In those days every industry screw, nail, and every part large and small was cataloged and displayed on microfiche film. Different agencies called us to research part numbers in our microfiche library, and then we'd order the parts for them.

I had a female boss at my new job. She was a pretty woman. Kind. Nice legs. The guys lived to look at her legs. "Gettin' a shot" was what they called it.

That day, I couldn't have cared less about gettin' a shot. All I wanted was to go back into the microfiche room where it was dark and quiet and to be alone. I went into the dark room, turned my machine on, and just sat. I couldn't move. By now I was in a state of total bliss, which had slowly been building since breakfast. All I wanted was just to sit there and be absorbed in all the love I felt inside, and the unspeakable stillness. I had never felt a love like that before, a love that had no cause. It just *was*. I couldn't think about it. I couldn't speak about it. All I could do was *be* it. It felt so damned good. I only wanted to be alone, in the dark, with *that*.

Someone so deeply wounded, and so deep into the darkness of life, can experience a profundity of awakening until it is very apparent and overwhelming. Just this one ray of eternal light from Gangaji was all it took to drastically transform me.

Before I knew it, someone was knocking at the door. "Time to go to lunch, man," a fellow worker informed me. I really didn't want to move, but I thought, *Okay, I'll go to lunch, then I'll come right back to the microfiche room and sit,* and that's exactly what I did. I wanted nothing else. I needed nothing else. I cared about nothing else. The bliss was everything. If I wanted anything at all, it was just to sit there and be quiet.

For many weeks thereafter, day in and day out, I sat in the dark solitude of my microfiche room. My boss got used to it. I'd make some excuse to go in. I'd say I was searching for parts, and then I'd just sit in the dark, reveling in the love and the bliss that continued to reveal itself inside me.

Whenever I asked myself, *Who am I?* and I looked deeply within, I honestly could find no one there. "Kenny" appeared to be just a thought in my mind, not the actual truth of who I was. And yet, there I could see myself, this body, this man I knew as Kenny Dale, sitting in the microfiche room, but I no longer seemed to be who I'd always thought I was. This new Kenny was joy. He was love. No longer did I have the usual limiting thoughts running around in my mind, labeling this "good" and that "bad," this "right" and that "wrong." There were no judgments of any kind, only an empty mind, resting in pure awareness, an awareness that was aware of nothing but itself. There was no need to think about anything, and that was the greatest gift of all. The old Kenny had ceased to exist. An all-knowing, all-powerful, all-loving power had taken over my mind and set up residence in my heart. I was free.

As I did what little work I had to do in my darkroom, every simple act of doing something was just that—"doing." My actions left no tracks in the mind, like someone walking down a beach and leaving no footprints in the sand. I could feel my humanness and at the same time this divine power coursing through my body, but I couldn't find any separation between myself and what I could only call the Divine. *That* force knew what to do when and why. I didn't need to know. I didn't even have to think about it. It knew what was best for me. It knew what was best for all beings, everywhere. I decided to trust it. I let go into it. I let it have all of me.

As I sat there day after day, I reflected on many things. I thought about grace, and I realized that grace loved me so much it had used whatever means it could to get my attention, which for me meant being locked up in a cell.

I had thought that this kind of grace would arrive at my death, or at very best through my going to church. In my imagination I had always seen myself struck by grace in the middle of a preacher's fiery sermon. I had envisioned grace blasting my sinful heart open, then walking up to take the altar call and give myself to the Church. I had even tried that strategy a few times at my family's insistence, on the rare occasions when I'd found myself home from prison. I would sit there in my pew, waiting on the Lord to descend upon me, and nothing would happen. Eventually I'd walk out of the church the same sinner I'd walked in.

Now, here I was locked up in a place with a whole lot of pissed off men of every race, each one actively sinning, yet grace had somehow made its meandering trek through the mine fields of my skepticism and into my waiting heart. Grace knew I was ready to receive this amazing gift of freedom, something I could have never known. To this day my heart spills over with gratitude for this unexpected and incomprehensible gift.

I contemplated the meaning of freedom. Up until meeting Gangaji, I still had this belief that positive affirmations were the key to my freedom. No one had told me that one day I would have to actually "let go" of the affirmations in order for them to work. My conviction was that whatever mind can conceive and believe, it can achieve. I had thought that if I could remember all of these great affirmations in every moment, then that was the ticket to my freedom. But I had also seen that reading spiritual books and having a few affirmations stuck on the refrigerator didn't cut it. I had already gotten out of prison loaded with thousands of affirmations and spiritual platitudes and landed right back in jail. I was starting to have a glimmer of understanding that all of those affirmations, as well as all the yoga and the meditation, had only been a preparation for what was to occur when I met Gangaji.

My definition of freedom had always been all mixed up in my mind—a few parts spirituality thrown in with the central desire to be freed from prison. Then a lot of other physical freedoms piled on top of that once I got out. Now I was starting to get glimmers of real understanding. I was beginning to see that first I needed to drop every *concept* of what freedom was. Until that happened, I was not going to realize the freedom I'd been seeking for so long.

Day after day I sat in the bliss of that darkroom, but eventually I started to feel uneasy whenever I'd have to leave the darkroom and go back out into the population. I no longer wanted to play tennis, which, until then, had been one of my main pastimes. I just wanted to go sit on a bench and gaze out at the Rocky Mountains.

At this point I was still hanging out with a few pimps and players, Icy Rivers, Walkman, Stuntman, and the like. And I was still running a pimp game of my own of sorts. I still had me a woman working on the outside. Her name was Lil' E. She weighed a hundred pounds soaking wet. She was sending me money in prison, and in return she was getting a few of my connections. I still had my macaroni, I was cute (or that's what she said anyway), and I was still Slim. To Lil' E, having a pimp in prison was better than no pimp at all.

One day, when I was sitting on my favorite bench, my buddy Stuntman came over and sat down next to me. The afternoon sun glinted off his shaved head and caused little shadows to pool up inside the pockmarks strewn across his cheeks. Stuntman's fingers were fat and swollen like little brown sausages. Pale scars dotted the backs of his chocolate hands from years and years of shooting heroin, continually searching out new veins before they burned up and collapsed.

"Come on, Kenny," he said, "let's go kick the pimp game around." Stuntman's voice was cottony smooth, melodious, always a pleasure to hear. Plus he always looked straight at me. He said what he meant and meant what he said, which was rare in a player and made me feel like I could trust him. It's why I liked hanging out with him. On that day, however, I just wanted to be left alone.

"Naw," I declined. "I'm just gonna sit here." I was feeling so still inside; there was so much peace. Walking the track building air castles about what we would do once we hit the bricks no longer held any juice. I was happy simply being silent, watching the play of my thoughts and witnessing how the mind was constantly in the process of creating some story to follow.

He glanced at me suspiciously like I was sick or something. Suddenly he leapt up off the bench and turned to face me. "What's up with you man? What's going on?" he asked accusingly.

"Stuntman, you know I've been going to regular meetings at the prison chapel, right?"

"Yeah," Stunt shifted uneasily, "what does that have to do with anything?"

"Well, man, I don't understand it yet, but this woman came in and talked to us. It's changed in me. I don't care about the pimp game no more. I don't care about the dope game either. I don't care about nothing but this peace, man. Can I tell you about this peace?"

"Kenny," he snapped, "whatever that is you got, I don't want none. You just keep it over there." He started backing away from me like a gunslinger out of the Wild West, as if we were two gunmen in a saloon with guns drawn. He looked certain that if he turned away from me, I might just shoot him in the back. His eyes said, "Don't you come out those doors 'til I'm on my horse and riding away." What I had found, Stuntman obviously considered dangerous to his hustling health.

Stunt had a woman waiting on him and maybe a hundred thousand in cash stashed somewhere. He was not going to let all of that go for what looked to him like insanity. It was like the rich man in the Bible who went to Jesus wanting to know the way into heaven and Jesus had said, "Go and sell all that you own and follow me." The rich man had walked away sad. Stunt walked away afraid. The same.

It didn't offend me. It didn't hurt me. It didn't even touch me. I understood. Losing Stunt's friendship wasn't a big deal. We never really spent time together after that, chopping it up, kicking it around the yard like we had so often done. I had shifted from "Slim the Player" to just plain Kenny Dale, and our last interaction had been a reflection of that. Those old conversations about pimping and robbing and selling dope led to nowhere, and those people were going nowhere I wanted to go, so we had to separate. Everything about my old life was already falling away, seeping out of my veins like sour sap being squeezed from a tree.

On impulse, I phoned my mother. I didn't try to tell her what was happening to me. What could I say? I didn't understand it myself. Yet I didn't have to. She could hear it in my voice. She could feel it in her soul. Her son had finally come home.

Right off the bat she knew something had changed because I wasn't asking her for money or to do something for me. I was asking her about herself. I asked her how it had been for her all those years I was a criminal in and out of prison.

"Son," she said, "there was many a day when I would get up off my couch and walk to the window. I would open the little curtain and I would look up the street, I would look down the street, I would look across the street, and then I'd look around the yard. In my mind, I'd be asking the Lord, *Where is my son? Is he okay? Is he in jail? Is he dead?* It was like looking through muddy waters, trying to spy dry land."

I, on the other hand, was often locked up in some kind of prison. I would walk to the bars of my cell and I would look up the range, I would look down the range, and if I had one, I would try to look outside my tiny window. I, too, was looking through muddy waters trying to spy dry land. We both had been looking for some kind of comfort, searching for an answer to end our suffering as a mother and a son.

Finally, I had met someone who could help me resolve that cycle of suffering. She herself had seen through the muddy waters. She herself had found dry land. By some inexplicable grace she had found her way into a Colorado prison, to share with us what she had realized, and to help us do the same.

Since then if I'd had one desire, it was to sit and be with the vast stillness that had overtaken my mind and heart. I didn't want to talk to anybody, not even to my spiritual friends. I just wanted to be alone with the peace and the love I was experiencing inside.

I liked to lay on my bunk, alone in the dark, or walk the track at night, a solitary figure in the shadows of the prison yard, gazing at the stars and the moon. My days were spent sitting on my favorite bench, simply being silent and watching the awesome beauty of a cloud drifting by or the tragedy of a newborn raven caught in the concertina wire between the prison's walls.

I reflected on many things, most especially on the mystery of grace. I realized that grace loved me so much that it had used whatever means it could to get my attention, and for me that meant being locked up in a cell.

What was this mysterious thing happening to me? I couldn't make any sense of it. What I did know was that I was okay. Deeply okay. More than okay. I was completely at peace. All I wanted was to be alone with this newborn friend inside me and to contemplate that relationship to the maximum.

To my amazement, gratitude had replaced all the old feelings of self-pity. Rather than feeling sorry for myself for growing old in prison, I was happy just to be alive. I was free, and I had found freedom in the last place I'd ever thought possible—behind prison walls. To this day it's difficult to put into words the magnitude of that initial awakening. Kansas City Slim was dying, and Kenny Johnson, the real Kenny Johnson, was being born.

Everything I was experiencing, I was writing to Gangaji. Mostly, it was some form of "God is this Love; God is this bliss." To this day it's difficult for me to put into words the magnitude of the awakening experience.

> Dear Gangaji
> With much love this letter leaves me and flees to you, My Self. For the last week I have not been able to talk to anyone. My mind and heart have been absorbed in YOU the whole time. Now it is starting to make sense why John was bowled over by your grace and then me.
> Then there are the times of intense headaches and total doubt about all that is happening to me, but the doubt doesn't last long if I pay it no mind.

There is one year left on my sentence and then worldly freedom shall be upon me. Gangaji, it brings me great pleasure to have one more year in prison. What I am experiencing is so subtle, and if this had happened to me in the so-called "free world," surely the ego would have won. What a blessing!

Meditation has changed drastically. Now I wake at 1:30am or so, clearheaded and anxious to meditate. While walking there is meditation. While sitting there is meditation. Just now, while typing this letter, there was a turning within. The question, WHO AM I? arises again and again.

John tells me to follow my heart. This takes courage because the ego is constantly at my throat and trying to take over my mind. I shared my experience of God's grace working in my life with a friend here and it bothered me a little.

John asked me, "Did it feel right at the time?"

"Yes," was my reply.

"Then it was right."

You can be sure that my eyes are always looking into my fellow inmates eyes to see the true Self.

It gives me great pleasure to write this letter to you. You are in my heart, and this is true. "I" is "You."

With much love, Kenny.

The Last Hustle

When I first met Gangaji, I was still a thief at heart, and that thief still had one last ace up his sleeve, one last desire.

She had told me unequivocally, "Kenny, God's grace is here now," but I hadn't been hearing her all the way because I was still holding on to that one last hustle, a plan that had always been there in the back of my mind, and it went something like this:

When I finally get out of the penitentiary, I'll cash a few thousand dollars of phony checks, get my little business together, get me a house with the white picket fence, get me a wife, get me 2.2 children and a dog, and then *I'll live happily ever after.*

As it turned out, even though *I* was the professional thief, it was *she* who stole that one last hustle from *me*. Consciousness Itself proved to be the Ultimate Thief. In order to receive God's grace, I had to surrender fully into *now*, with no promise of a future or nothing in return.

When she stole that card from me, in its place she left *nothing*. That's the truth. Absolutely nothing. And that nothing was the bliss of an empty mind; a mind willing to step into the unknown. It was the bliss of an empty heart; a heart willing to bear whatever life on the outside was going to throw my way without my knowing a thing about how I was going to bear it.

I had witnessed John Sherman suddenly awaken to the realization, "God is love, and nothing else matters," but for me it took some time to sink in all the way. I had still been anchored in the belief that physical freedom was what mattered most. Plus I hadn't just wanted freedom from prison. I'd also wanted the power to read people's minds, to walk through walls, to have sex with as many women as I wanted for as long as I wanted. That was what freedom had meant to me. To my utter surprise, freedom revealed itself to be something altogether different.

In a miracle beyond my wildest imagination, I had found freedom behind prison walls. I had thought freedom outside prison was it, yet here I was, still in prison, and I was happy with *everything*. I was happy with the guards, happy with my cell, happy in all situations. I was in prison, yet I was totally and completely free.

The irony was that as the day of my release approached, fears started creeping in about being on the *outside*. How was I going to make it out there in the world? I had no real job skills. I had no money. How was I going to survive? In prison I'd been reading, meditating, learning yoga, playing tennis, and playing the saxophone. But I hadn't learned how to be an electrician. I hadn't learned how to be a cabinetmaker or a stonemason. I had been trying to find God. Now how could God be a viable trade? How could that feed me?

Eventually, those questions would get answered. Through Gangaji's example I would one day come to realize that what I wanted more than anything else was to serve others. If I shared with them what had happened to me in prison, then maybe, by the same grace that had touched my life, they would find it for themselves. I didn't know how that kind of work could support me. Still, it's what I would be called to do, to trust Love, without yet knowing that Love would indeed take care of everything. Yet before all that occurred, there were a few more tests to pass.

Window Cat

I got paroled from Englewood Federal Prison in December 1995, just a couple of weeks before Christmas. I had hoped that I would be going home to Kansas City, but the state of Iowa still had charges on me. At the last minute I was informed I was being sentenced to fourteen months in an Iowa state prison. I was going to have to face the music one last time. They took me to the Golden, Colorado, county jail and threw me into a holding tank.

I put in my one free phone call that day to Maitri at the Gangaji Foundation, and I told her that I would not be able to make it to Boulder. I had been looking forward to going there and hanging out for a while with the *sangha*, my newfound spiritual community, and then making my way home to Kansas City. Everyone in Boulder was expecting me.

"Oh, Kenny," she said, "I hate to hear that. You're not going to meet everyone at the Foundation, but what a great opportunity for you to just sit in that and find peace."

At first her lack of anger and disappointment with my "fate" took me by surprise. Naturally I wanted her to commiserate with how I was getting fucked by the prison system *one more time*. Yet I had to let all that go. I realized that it *was* a great opportunity. It was a test I was willing and ready to embrace.

Back in the holding cell, this guy with fire-engine-red hair and huge freckles was bouncing all over the place. The hair and freckles made him hard to miss. He had a smile so toothy you might swear he had an extra set in there, and he was using every one of them to let us know he was not a happy camper this holiday season. He was complaining at the top of his lungs that he wanted out, he wanted this, he wanted that. I decided not to respond to him. Why pour gasoline on a raging fire?

I resolved to just sit and be quiet. I quit trying to make phone calls. I quit trying to fight anything at all.

After getting booked in and fingerprinted, they took me up

219

to a one-man cell where I was to live for a few days before they let me out into the general population. They had to check out all the newly incarcerated to try to ascertain the level of danger they might pose to the rest of the population.

Every morning I got up at six and wrapped my head in a towel because it was so cold. They had the damned air-conditioning on even in the wintertime. It was literally freezing, the whole jail hermetically sealed like a meat locker. Next, I got my blankets and pillow and climbed up onto the window ledge of my cell, which had just enough room for me to sit.

And sit I did, all day long like a cat on a window perch, watching life move and flow outside my window. My view looked out onto a horse barn, a pasture, and a wide expanse of the Rocky Mountains. I watched the horses eating on three legs, their butts turned into the wind. I watched the prison vans bringing their arrests in. Later, I would see those same people make bond and walk back out with their loved ones. I watched people coming in to court. I watched the clouds drift by. I did nothing but sit on my perch, day in and day out, watching the life happening outside my prison window and the thoughts that came and went inside my mind.

I was happy to be alone in my cell. I didn't want to read. I didn't want to study. I just wanted to sit in the window like a cat and watch life. On the fourth day, about eight at night, a guard came to my door. "Are you all right?" he asked. "I've been observing you for four days, and you've been sitting in that window the whole time."

"Man," I replied, "I have never been happier. I am totally at peace."

"Okay," he whispered, looking puzzled, and shut the door.

For the first seven days mealtimes were the only times I had contact with other human beings. Finally I was shifted to a group cell with other inmates.

One day Randy, this young white guy, came knocking at my door. "Can I come in?" he asked. His bottom lip had flakes of dried skin sticking out in the places where he'd been chewing on it. His hands darted all over the place while he talked, but when they did stop every once in a while for a split second, I noticed he had nubs for nails. They had been chewed all the way to the quick.

This guy is a wreck, I thought, but to not let him know, I gave him a big smile.

"Sure man, come on in," I invited. He sat down and immediately started telling me his troubles.

"I've got a girlfriend out there, man. She's been stressing about my robbery case. I don't know what the hell to do. Those other guys hanging in the rec room, the one's watching TV and smoking cigarettes, they were trying to help me, but I could tell from their tattoos that they were all skinheads. I didn't trust them."

Why is this complete stranger telling me his troubles? I was thinking. *I don't know anything about his girlfriend or the terms of his case.* But to my surprise, once Randy had run down his predicament, the perfect answer appeared.

"You know what man?" I said matter-of-factly. "What you need to do is call your attorney and tell him what kind of deal you want. Is this your first offense?"

"Yes," he said, chewing on his bottom lip and drawing blood. *If he keeps this up he's gonna need a transfusion*, I thought.

"Are you able to live your probation down?"

"Yeah, my boss still has my job open for me."

"Tell your attorney you want probation as soon as possible, and that you have a family that needs you. Be honest with him man. Then call your girlfriend and let her know that when you get out of here, you're gonna do everything she asks. Every time I didn't listen to my woman I went to jail. Listen to your lady, man. She won't give you bad advice.

"Lastly, ask God for help. God will hear your heart, and God will take care of everything." Here I was, giving him advice that I hadn't yet time-tested on myself. Even so, I saw him visibly relax.

He came back a couple of days later with good news.

"Man, guess what? All they're giving me is probation, and I'm going home. My girlfriend appreciated my phone call, and everything is great with her. Thank you so much."

Something new was starting to happen in my interactions with others. I had never given out advice before. I had always been the one looking for advice. Something about the way I was seeing things had been rearranged. People started coming to my cell to tell me their troubles, and I had no idea why. I wasn't soliciting. I wasn't pimpin'. I wasn't hustling. I was just staying quiet, alone in my cell.

Throughout my life there had been a whole slew of men who had wanted to be my mentor, and they were; yet they had all been criminals. The preachers had never really gotten through to me simply because I had very seldom made it to church to be mentored. I had met some good people along the way, such as that guard, Officer Ricks, who had told me my light could never die. Then there had been my friend Brown, who had refused to sell me more cocaine when I'd been standing on his porch in the middle of the night trying to trade my shoes for one more hit. There had been the Black Israelites, and there had been Pops, the one who had been the most unforgettable human landmark on the path before meeting Gangaji. There had been many books to help me along the way, but few humans had affected me as much as Pops had. Maybe it was because we had been locked up in the same cell day and night, but most likely it was because Pops had an honest, natural way about him. His devotion to the arts and to truth was real and unpretentious.

Now, in our work in the prisons, it is really strange to have people thank me for being who I am. I did not start out wanting or trying to be a light for others. My one desire had been just to get out of jail and stay out. Now, this being a role model is what I call "icing on the cake." It is really humbling to come from the streets as one who brought destruction to everyone he met and now to find myself trying to bring as much love as possible to all whom I meet. It is a joy to speak of the glory of this mysterious force that is always present and available to us for the greater good of mankind. I am doing for others what Pops did for me. Simply by being my natural people-loving self, and by doing my practice of rightly dividing out the good from the bad, I am an example for men and women who are looking for a Pops in their lives. After all this time I can finally say that I am *a workman that needeth not to be ashamed, rightly dividing the word of truth.*

One Heaven, One Hell

Just before Christmas, the authorities from Iowa came down and loaded me up in another van. They shackled four of us together, two white guys, a Mexican dude, and me. We were a pitiful sight, the four of us shuffling out together and barely managing to climb into the van. Everyone's stress, all of the confusion and the anger, climbed right on up inside that van with us. What followed was one of the biggest tests I had ever faced in my thirty years of incarceration. I wrote to Gangaji about it after finally arriving in Iowa.

> *Dearest Gangaji,*
>
> *I was paroled on December 8, 1995, to Kansas City, Missouri. However, my going home to be with my family for the holidays was not to be. The state authorities of Iowa placed a detainer on me, and this body was re-incarcerated to a county jail. I called Maitri and my daughter to tell them that freedom for this body would not be forthcoming this day. Maitri's plans included my seeing all the volunteers of the Gangaji Foundation and staying in Boulder overnight before going on to Kansas City. My daughter had visions of my seeing the grandkids in their first Christmas play. This one call to them dashed those plans upon the rocks of expectation.*
>
> *Gangaji, I love you. This love is so deep until I truly can see no end.*
>
> *ENDLESS LOVE!!!*
>
> *While in the county jail, sitting all alone and looking out the window, gazing at the mountains, I thought of what Maitri had said to me earlier: "Kenny, what a great opportunity to go deeper into THAT."*
>
> *After thirty-two months of incarceration, the last thing on my mind was to be in another jail for at least six more*

months. However, it was apparent that Maitri was right, so I assumed my seat and sat.

For hours on end, I just sat and looked at the mountains, entertaining no thought. One officer became so concerned that he opened my door to see if all was well with me. This man had never been happier.

So many thoughts arose to shake my resolve to be present in the moment. At such times, I would reflect upon how Ramana had lived deep in the basement of the thousand-pillared hall, being eaten alive by rats, and yet he never moved. Surely, I could endure whatever came forth.

Gangaji, I love you so much because you came into prison and visited me with your sword of Compassion. You slew the demon "delusion." There are times when I want to be with you so bad until it hurts, but when I looked into the truth of even that desire, surely I cannot find even a Gangaji.

In prison there is so much pain. Everyone is creating some scheme to get out of jail and some plan to get rich. There's nothing but hate and hurt. There are excuses for everything, and the guards are the enemy.

Back in the county jail, I was awakened by a voice over the intercom in my cell, telling me to pack my stuff, people were there to pick me up and take me back to Iowa. Once I was in the lobby, there stood four pitiful looking inmates, shackled heavily around the waist and feet. We were all led to a white utility van, which would be our home for the next six days. This van, at most times, would hold ten inmates, eight men and two women. There would be no heat or fresh air, so the smell became oppressive. I will not go into the grossest aspect of why the smell became so bad. The men sat facing each other on these benches welded against the wall. The women were in their own cages. There was never any room to stretch out or relax.

There was nothing but pain. We rode in this van for twenty-four hours straight, and then rested for twelve in some county jail.

Gangaji, the words of Maitri drove me to do one thing—assume my seat and sit. The inmates complained about everything: It's hot in here. When will we eat? Who farted? I want some water. Can we stop and have a cigarette? These ongoing mantras lasted non-stop the whole trip. There was only one thing I could do, and that was to just absorb this pain.

I ABSORBED ALL THEIR SUFFERING AND GAVE IT TO YOU.

It is only now that I can actually shed tears. It hurts so bad to know that my fellow brothers and sisters are crying out, all over America, in these vans of pain, and there is no Kenny in each one to absorb that pain. Please forgive me, but I must cry. These are HUMAN BEINGS, transported like cattle for slaughter. Plus we were and are made to sit in our own filth.

What became increasingly clear was that your grace was with us. What a blessing!!! We were placed in this county jail for twelve hours of rest, and this one inmate kept looking at me, and how I was just kicking back and enjoying the ride.

"Why are you so relaxed and content?" he asked me. We were in a room the size of a living room, and there were seventeen men packed in this cramped space. We were located in Santa Fe, NM. The stench was oppressive as usual.

My answer to the gentleman's question was simple. "I am just being here now, and that is it."

I went on further to tell him a little about my teacher, and how she can lead one to a deeper state of awareness. The most incredible thing happened. I was asking him to find his mind, and we looked into each other's eyes. For one instant he stopped and WOKE UP. I was so amazed and thrilled at the same time. Now I had an ally. For the next two days we just looked at each other and gave a knowing smile or nod. There were so many questions to be answered, but by your grace, all was perfect.

There was also this twenty-year-old kid who was lost, and right before I was to depart, we had a long talk in the van. It is clear that he will get out of prison and take care of his daughter who has been abused by another man.

I love you because you have given yourself to mankind. I can remember my last days in Englewood. Every day, I would go to the chapel and watch three videos over and over—your video, River of Freedom, Ramana's, The Sage of Arunachala, *and Papaji's,* Call Off the Search. *All three have given me the strength to aid and assist my fellow brothers in prison. I can see why you have* satsang *daily. There's nothing but* satsang *anyway.*

When I look at women, I try to see only YOU. Much love, much respect to you, Gangaji.

It is Christmas and I will not be home to enjoy my family. There is so much work to be done, and so few workers. Sometimes I wish I could wave a magic wand, and all the inmates in prison would wake up. But if my presence here can be of service, then what a wonderful Christmas.

One more thing. Whenever things got rough and my resolve seemed to waiver, I would just think of seeing you one day in satsang *on the streets, laughing as you do. Everything seemed worth it after that. So until then, I will just assume my seat and sit.*

With great respect and love, I welcome you into my heart always.

—Kenny

Spontaneous Evolution

Before long it became obvious why those two years for the Iowa tire theft hadn't run concurrent with my federal charges. It was the one loose end that I was always hoping would miraculously disappear, but God had a different plan for me. I was to go back into the Iowa state prison system and minister to the inmates incarcerated there. For the next sixteen months I would be sharing my spiritual experience with men who had never heard of anything like it.

Inmates began to gather in my cell where we had spiritual conversations long into the night. We read books that the Gangaji Foundation sent in by Gangaji, Papaji, and Ramana. Gangaji's own teacher had been H.W.L. Poonjaji (affectionately known as Papaji), who passed away in 1997 at the age of 86. Papaji's guru, Sri Ramana Maharshi, was one of the most renowned Indian sages the world has ever known. Just as I had come from the lineage of Iceberg Slim, The Magnificent Seven, Fillmore Slim, Minnesota Bob, and Sly Ryan, now I was of the lineage of Ramana, Papaji, and Gangaji.

We walked the yard and talked about God, about consciousness. I felt like I was in heaven. Never in my life had I been used like this. I even stopped caring about going home. Men needed me to be there for them, and I was happy to be needed.

When my bunkie saw me meditating, he asked, "Kenny, man, what's all the meditating about? What does it do for you?"

"You really want to know?" I asked. "Let's start meditating together." And so we did, every day. I wasn't consciously ministering, I was just being myself, but guys kept seeking me out. We might be up at two in the morning, smoking cigarettes and hanging out, and before I knew it, I'd be talking about Gangaji, my spiritual experience, and all the books I was reading. We'd speak about spiritual matters for hours. Word got around that if you wanted to talk some heavy shit, I was the guy to talk to.

Guys who wanted to turn their lives around began coming to me for books to read.

Naturally it was the guys having the hardest time in jail who started coming to learn to meditate and let go of their suffering. I didn't know it at the time, but those interactions were the genesis of what would one day grow into my own nonprofit prison program, This Sacred Space. Together, in prison, we were finding a sacred space, a place where we could speak of God, of peace, of spirituality, and each man was having the opportunity to discover that sacred space inside himself. They all knew the suffering of prison intimately, yet now they were discovering that this sacred space within them was free from suffering. I shared with them only what I found to be true in my own experience.

> *This sacred space is always here. It's never not here. It's everywhere, in every moment, and once you have the experience of that, you cannot really say that you don't know the truth of the matter. You cannot ever completely go back to your old ways of thinking and being. You are changed forever. If you tell the truth about what is here now, what is always present, you cannot deny its existence. Having that awareness will constantly challenge you to let every story of suffering go. It will call you to let go of every unnecessary fear, every unnecessary painful emotion, every unhealthy desire or addiction. Once you have that initial experience of the peace that is always here, that's your initiation into Sacred Space, and it will never leave you. You will find that you can let go of anything, no matter how big it seems or how difficult, because you will want to let go of it more than you want to hang on to it. Each time you let go of some burdensome story about yourself or anyone else, you will be filled with gratitude because each instance is an opportunity to realize that you're okay, God is still here, peace is still here, love is still here.*

One day, the prison chaplain came to me and said, "I've been hearing about you Kenny. You're having all these books sent here. I've been approving these books. What's this all about?"

"I was locked up in a federal prison," I told him, "and I met this spiritual teacher, Gangaji. She had a pivotal effect on me. When she came in, I asked her about God's grace, and right there on the spot, my life changed for the better. Those books coming in about Gangaji, Papaji, and Ramana, those folks are from a lineage of awakened people who speak about the truth, about the oneness of life. The teachings of Christ, the teachings of the Buddha, Mohammed, they're all one, sir. I serve that oneness now. I try to share that with the men so that they also can change their lives. It's what I do now."

Looking me over skeptically, he replied, "You look thoroughly convinced of this story you're telling yourself."

I didn't mind his skepticism. "However you want to see it is fine by me," I said. "I'm grateful for the life I'm living now." I couldn't have been more sincere.

He had no reference point for this concept of awakening, so all he had to say was "It's good that you're not causing trouble here."

I didn't expect him to embrace my point of view, and I didn't need him to. I never knew who would be attracted to this. But since he was asking, I shared my direct experience with him. Because he could find nothing to refute my experience or to doubt it, in the end he just said, "Whatever books you want, whatever material you want, I'm fine with that."

I had to keep asking the Gangaji Foundation for more books for the guys. They were learning to let each stressful thought go as it came up until they were finally in a place where their minds were empty of stressful thoughts.

"Explore that emptiness," I encouraged them. "Rest in that spaciousness. It's what is always present. We don't usually notice it because of the constant activity of our thoughts. Let the thoughts stop and there it is. Stay there. Stay there and explore the spaciousness.

"Once you are able to drop everything and just for an instant feel the truth, the love, the richness that is present in every moment, you can begin to explore that, to play with that, and to allow that experience to grow. There will be no doubt that it is real for you. It is as real as a mountain, yet you can't put your finger on it because it is everywhere. It is in your heart, in your awareness, in your thought processes, looking out through your eyes. You will experience it as something living inside you and you living inside it."

Men were waking up all around me, popping and breaking through. It was a truly amazing, magical time, one of the most beautiful times of my life.

When I got transferred to another cell in another part of the prison, my little group of guys was devastated. "You can't go Kenny," they wailed. "What are we gonna do without you?"

"Everything you need, you got right here whenever you let everything else go." I reminded them of their own spiritual experience. "You know how to let the story go, which means you also know that you don't have to suffer. You have a choice."

I understood that they had to realize and to trust that their own spiritual experience was their refuge. The peace they were finding had nothing to do with me. Over time I had come to understand that my true teacher was always inside me. I knew that their true teacher was always there for them, and within them, because I was finding that mine was always there for me.

As soon as I set foot in the new dorm, I saw nothing but suffering all around me. I spent time with the child molesters, the guys considered the worst of the worst at the very bottom of the prison hierarchy. "Baby rapists" was what the other inmates called them. They were always taking a beating from someone in the prison, and they were in so much pain. They latched on to me quickly after my arrival in the dorm. I embraced them all. We too started to have long conversations into the night about consciousness, about oneness.

I got transferred a few more times in this last period of my incarceration. Each time the guys would get depressed and plead with me not to go. As if I had a choice! "I got to go, man, but you're going to be all right," I assured them. "You're going to be okay. Everything you need is right here, remember?"

Finally I was assigned to a work program at a plastics factory and was released to a minimum-security prison in Newton, Iowa. There I witnessed something that made a lasting impression.

Housed four to a room, we all had to share one tiny little metal sink in the corner for washing up. Whenever this one guy, Karl, would use the sink to shave, brush his teeth, and comb his hair, he carefully cleaned up the sink and the mirror after himself.

I was continually amazed by the fact that he cleaned out the sink every time he used it. It told me so much about that gentleman. Here he was, a criminal and a convict, yet he cared not only about his personal hygiene, but also about the next person who would be at the sink after him.

I was so impressed by this simple act of respect for others that I began to imitate him. He wasn't trying to teach me anything. He never even knew I was watching. Yet to this day, no matter where I am, I clean the sink up after I use it. I have never forgotten the power that one simple act can have, and its unlimited, unknown, reverberations.

Though I had some painful but productive lessons still to learn, Karl was a role model who taught me a profound lesson about love in action, without saying a word.

Redemption

Working at the plastics factory for minimum wage while living at the Newton Correctional Release Center was part of my reentry program. I went to anger management classes. I went to NA and AA. The program that impacted me the most, however, was the victim/offender program.

The heart of most victim/offender programs is a face-to-face sit down between victims of violent crimes such as robbery, rape, and murder, and their perpetrators. We inmates listened while the victims told us how our crimes had affected them. It was often a transformative process for both parties, because the victims got an opportunity to understand that the perpetrators were human, and the perpetrators got an opportunity to see that the victims were human. Sometimes the victim's actual perpetrator was in the room, sometimes he wasn't.

One Caucasian woman, Nancy, had been the victim of a violent black boyfriend, and she singled me out, I suppose mostly because I was black. Even though I wasn't "her" perpetrator, I was expected to play that role. My job was to simply sit there and listen, not say a word, not defend, not justify, just listen. We started by sitting down as a group while she told us her story.

"He was my boyfriend," she began, "and I kept trying to take care of him, but he just kept doing drugs. Then he started beating me, and I kept helping him anyway. Then he started raping me. He was in the military, and he was a very tough black guy. I was afraid of him." As she said that last part, she turned to me, eyes full of tears, and looked me dead square in the eye.

She's accusing me! I realized. I wasn't the black man who had hurt her, but I was sucked into her pain anyway. I could see that she was transferring all of her hatred onto me. As far as she was concerned, I was the guy who had done this to her.

It was hard. To this day I think I'm still dealing with certain aspects of that encounter. On the one hand, I felt defensive, like,

Hey, I'm innocent here! Yet on the other hand, I understood her pain, and I felt so much love for her.

I apologized. I told her I was sorry that this had happened to her, and I asked if there was any way I could help. I felt so much compassion for that woman that day. I'll never forget her. By the time she left, we were both feeling a lot of love. This was my first experience of witnessing a person healing their trauma.

At the time, I wasn't connecting what had happened to Nancy with the way that I myself had treated India, Ollie, and Clara and so many other women. I was still experiencing some shutdown in that area. None of the women I'd hurt in the past had ever confronted me with their pain. I don't think they even understood they'd been damaged. Those women never had the opportunity to see how much they'd been hurt. I wonder if, like me, they were shut off, numb and out of touch with themselves. So although I was able to feel Nancy's pain that day, I still wasn't particularly in touch with India's pain, or Clara's, or Ollie's.

For the longest time after I met Gangaji and had the awakening, it felt like all my past actions had just been wiped away, and along with them any awareness of remorse, shame, or guilt. I was just this empty guy. My whole past was simply gone. There was no attachment to the old Kenny. I had been born again, and all those hurts and pains and crimes were like they had never existed. I hadn't robbed that bank. I hadn't hit those women. The guy who had done all of that was gone. This new guy, he didn't do that stuff. I was only conscious of the present moment. It had been a near perfect redemption.

Pimp? Dead, gone. Sneak thief? No more. Violence? Gone.

Yet the truth was, it wasn't over, not by far. It was not what it had seemed to be. There were many more layers still to be peeled.

It took some time for me to feel remorse for the hurt I had caused in my past, but when it finally dawned, it hit like a freight train. *Damn,* I thought, *what was I thinking? Who was I back then? How could I have hit those women?*

Until then I had never really begun to face all that pain, or even acknowledge its existence in the first place. I felt I had just been a young man trying to play the role he thought he was supposed to play. I wasn't doing those things anymore, so why look back? I didn't see any point in wallowing in the past. I felt that God had forgiven me for of all it, and it had just simply been wiped out. I didn't realize that to some extent, I was still pushing it under the rug.

Of course *God* had forgiven me. The last step, however, was for me to let that forgiveness in all the way and finally, consciously, to forgive myself.

When the forgiveness finally happened, I had been out of prison for some time. I was having a conversation one day about the women in my past with my good friend Dia, and she had the courage and the insight to ask me, "Kenny, have you forgiven yourself?" When she asked me that, I was forced to look inside and ask, *Have I forgiven myself for all the pain that I've caused? I know that God has forgiven me, but have I forgiven me? God has wiped everything clean, but have I wiped everything clean?*

Instantly, I knew that I hadn't. I had still been making a separation between myself and God. I had still been defending against something that I didn't want to feel. I had actually been protecting against forgiving myself because it meant I would first have to really feel the pain of having hurt others. I had been telling other people to love themselves first, that only then could they truly love another, but I hadn't been taking my own advice. It was *my* healing that needed to happen. If I hadn't healed this all the way inside my own heart, then how would I truly help others to heal?

Most inmates never reach the level of forgiving themselves, of making amends not only to their victims but also to themselves. Consequently, when they get back out, they start doing the same crazy stuff all over again because all of that actually feels easier than facing their pain.

Today I tell inmates, "Don't be discouraged if you find yourself coming up short. Forgive yourself, truly forgive yourself, and move on. The next time that challenge arises is a blessed chance to do it differently. You always have that choice. Awakening never ends."

The only way I could hear the message that I had a choice was to meet someone who could see far deeper than I could, someone I was able to recognize as coming from a real, true, and deep place, a place of eternity. Everybody else had been talking to me from a limited perspective. When I met someone who was talking from an unlimited perspective, I could begin to see the unlimited possibilities for myself. I saw that I never had to be a criminal again, never had to beat anybody up again. Again, I thanked my lucky stars for having met Gangaji.

This is why victim/offender programs are so powerful. It's an opportunity for victims to wake up out of their pain and for perpetrators to wake up out of their shame. It's an opportunity to step into this limitless love.

When I talk to men and women today, it's from a place of limitless love. I know that it's possible for them to catch that and live from that, because it happened to me. I know that I am just like them, and they are just like me. That's where the healing is. God's grace is here for each person just as they are, whether a murderer, a rapist, or a thief. I know that if they are somehow able to taste this place of limitless love, then perhaps they will be able to change.

PART 7

Fire of the Unknown

*"What is enlightenment? Awakening? It is going home,
being home, and in your home, you have
all you could have ever asked for."*

—K.J.

Choosing Freedom

My final parole was February 1997. Never again would I be incarcerated or participate in an illegal activity. This miracle has never ceased to amaze me. There are still times that I almost feel like I don't deserve to be free. I still ask myself, *Is this really happening to me?* Not a day goes by that I don't thank the universe and the grace of God for my freedom.

Back out on the streets a free man, I was entering unknown territory and I knew it. I had no idea how I was going to survive. I vowed within myself to take it one day at a time, one hour at a time, one moment at a time, and there have been many times I've been sorely tested, like walking straight into a fire without being able to see what's on the other side.

That first day walking out of prison felt so damned good. Just to sit in the car with my sister and her boyfriend and ride back to Kansas City was pure heaven. I smoked my last cigarette that morning while they were driving up the hill to get me. As soon as I'd heard I was getting out, I said to myself, *Okay, Kenny, now you're done with that one too.*

While at Englewood prison I had written to a Zen priest named Patrick about my addiction to cigarettes. I had told him it was my understanding that a person on the spiritual path needed to be free of habits. Smoking was a burden. His response floored me. It was something I had never considered.

"Kenny," he wrote, "each time you get ready to smoke, stop, go to a quiet place inside yourself, and then *really* smoke. Watch yourself take out the cigarette, then the matches, and then feel how it really feels to smoke. Taste the smoke, feel it go deep into your lungs. Smoke totally and completely." Here I'd been wanting some deep spiritual teaching that would immediately cause the habit to fall away, and what he was suggesting was that I go deeper into my addiction.

For the remainder of my time in prison, I always took special pains to pay total attention whenever I smoked. Now I was throwing away my last cigarette, watching it smolder on the ground in front of me. I knew I was done with it.

I also knew I never wanted to be handcuffed again, and that I never wanted to go back to jail again. No longer was there any attachment to the street life. I had no desire to go to a nightclub. I knew my happiness didn't depend on what kind of car I'd be driving. My attachment was to being at peace. It was unknown, and yet it was known. I didn't know *how* I was going to be okay, I just knew that I would be. I trusted that I would somehow be guided and taken care of. I wasn't afraid of the world.

Soon after I arrived back in Kansas City I ran into Lil' E, and she tried to seduce me. It was obvious that she wanted a booty call, but I wasn't interested in that. As it turned out, what she *really* wanted was to tell me all her problems, and I was fine with that.

I asked her, "Baby, what do you really want?"

"Kenny," she replied, "what I really want is to be happy."

I felt so much peace and compassion for her. I looked her straight in the eye and said, "You want to be happy? You already got all that, and deep inside, you know it. Happiness is here right now. That's the only place it can be. If you let the story of your problems go, even for a moment, then what have you got?"

With those words, she just dropped down inside and relaxed. She had to go into the bedroom and lie down. Whenever you let your story go—the story you've been telling about yourself and your life—that's usually what you want to do. You just want to lie down.

Lil' E called me back the next day and said, "Kenny Dale, you a bad motherfucker. I feel soooo good."

I was glad I didn't take advantage of her ignorance and go back to the old ways of two people using each other for their own advantage. The feeling of peace and compassion was the true gold that stands the test and lasts. My old way of connecting was like the "brass and glass" – it looked good until it was seen for what it was. After the act I just wanted to be shed of that person pronto. There was no more attraction. The sweet nothings had been simply that: sweet empty promises to get what I wanted. No hugging and kissing afterwards, no talking about what came up before, during, and after the intimate connection.

I lived with my mother that first year out, but my daughter Chanette and I were constantly with each other. We went everywhere together. It surprised me how much we were alike. We also had our issues to work through, however. By this time she was thirty-two years old and I was forty-nine. We had never really had a solid father-daughter relationship, so now there we were, her acting like a three-year-old and me acting eighteen. We were both trying to find a place to be reunited as father and daughter. She was clutching on to me every chance she got. Her previous conditioning told her that surely I'd be leaving soon. That had always been my modus operandi. In the past, whenever I'd come to town, I'd hang out with her for a short while and then take off.

This time around was a hundred and eighty degrees the opposite direction. Most mornings found me sitting around the table with my daughter and all my grandkids, eating breakfast and joking around.

The happy state I was in was evident to everyone. I was truly okay with life. I was okay with having a job that didn't pay much. I was okay with the fact that my new girlfriend was handicapped and had a limp. I was okay with going back to church and getting baptized by the preacher.

During that time, I was working at the Sheraton Suites Hotel in Kansas City, setting up conference rooms for meetings and parties. The other guys I worked with were younger than me, in their late twenties, and they were all on parole. They called me "OG," short for "original gangster," which was what all the old players got called.

This one guy, Mack Honey, was a marijuana dealer, and he was using his job at the hotel as a front for his real game, which was selling weed. He invited me over to his house. He said he wanted to help me out, give me a gift. I figured it was most likely some marijuana, which I didn't want, and I was trying to figure some gracious way out of accepting. But when I got there, he gave me ten one hundred dollar bills. All he said was, "Here man, take care of yourself."

Now I had me an extra thousand dollars. There it was, sitting on my dresser, and I started thinking how I could flip it, turn it around and make more money with it. I could go to Chicago and buy some cheap clothing, some watches and rings, come back and sell it all for a huge profit, and then go back and do it again. The old hustling nature was still there inside, and now it was whispering in my ear. But I didn't move. I just kept sitting with it.

Suddenly, blessedly, I had a conscience about it. I knew that the money was drug money, and if I did what I'd been thinking about, I'd be saying yes again to the game. I'd be back out there hustling. I'd be saying yes to lying and conning people, and it was clear I didn't want to go down that road again. I put the money back in the envelope, and when I went to work that evening, I gave it back to Mack.

It was such a relief not to succumb to the temptation, and to feel secure in the knowledge that the old nature hadn't won. It was the final breaking of the biggest addiction of my life, the addiction to hustling.

I have never come that close to succumbing to the temptation again, but that's because I've come to understand and accept that the old nature is always just right there, biding its time, waiting to find just the right moment to whisper in my ear again.

In Islam it is said that there is a Jinn (companion) sitting on your shoulder, whispering to you, encouraging you to follow base desires that will get you into trouble, and only through service to our creator can we repel this whisperer.

By some mysterious grace I had finally found a conscience, a true means by which to "rightly divide." I was beginning to have some real awareness about the choices I was making. The path of conscience is the same as the path of choice.

My greatest joy now is the path of awakening. My greatest fear is going back to prison. Put the two of them together, and they keep me real.

Anger Management

In 1999, I got married, and my issues regarding domestic violence came back up in my face full force. I had moved from Boulder, Colorado, to Marin County, California, so that I could live closer to Gangaji.

For many years after meeting Gangaji, I was in such a state of bliss that even in my day-to-day awareness it was very clear that I was love itself. That high state, however, had begun to fade into the background somewhat because there were still issues I hadn't totally dealt with. It had taken some time for them to come to the foreground so that they could be cleared. One of the biggest issues was that I had yet to make real peace with my anger.

It was a complete surprise, but there it was coming back again in this marriage, and I found that I still had a lot of rage inside. That's when Gangaji and her husband, Eli Jaxon Bear, suggested that I attend anger management classes. Gangaji had written me a letter in which she'd said, "This time, Kenny, really do the work."

I was in that class for eight weeks. It took me a long ways toward healing my anger, but the marriage was beyond healing and we divorced soon after.

At the classes we learned to hug ourselves and to give ourselves love. I started learning to appreciate myself. I began looking in the mirror and talking to myself. I learned to hold myself and to give myself relief, to allow myself to feel the impulse to hit, and then to calm down and hold myself. Finally I began to realize that I didn't have to lash out when I was angry. I had found an alternative to violence.

After learning to give myself relief from my anger, I experienced just one last episode of losing control. It happened in the early years of my relationship with my cherished partner, Rupam.

We were having an argument. She pushed me, and I grabbed her. When I did I accidentally scratched her ear with my fingernail, causing it to bleed. The sight of that blood on her ear stopped me in my tracks. Immediately the argument was over. Done. Finished. At the time of this writing, nearly thirteen years later, we've had no further violent episodes.

I am respectful of my anger because I know where it can lead. Now when inmates ask me how to deal with their anger, I tell them not to try to get rid of it, but simply to acknowledge it. At least then there's some conscious awareness about the anger, rather than allowing it to run the show unconsciously, and that's the first step.

I used to think I could somehow pull anger out of my body and be rid of it forever, but I found that to be an impossibility. Anger is a natural part of being alive, and in some cases, necessary for survival.

My violence was a symptom of a sickness, and that sickness was a lack of love for myself. Now I simply acknowledge the fact that I'm angry. Then I ask myself, *Are you loving yourself?* Since I've learned to love myself, to calm myself, and to give myself relief, there is more tolerance, both for myself and for the person I'm angry with. But it had to start with me, with my loving myself, which is something I had never before considered. I had to find my own worth, my own lovability, in me, Kenny, the conditioned human being. There is no specific formula for finding that, just the *willingness*. Rather than lamenting that my mother never hugged me, or having the hopes that my girlfriend *would* hug me, I had to become willing to love myself, and that willingness created a huge internal shift.

As I look back at myself as a young child, I see a boy who was desperately searching for attention, for kindness, for love, for a genuine smile. My robbing and stealing, driving a flashy car, had been my way of getting people to pay attention to me. I had thought I was desperate for the money or for the "thing" I was stealing, but my real desperation had been for someone to take time out of their life and see me as someone having value and worth.

The more that people had failed to truly see me, the more crimes I had committed, the more frequent they had become, and the more life-threatening for the people involved. I had thought I could buy my way out of the pain, hustle my way out of the suffering, steal my way out of loneliness. I had felt isolated from the rest of the world, and I had tried to insulate myself from the pain of that. That insulation was my anger, my rebelliousness, my "fuck you" to a world that didn't seem to recognize Kenneth Dale Johnson as a valid human being.

Now, I am a man of sixty-two, and as I look back at that hard-headed boy of eighteen, I want to say to him, "Stop. Let your anger go. There is another way out of the madness. The way out is love. Choose the path of love. Choose peace."

If I could, I would hug that boy and hold him. I would make time for him when there was no time. I would go out of my way to let him know that his words had merit, that his ideas were valid, that his thoughts were relevant.

A couple of years ago my beloved partner, Rupam, and I were in the kitchen, making our breakfast. The name Rupam, in Sanskrit, means "beauty." We were about to eat breakfast.

I had just been to a spiritual retreat where I'd been pondering this book and the question: "Who gave me good advice as a young kid and teenager?" I found myself asking Rupam what type of relationships she'd had with the adults in her life as a young girl.

She was bent over the kitchen counter, her hair covering her face, but the tone of her voice left me no doubt she was smiling.

"My grandpa taught me about flowers and how to cut them," she said. "He taught me about medicinal herbs. I come from a long line of herbalists."

I could feel the joy and the gratitude coming from her as she reminisced, and at that moment the reality of my own life hit me right between the eyes. Out of nowhere, the tears started to flow. All I could choke out was, "No one talked to me. No one talked to me. No one talked to me."

The magnitude of that realization was so powerful that I

244

went out, sat on our front steps, and hung my head and cried. Rupam followed me. She put her arms around me, and she cried too. There I was, sixty-two years old, crying my eyeballs out over the fact that no one really thought me important enough to sit down and teach me at least a few of their facts of life. The fact that I never had a father to teach me how to play baseball, hammer a nail, or approach a girl was a hard reality. Sadly, almost every single one of the male role models in my young life had been alcoholics and criminals.

At this point in my life, I can feel grateful for every bit of pain and confusion I experienced, because I see how it ultimately served my quest for true self-knowing. Maybe as a square I would have had a more steady, productive life, but would I have come to long for a different life so intensely? Would I have vowed to overcome my conditioning? Would I have found God? Who can say?

Now when my partner and I argue, and the potential for violence is present, I am fully committed to not crossing that line. Anger can still come up like a volcano, but when it does, I don't move. I just let it have me. I sit quietly, fully in the awareness that I'm mad. If I don't act on it, if I stop telling stories inside my head to justify it—such as why I'm angry, who's doing what to me, and why they shouldn't be doing it—then the anger dissipates on its own. It leaves me in peace, and anything that leaves me in peace I consider a gift.

I've also had the opportunity to experience the violence that words alone can impart. She and I were at a hot springs resort one day. Rupam and I were in beautiful surroundings, we'd just gotten a beautiful room, but I was angry about something silly, and I was going off about it.

"Can I help?" she asked. She was sitting on the bed, looking at me with eyes full of love and innocence.

"Hell no, you can't!" I blasted. "Leave me alone!"

Her face fell. I saw the hurt in her eyes as they dropped to the floor. It was as if I had hit her in the face with my fist.

Oh my God, I thought, *now look what you've done.* I felt her surprise, saw the look of devastation. Horrified, I ran over to her, kneeled down, and said, "Honey, I am *so sorry* for yelling at you like that. I truly, sincerely, apologize." Before that day, I had never clearly seen how words spoken in anger could be just like a fist, how they had so much power to make another person hurt. Here she was offering to help me, and I had just slammed her in the face with my words.

I held her. I continued to apologize. My heart broke open in my desire to shield her from my own pain and rage.

Addiction Revisited

As soon as I'd dealt with the anger piece, then sure enough my alcoholism came back to get me.

When I've told the story of my alcoholism to groups outside prison, many people have been astounded. There is a belief that once someone wakes up to the truth of themselves as the totality of love, then that's it, end of story, no problems, no vices, nothing but love ever after.

My experience, however, is that awakening is a process. It doesn't just happen one time and that's it, you're finished. Whatever is unresolved will reappear to be seen in the light of love and consciousness, and whatever is unresolved must be seen. It's a continual awakening, fresh in every moment, infinite and eternal.

By the second year after being released from prison, I was drinking like a fish again. I was driving drunk and fighting with my girlfriend. For five more years I just could not let go of that bottle. I continued to meditate, and I was able to speak eloquently and clearly to others about awakening, but I still found that I needed some kind of medication to handle the stress of learning how to live a different life back on the streets, and mine was in a bottle.

After about the hundredth time of getting drunk, spending all my money, throwing up, and waking up with a horrible hangover, I went to my closest spiritual friends and asked, "How does my drinking affect you?" They were willing to be honest with me. "Kenny," I was told, "I don't like you when you drink because you're not your beautiful loving self that I know you can be. You're not present. You become loud and boisterous and sometimes even ugly. It just doesn't feel like the real you." Again, I was up against a choice.

On New Year's 2002, I got completely wasted at a party and woke up the next day totally torn up. When I asked my girlfriend what had happened the night before, she said, "You were embarrassing and despicable. It was horrible. I wish you would quit drinking." I still wasn't ready, however, to let this thing go, so I drank for another year.

New Year's came around again, and this time I was alone. My girlfriend and I had temporarily broken up. I began drinking while I was getting ready for the party, and by the time I was ready to go downtown and celebrate, I was already drunk. I started down the steps of my porch, but I was so drunk I had to sit down. My head was spinning. I knew I wasn't going to make it to the party. I went back upstairs and laid on my bed, telling myself I was just gonna lie there for a moment and then go to the party.

At 12:01am, my friend Diane called with a cheerful "Happy New Year, Kenny!" I was still drunk and mumbled something unintelligible. The next morning I woke up fully clothed with a huge hangover—mouth like the Sahara, head bursting, stomach on fire.

I'm done, I said to myself. *I am so damned tired of this same old mess. Fuck this! I'm through. I'm finished.*

This thing had kept coming back to me and kept coming back to me. People I loved and respected had told me they preferred being with me when I was sober. Finally, I was able to take that all the way in, to wake up to the fact that I couldn't drink alcohol and that drugs ultimately caused me suffering. No longer was there any juice in those activities. No longer did I see any real life there. Real life was in *not* doing those things. I could live a life of sobriety and commit to a different kind of medicine, the medicine of inner stillness and true love and companionship. I have not picked up the bottle since.

It seems I had to keep visiting that place until I finally got it. The same grace that had been there for me through every trial, every tribulation, and every breach of faith since I'd gotten out of prison was with me still. It was the grace of wanting to be close to my creator, of continuing to pray for real and lasting freedom that helped me to finally make the choice for sobriety once and for all.

I am now consciously choosing to have intimate connections with my own inner feelings and emotions and with other human beings, rather than an intimate relationship with a joint, the bottle, or a cigarette.

True Intimacy

When I got out of prison at the age of forty-nine, I still had no clue what an intimate connection with a woman was. I had always fantasized about being with a square woman, a woman who wasn't in the game, but how would I talk to her? What would I say? The deepest connection I had ever felt with a woman had to do with sex, but even my sexual relations had not been all that intimate. Whenever I'd done something nice for a woman, it was usually to get her in a position to do something for me in return. It was all about manipulation. If I told her she was cute, it was because I wanted her to do something for me. Everything I said was designed to get something for myself.

I had used women to cash checks for me and to sell their bodies for me. They had used me for attention, for protection, and for self-importance. We had used each other for notoriety, sex, and to survive off each other. If a woman said she loved me, it hadn't really meant anything. She could be off with my brother tomorrow. I felt I had to constantly watch my women to make sure they were doing right by me, the same as I had to watch my buddies. That fog of mistrust tainted all that we did to and for each other.

To this day that mistrust can show up. I can still smell it sometimes, even in the smallest of interactions. Realistically, our conditioned ways of being and living can take some time to turn around. It's a process of vigilance.

Now I can appreciate women. My partner is a dream come true, the kind of woman and the kind of relationship I had always wished for. I appreciate her openness and the consciousness she tends to bring to a conversation. When she speaks, more often than not, it's from a place of love, compassion, and honesty.

The way that I relate sexually has also changed beyond my wildest imagination. I have come to have a true appreciation of the power and the sanctity of sexual intimacy. When I started to bring all my awareness to the act of making love, it became an opportunity to experience God as awareness and energy, in myself, in my partner, and in the lovemaking. Being present in the act invariably brought up so much energy until just touching my lover's finger was orgasmic. This energy field would rise and fall over the hours of our lovemaking. We simply rode the waves. Lovemaking was no longer friction-based but energy-focused. Staying totally present in the moment was our goal, the lover and the loving merged as one.

I discovered that to be fully intimate with a woman was to be fully intimate with myself. When I was able to look into my partner's eyes and see the depths of infinite love totally and completely, I realized I didn't need two, three, or more women. I only needed one. When I started to consciously put all my attention on just one woman, my sexual relationship with that woman immediately became more satisfying.

At the time I had first learned to meditate, to quietly watch the in-breath and the out-breath, I had seen how my mind naturally drifted away, and I learned to bring it back to the breath. I stopped being discouraged when my attention drifted away because I realized that I could always come back to what really mattered. I find the same to be true in a relationship.

As a man it seems natural for my mind to sometimes drift to other women. It's human. The mind wanders all the time. The difference now is that I am conscious about my mind's wanderings, and I know how to bring my attention back to what really matters, my one committed relationship. I know that I'm not missing out on anything by staying with just one woman. In the past when I was busy wandering from one woman to the next, I was missing out on what is truly possible when staying totally present with one partner.

In the past, I had learned to cut off my feelings so that I could do what I thought I had to do to survive and be safe. Eventually, when I became able to bring my consciousness to my thoughts, to my relationship, and to my lovemaking, I started becoming aware of all the ways I moved away from love, away from intimacy, away from real connection.

One of those strategies of protection was an ingrained habit of being suspicious of everyone and everything. Doubt and mistrust is something that poisons a lot of relationships. I went through a period where I was plagued by thoughts that Rupam was being intimate with other men or women.

These scenarios of betrayal that my overactive imagination continuously conjured up were very painful, and I searched desperately for any way I could find to feel safe. I believed that if she were to leave me for another man, it would mean that I was worthless, that I was no good, that I had nothing of value to offer her. Blessedly, I saw that all my projections were blocking me from being able to love her completely. I opted to grab on to the love and to get to the real truth of the matter, which was this: I was terrified of her love, her devotion, her dedication to me, and I had been afraid to let it in. No one had ever expressed that kind of love toward me, or if so, I was too blind to see it, so I wasn't able to believe that she could love and care for me so much.

Letting this old suspicious guy go was painful because I was very familiar with that person and his way of doing business. In order to create something beautiful, to birth new life into the world, I had to let the old life go no matter how painful the process. The more I am able to be open and truthful with her, the more she is available to me. Vulnerability is a powerful force. When I was able to finally talk to her about my jealousy and fear of abandonment, the trance was broken. I realized, *Oh, this is what deepening together is about, sharing our feelings, talking it out*. When the spell of this past habit fell away, our relationship moved into a place of deeper intimacy. Now this deepening is transferring into my business relationships and to all other aspects of my life as well. This trust spills over into the world, and it is medicine for all, not just my partner and me.

There are times when I look at her, and all I can see is innocence and sweetness. A love so fierce wells up inside, and I realize, *Holy shit, I love this woman just for who she is*.

Taming the Dragon

Back out on the streets, I could find no reference point for the old Kenny/Slim. I really had been born again, and I had a new appreciation for the phrase: *All things have become new.* The ego that had been identified as a pimp, thief, hustler, and player had died on the killing floor of the church where Gangaji's sword of truth had inflicted a deadly wound. Yet with that death had been a rebirth of a newly forming ego, and a new driver was behind the wheel. It still took me many years to learn how to be back in the "world" with this new egoic self.

One day after being freed from prison, while working for a fellow lover of truth as a painter for his company in Boulder, Colorado, I saw how different our lives were from each other's. This was just a year after getting out. He was my age and he had all those things I feared I would never have. Each day he came to pick me up and take me to work, and I would look at him and think, *Dammit! Here I am out here living amongst people my own age who own homes, have businesses, have families, and I have none of those things. And I may not ever be able to have that simply because, in so many ways, I still feel like a teenager.*

This line of thinking eventually threw me back into deep suffering, and each day it got worse. My friends in my spiritual community would look at me and say, "Kenny why are you suffering so?" All I could say was, "It's hard being out here at fifty years old, not having anything of value, knowing that I cannot pay my bills and that I still haven't been able to have a real relationship with a woman." The reality of who I was as a man, as an ex-con, and as a new card-carrying member of society hit me right between the eyes.

People tried everything to get me out of this fog. It was like the fog I used to feel when I had landed myself back in prison, or even worse than that, the heavy oppression I had once felt when I'd wanted to commit suicide. I began to feel certain it would never lift until death had arrived and completed its assigned duty. My body was free from prison, but I found myself back in a mental jailhouse of monstrous proportions.

Later that first summer, Gangaji came to do a weekend intensive and fundraiser event. For me, intensives were like down-home country revivals that Christians have when a country preacher is coming to town, though what Gangaji was offering I wouldn't call "preaching." Still, that time together as a spiritual community breathed life into deflated and wounded spirits, celebrated rebirth, and gave spiritual sustenance to all. I was scheduled that weekend to speak at a Gangaji Foundation fundraiser being held in honor of Gangaji's prison program and the men and women in prison. Gangaji wanted to keep the prison work alive, and what better spokespersons could there be than John Sherman and myself? John was his ever-loving self, seeing nothing but Gangaji and showering love on her with every breath he took. As far as he could see, there was still nothing but her.

By contrast, I found myself in the pits of wanting what I saw as a better life and realizing that it may not happen. Depression had set the hook deep and was reeling me into the boat of despair. At the Saturday morning meeting I was sitting in my chair with a hangdog look. The meeting went on as usual, but I heard nothing, nor did I feel anything but my story of sorrow.

Susan Carabello, my trusted friend and therapist who had come with Gangaji into Englewood FCI and had taken personal interest in my suffering, whispered in my ear, "Gangaji wants to see you outside." Her words barely made it through my fog of self-pity. Once outside, Gangaji took one look at me, put her arm in mine, and said, "Let's walk!"

As we walked I told Gangaji how hard it was living on the outside. "It was easier in prison," I told her. "Now, I'm out here competing with people who have been free all their lives. They understand how it works out here."

I felt ashamed and was fully expecting her to admonish me. Instead, she just simply said, "Oh Kenny, I see that you are suffering!" This simple recognition that I was in mental anguish floored me. Looking into her eyes, I once again saw the truth of myself. In a matter of seconds Gangaji had somehow managed to annihilate my attachment to the story of self-pity that had begun to imprison me all over again. Again, I was set free, simply through her *seeing* me, accepting me, and acknowledging me as someone worthy of being loved and respected. There had been no attempt to brush my feelings aside as if I should not be depressed. All she saw was a man who had been freed from prison after many years and was suffering from growing pains.

By the time I had walked her to her hotel, I was all smiles. There was joy in my heart. Laughter returned. Gangaji's love had once again invited me to live in the here and now. It was exhilarating, freeing, beautiful beyond belief. I realized that I did not have to carry around the baggage of the past and all of its dead stories and concepts, woundings and craziness. As well, I could drop the stories of the future with all of their hopes, wishful thinking, expectations, and fantasies. They were a weight that I needlessly carried around. Just the dropping of those two imaginary burdens was such a relief. God's Grace is here now, not in the past, not in the future. There was so much to understand in Gangaji's simple utterance, and it has more and deeper meaning every day.

I was being given the opportunity to directly experience the symbolism of being in prison even while living outside prison walls. This is the prison she frees so many from each day of her life. What a blessed gift this freedom is. I was deeply humbled by seeing how much more I still had to learn and just how endless is this surrender.

That evening at the fundraising event, I found myself getting up on that stage and speaking eloquently to hundreds of people about the prison work that the Gangaji Foundation was doing for those in prison. As I stood and looked over at a beaming and smiling Gangaji, I was thinking, *It is not just the iron bars and concertina wire she has freed me from, it is the layers and layers and*

rows upon rows of negative stories that the ego spins to try and draw
me back into suffering.

It seems that so many people are afraid to do the real work or admit that they are terrified of facing their dark stuff and old trauma that still persists after they've had some degree of awakening. Pain is not bad. Pain is good. God can be found in the pain. Freedom can be found in the pain. I have seen this so clearly that now I am truly okay with all kinds of discomfort, and I don't need to know what the outcome will be. The outcome is a mystery. You never know how it's going to come out because you're not in control; God is in control. All I know is that whenever I let go the controls, the gift in the pain reveals itself, and there is peace.

We all have a shadow side, and we can't afford to be unaware of it, or to run away from it, or it will come back and bite us in the ass.

That initial awakening in prison was not the finale of this show called "The Life of Kenny Johnson." Waking up put me on the path of opening to grace and learning to listen to the voice of the guru within, the guru who is always close and ready to assist. This awakening is a getting to know your creator and sustainer intimately. I don't know what a final awakening will mean for me, but I do know that Kenny Johnson is a far better and more content human being whose greatest desire now is to serve that awakening. He is no longer hustling and thieving, beating on women or giving the judicial system hell. He gets up each day and makes an intention to live a life of peace as best as he can and to try to guide others to do the same. Yet he's also mindful and respectful that any moment he could re-experience all of the old anger, sadness, mistrust, delusion, and denial of the truth of his being.

In awakening you don't have to have an answer to every problem. All you need do is wait for the right answer to appear at the right time. You don't have to know everything beforehand; you just have to recognize that there are unlimited options at your disposal each day and each moment. There will be insight, and the mind will reopen to the truth of consciousness for a moment, a flood of light will come in, and then you have to digest it like food. Most human beings cannot surrender to all of consciousness in one single inner event. It takes time, slowly, slowly, until you begin to realize that there's no other place in your mind and heart that you'd rather be.

Stayin' Free

All these years since being released from prison I've had to continually ask myself, *How do I live life now? What do I have to do to stay out of prison today?* By earnestly asking those questions, and staying open to the answers, I have been guided from one job to the next, one person to the next, showing me on a day-to-day basis how to stay out, stay free, and not imprison myself again.

I've also found that no magic bullet exists that is going to once and for all put an end to all my old tendencies. The magic bullet is in being willing to meet each new situation as it arises, and to continue to tell the truth about what really matters.

Along with each awakening experience comes an unknown way of being, and ultimately, this was what I had always been afraid of the most—the unknown. Fear of the unknown, of not being in control, was why I drank, why I hit, why I stole.

Most people are terrified of the unknown, so they keep running back to the known. If an ex-con has no experience holding down a job or having a healthy relationship with a woman, going to church or to the mosque, to the temple or to a meditation group, how are they supposed to do all those things? Most of them go back to robbing, pimping, or selling dope because that's what is known.

I didn't know how to not drink alcohol on the streets. I had been drinking since I was a fourteen-year-old boy. Through grace and through the support of a spiritual community, I realized I could step into that experience of the unknown one situation at a time. I found that no matter how hard the situation felt, the truth was, I was okay. I began to trust the unknown. I began to get comfortable there. Each experience of letting go turned out to be nothing but grace on the other end.

Living in this sacred space of the unknown continues to be an experience of pure joy. Now I want this state of happiness for all beings. I want everyone to realize that their true nature *is* this happiness.

Until I woke up, I didn't know what real happiness was. Now I know that happiness *is life*. Now I am grateful to have an old 1992 Volvo with no air conditioning when it's 99 degrees outside. I'm happy to be doing the hard work of relationship, happy to know that I can share my experience with men and women in prison, happy to see that they can catch this from me. What I know is that if they taste this happiness, they most likely won't be going back to prison again.

Yet the prison that everyone must eventually be freed from is the prison of his or her own mind. Our own minds are the greatest creators of suffering, regardless of our circumstances. Everyone faces challenges in life. The central issue is *how* we face those challenges, *how* we deal with it all in our minds.

Like most of us, when I was in prison, I was always focused on what I could change outside myself. What kind of trade I could learn, what kind of positive affirmations I could spin. It was all external. I had yet to turn my attention to the inner sanctum and take stock of my thinking. I had yet to ask myself, *What kind of world am I creating with my thoughts?* I had yet to look at my prison surroundings and realize that my predominant thought processes were what had led to my being locked up. Once I went in and investigated those inner thought processes, I began to get a glimmer of understanding that my outer world was simply reflecting the thoughts in my mind. Whatever I was projecting into the outer world was simply reflecting back. I began to understand that only when I changed my thinking would my world begin to change.

I began to ask myself, *Where do my thoughts come from? Where do they go? Where does my love come from? Who am I?* The inner answers to those questions changed my life forever. Whenever you sincerely inquire, you will most surely be answered, I guarantee it.

"Waking up" can mean something different for each person. For some, waking up can mean the deepest possible self-realization, total and complete liberation from egoic suffering. For others, waking up may simply be the realization that the life they've been living is no longer satisfying. Whatever type of awakening it is, it's always for the good.

Awakening, insight, never ends. Since who we are is consciousness, and consciousness experiences everything, we have the capacity to experience anything and everything, including consciousness itself. Consciousness is endless.

The truth is that if anyone wants this truth, they've got to get out of the shallow water and dive into the deep end. They've got to be willing to drown. The deep end is the willingness to be humbled, to have the ego totally busted, in each new moment, in each new circumstance. The deep end is the willingness to be vulnerable and to allow oneself to be seen just for who one is. The deep end is the willingness to keep an open mind at all costs, and to keep telling the truth about what really matters.

This Sacred Space

W hen I first got out of the joint in 1997, I never wanted to see another prison. If ever I found myself driving by one, I'd turn my head the other way, refusing to even look at it. Yet I had continued to have these dreams about being back in prison. I'd wake up in a cold sweat, confused and groping around in bed to see if I had a gun next to me, or maybe some drugs, always in a panic. The dreams were telling me, "You haven't done all your time, Kenny. You're going back." And they were right. I was going back.

Eight years later, when I found myself going back into prison as a volunteer, I felt I was paying off my final debt. Even though I was going back in a free man, a part of me was terrified, and I remained scared for quite some time to come. I knew the kind of rough crowd I was talking to, many of them murderers.

In 2005, I was granted 505(c)3 status for the founding of *This Sacred Space*, the nonprofit prison program through which I and other volunteers offer silent meditations and healing circles to men, women and adolescents in all types of correctional facilities. Our work in prisons, jails, and youth facilities provides a safe container for inmates to experience meditation and to share both the pain of their past and the pain of their current imprisonment. It's an opportunity for them to realize that in the very heart of their pain is peace, beauty, wisdom, insight, and freedom from feelings of horror and hopelessness. They begin to realize that their stories are not the deepest truth of who they are and that they have options other than a life of crime.

The men and women incarcerated in our prisons are just like everyone else. They have the same confusion, the same shame, the same guilt, and the same feelings of un-lovability as those of us supposedly not in prison. They are no different. Whenever I speak to groups of people who have never been incarcerated, I hear the same horror stories from those on the outside as I do from those on the inside.

I never imagined that the work of *This Sacred Space* would come to emerge. All along I had just kept praying, "Here I am Lord. I'm available. Send me in." By staying true to that prayer, the money and the support for the program continue to show up to this day. Doubts and apprehensions certainly enter my mind from time-to-time, but I have learned to fully trust that if I just keep doing the work, including my own personal work, the support for the prison program and for my own survival will always be there.

All those years ago when my Aunt Equator used to tell me "the Lord has a work for you, son," I always wondered what she meant. Now I know. Even when I was a thief, Aunt Equator saw who I really was, and I will always be grateful to her for that.

I now have a purpose, a prayer, and that is for God to take this wondrous new life I've been given and to use it to the fullest. My greatest desire is to help every being across this planet find freedom from imprisonment, whether that prison is one of brick and mortar or one of their own unexamined thoughts. I want every person who is suffering to know that they have options. They have choices. There are other ways of being in the world. Ways that are deeply fulfilling. They can be free.

From the moment I was able to receive the message: "God's grace is here now," my life has only gotten better. Each day is a deepening into a newer, cleaner way of being in the world. I have learned how to be happy with myself, with life as it is in all its vicissitudes and confusion, rejections and deceptions. There's nothing like this grace.

By that same grace I now know that there is a power available to us all. That power loves us, wants the best for us, and will do whatever it can to reveal itself to us.

There are a lot of things that bring me joy, but the greatest joy comes from the certainty that no matter what happens, I will be okay. This, I know, is the fruit of waking up, of drinking deeply of my natural self. I say natural because it is natural to live in a state of surrender. It was my unnatural way of living that had kept me incarcerated all those years, and which now has a hold on my brothers and sisters in prison.

Not surrendering made me a wild man. I would wake up each morning and find some way to terrorize my fellow citizens in the named of getting paid. My gratitude will never cease for the miracle of meeting someone who could tame that wild man, tame him in the spirit of peace and real love and compassion. It was compassion that healed me, and which continues to heal me to this day.

My gratitude for that fortuitous meeting with *grace* in the form of Gangaji is unspeakable. I have little doubt that if I had not met her I would be dead at this point or doing life in prison. I feel like my real life started in 1994 when I was finally captured by grace.

Slowly, little by little, again and again, I have come to realize that I am all things. There is nothing that is not me, nothing that is separate from me. Our creator, which is eternal, lives through us and has its being within us. This creative force does not die. It cannot die. It will never die. It is who I am.

If ever I find myself experiencing a problem, I know that I must be identifying with myself as a person, rather than this mysterious creative power that causes me to be alive. If I allow myself to be guided by this power, then all is well. This divine wind blows me wherever I need to be in order to bring about whatever needs to be accomplished.

It is possible to discover our divine connection to ourselves and to see that our disconnection from that is the sole reason and purpose for our suffering. The truth is that suffering is God's greatest gift, if only we would but open to it.

I've faced some challenges in writing this story. For years people said to me, "Kenny you've got something to share that will help others. You should write a book about your life." I didn't want my ego to get puffed up. Plus I didn't put any value on my past, and I didn't want to spend a lot of time focusing back on it.

I felt that all of that was behind me, and now I was a completely different man.

Finally I allowed the possibility to come in. What if my story could actually help others find their way out of prison, whether that prison be a correctional institution or a prison of their own making? I decided to take the leap.

Throughout the process of telling my story, I've come to have a deep appreciation for every experience, however wonderful or heartbreaking, because I understand that all of it was necessary to bring me to where I am today.

Now I speak the truth of Aunt Equator's words to men and women in prison. I speak to the spirit in them just as she was speaking to the spirit in me. I don't see them as criminals. I don't care anything about their past. It doesn't matter to me that they're in prison. I see each one as having their own mission in life. I see them as going somewhere. I know they have a purpose.

Those of you reading this book who happen to be in any kind of prison, I say the same thing to you that I tell every inmate in my programs:

The Lord has a work for you.
This light inside you cannot die.
I love each and every one of you. I do.
I want the best for you.
I see no difference in you than in myself.
I know you can change because I changed.
We are One.

Epilogue

In conclusion, I offer this interview excerpted from the book, *The Awakening West: Conversations with Today's New Western Spiritual Leaders* (Fair Winds Press, 2003). I do so with the express permission of the authors, Lynn Marie Lumiere and John Lumiere-Wins, who interviewed me by telephone in 1996, my last year in the Iowa state prison.

᠅

Kenny, how would you answer the question: "Who are you?"

I am That which was and which is and which will be. Simply put, this means there never was a time when what I am, eternity, did not exist. When you realize that you are awareness, you come to know that you are eternity and will never cease to exist. All you have to do is simply STOP and LOOK and you unerringly know that you have always been here, now, and you will always be here, now.

What do the words enlightenment, realization, awakening mean to you?

People always want to know what is realization, what is enlightenment, what is awakening? It is going home—being home—and in your home you have all that you could ever ask for. It is your natural state. You are no longer sleeping the sleep of delusion. You are always worshiping the divine form of the Beloved. You see Her in the squirrels, the trees, the rocks, and in every human whose eyes you gaze into.

My reward is only a chance to kiss Her, to hold Her, to embrace Her. She is me and I am Her; you can see that we are One.

I have no life as Kenny any more. The Beloved has destroyed the false concepts of "I," "me," and "mine." There is only the spontaneity of just being in the present moment and doing whatever job needs to be done. Just being!

I notice that you speak in terms of the feminine, "Her." Could you comment on this?

This is coming out of my amazement at how all things spring forth from the earth, nature that is. When you contemplate this miracle of life, you automatically recognize the feminine aspect of God—the causeless cause. When absorbed in Awareness, love continually flows from the heart. Since the Beloved cannot be captured in any manner physically, there is a longing. The Beloved is everywhere and yet nowhere. You see the impossibility of possessing Her, so you just adore Her in all things. We are married in the "no thing."

You speak in a beautiful, devotional manner. Could you please say something about devotion when there is a realization of non-duality, of not "other"?

For the longest time there was this sense of separateness within my mind and in the way I dealt with people. However, after realizing the Self, I became aware of the unity of all things. In this unity I realized that I, too, was the loving hand of the Creator. I saw that everything was perfect. There were truly no problems in a perfect creation. There was no need for schemes or deceit. Everything just took care of itself marvelously. This revelation made me happy, ecstatic with joy and gratitude. I came to see how nature praises the Creator. How the sun rises and continually submits itself to the will of Father God. How the moon also does its duty with no complaint. Wherever I looked I saw everything embracing and submitting to the Self.

So, I became like the sun, each morning embracing the mean

guard in my heart, or the angry inmate. At night I would become the moon and embrace the dark moods of the prisoners who longed to be with their loved ones. My heart sent forth torrents of love to them. Even in my dreams I would find myself telling others to let go of all conceptual thoughts and become filled with this love, this bliss. Just by being focused on the Self every hour of the day, the child of devotion was born. My every action became devoted to the Self in all its manifest form.

Kenny, how has this awakening changed the quality of your life?

One's quality of life improves immeasurably. The best part is that you no longer have any question about people, life, God, and so on. Each time a question appears, the answer is right along with it. It is sort of like having this "Wish Fulfilling Tree" inside of you, and there is never a sense of lack. You are always full. Wisdom is your best friend. You are no longer a victim. No game can be played upon you. You no longer play games with people. You value your fellow human and want only the best for him or her.

Before this awakening, there was a distinct feeling of hollowness in all my pursuits. I would buy a new car, believing that the car would bring me much joy. But the opposite happened. There was a longing for something else to make me happy. So I would go shopping and buy some new shoes. Again there came the longing for something else to fill this hollowness. After experiencing this awakening, all desires have been quenched. If I get a new pair of shoes, so what. If a new car comes my way, so what. I am full always. Being here now is all that is. Since joy comes from the immaterial awareness, then it is only natural for me to remain in the place where all happiness, all joy, all peace emanate and pervade this universe.

When one turns the searchlight of awareness on the field of desire, there is nothing.

What do you see as the source of suffering in the world?

So many suffer because there is identification with the thoughts that arise in the mind and because of attachment to these thoughts. Prisoners suffer a great deal because they are attached to loved ones on the outside who they can't be with. Whenever I ask someone to simply inquire into their mind and find the source of a thought, they find nothing and instantly realize that all thoughts are empty and have no power but the power we give them. A question I ask others here in the prison is, "Where does the thought come from and where does it go or return to?" A lot of the brothers say, "Wow!" They can't believe it is so easy to be free and yet be able to live a productive life. They come to realize that if they are sweeping the floor, they are here. If they are shoveling snow, they are here. There is no place where they are not here. When in a group of people, there is the Beloved! Laughing, talking, lifting weights, or jogging.

It seems to us that more Westerners are waking up than ever before. Can you comment on this?

It is the perfect season for Westerners to "wake up." When the fruit is ripe it shall be harvested! We Westerners have inundated ourselves with material things, which have left us hollow inside. The drugs get us high for a while, and then we pursue sex, which leaves us drained. Then after years and years of searching for permanency in impermanent things or feelings or relationships, we are ready! We come to know that all created things can only give us temporary thrills. It is the perfect time for Westerners to experience the awakening. We have prepared ourselves well with all the suffering that we have inflicted upon ourselves.

Is the awakening for everyone or just a rare few?

It is my experience that anyone can "wake up." No one is excluded. They must simply desire to be free. The Beloved is patient and has eternity to wait, so all can and will be free. No one will be lost—for how can the Beloved ever lose Herself?

Do you see spiritual practices as necessary in order to wake up?

As I stated earlier, there is no requirement to being free. After experiencing this awakening, some say that they need a practice. I ask them, "When are you not doing the practice? *Who* is doing the practice? If you sat on the meditation cushion and meditated all day, what would be gained or lost? If you worked hard at your job and you were aware of your True Self, what would be gained or what would be lost?" They say, "Nothing." "So, please tell me when are you not in meditation?" And always, they stop. They realize that it is the ego-mind still fighting to stay alive. Finally, there comes an understanding that thoughts are not able to stick to the mind. Ultimately, in Truth, there is no mind.

How do decisions get made and things get done without identification with the ego, a separate "I"?

All duties, all performances, are done spontaneously. There is no conscious planning on my part. There's no looking for reward. While working, there is only the consciousness of being here. There is only serving the Guru in all activities. When one has submitted to the Guru, there develops a single purpose. That purpose leads one to work unselfishly and contentedly. You come to know that pleasing the Guru is in essence the best service. In Truth there is no work, no Guru, and no one doing the work. You are continually established in the present Now, Totally Aware. Totally Pleased. Totally Rewarded. Totally Devoted to this Love.

When you say the "guru" to whom or what are you referring?

The Guru is not a person you are submitting to. People fear submitting to another person or institution, simply because they fear abuse, misuse, or mind control. There's a fear of having their freedom to think and to be themselves limited. But once you submit to the True Guru, the Sat Guru, you are in reality submitting to your True Self, what you truly are. You are the Guru. God, in His/Her infinite mercy and wisdom, gave everyone their own Guru. He/She is you as the Guru. So you are able to experience all the blessings of the universe. You possess your own magic lamp and every wish is fulfilled. Even before you can formulate a wish—behold—it is here, a gift from you to you! Do not waste another second of your life looking outside yourself for your Self.

How do you experience relationships with others since this awakening?

When dealing with others, one sees each person as himself. One wishes true enlightenment for each person. If a person speaks about life being unfair, instantly there comes the realization that they are in suffering. But how can there ever be suffering when there is nothing but Love everywhere? Love is the cry of the baby for food. Love is the cry of the grownup for better wages to feed his family. Love is the essence that causes the baby to cry, the grownup to cry, and Love is the satisfier of all those who cry. From Love comes the cry and from Love comes the responses to the cry.

We are continuously reaching with our minds for something other than the present moment of Now. We reach into the past for those good old days. We project our minds into the future for visions of happiness in some event. Whenever we perform such mental gymnastics, we are always doing them Now! So, my brother, my sister, Be Here Now!

Anything else you would like to add?

As a lover of the scriptures, I once read the word and could only gain a little solace from what was being conveyed by Jesus,

Muhammad, Krishna, and Buddha. There seemed to be a missing element that evaded my grasping mind. I would go to the churches, the mosques, to hear the preacher preach on these sacred texts; still there was no rest for the weary mind. Then came the awakening! The mind was slain. Awareness was revealed. Now, each scripture only confirms that inner awakening; each word, each verse points to this spiritual experience. You come to know that the books come from the very same source that is you. The book, the Source, is you, no difference.

Acknowledgments

There are many people to thank who made this book possible. All gave precious time or invaluable assistance so that men and women around the world might hear this tale of hope and freedom. It humbles us to know that so many people from diverse walks of life and varied religious and spiritual persuasions believed in this project so fully. We thank you all from the bottom of our hearts. Many blessings to each and every one of you, and may our precious creator and sustainer continue to keep you close to this glorious gift of freedom.

The unconditional love of those who have supported this endeavor has been amazing. When we started this project, out of nowhere came people who simply said yes and did not stop saying yes to this giving. Such generous hearts you are. Your devotion to wanting the best for all causes me to pause in deep gratitude. We truly and humbly thank each and every one of you.

An especially deep bow of gratitude goes out to Peter Kyne, Robert Leathers, and Gary Stokoe. The depth of your hearts is enormous. May many blessings come to you in so many varied ways. Thanks also to Sheila Waugh, Penelope Moore, John and Terry Stalp, Robert Cheatham, Maureen Claire, Candice Ellingham, Ben Snyder and my brother Michael Daole. gems you are.

Our sincere thanks to Dia Paxton, God's love offering to this project, whose insights contributed immeasurably to the content of the story.

Roslyn Moore, the gift of your editing expertise and your generous and gentle heart were instrumental in bringing this book to completion. Thank you so much for your openness and unconditional support.

Much went into the beginning stages of the book, including tape transcription, interviewing, and the reading and lending of invaluable insights to the manuscript. To all those involved who stopped and gave of yourself without hesitation, know that your dedication to this book will provide spiritual sustenance to men and women in prison who are without the freedom to get to a church, mosque, or holy place of inspiration. Your support is bringing them all a mountain of love and light in some dark places. Our deepest thanks to these lightbearers: Meera Censor, Mariana Caplan, Patty Klauer, Bruce Moore, Joel Orr, Susan Rouzie, Pat Righter, Jane Sterling, Bev Collins, Sudha, aka Nancy Marsh, Jennifer Nichols, and Celeste Walker. David Gabriel, may your vision be visible. Cynthia Volpi, keeping me straight seemed so easy for you, thanks for the patience. Stace Hirth, couldn't leave you on the sidelines my sister; thank you.

Barbara Denempont, you saw the players that could make this amazing gift come to life and your vision brought us all together to make it happen. Thank you so much for seeing so deeply.

To Julian and Catherine Noyce of Non-Duality Press, when you said yes to this book, everything I had envisioned in a publisher came true. You made me feel that whatever my vision was, it was yours also. Working together has been amazingly sweet, easy, and joyful, just what this project needed. Thank you from the eternal depths of my heart.

To my brother Chris Hebard and his wife Astrid, you two are truly angels. Blessings to you both.

John and Yoko Raatz, thanks for the words of encouragement, and also your open hearts.

Toby and Amber Terrell, when it looked bleak your inspiration was right on time to guide me through. When things looked dark, and the book seemed stalled, you were the shining light of experience that brought a wisdom to the project.

Then there are all those kind and loving souls who have been working in the trenches, going into prison daily and giving of themselves completely and selflessly. You are the change-makers. I would like to give honor to you from this unspeakable place in my heart. Day in and day out you have shown up and continue to show up for your brothers and sisters in prison who thirst for this "water of life" that you bring in. Working directly or indirectly with This Sacred Space are Susan Carabello, Chris Mohr, aka

Satchitananda, Michele Sondheimer, James Fox, Frank Williams, Lisa Mansfield, Lisa Leeb, Karl Frederick, Richard Charles, Joy Ravelli, Ron Caracter, Jacques Verduin, Katherine Coder, Adva Mey, Jenny Overman, Melanie Derynck, Judy Cangiamilla, Monique Martineau, Adva Mey, Bo Lozoff, and the very first volunteer for This Sacred Space, Mike Katz.

To Elizabeth Samet, you are a dream come true; never stop dreaming those big dreams. All things are possible for you.

Suzanne Werblin, I can't say enough. Thanks, for the genuine love that is always flowing through you, Sis.

Diane Peterson, for years you were right there beside me, aiding, assisting, helping me to get re-accustomed with society, asking nothing from me but one thing: "Stay true to your spiritual experience and your connection to God." You are a true friend. Thanks Di.

Here I must take a moment to say that I am especially pleased to have worked with Dania March Sacks at Downtown High School in San Francisco, CA. I want to express my gratitude to Rob Schwartz for this fortuitous introduction. Those years there were definitely humbling. Living in the moment was the only way to work with the young men and women who wanted only one thing from us: honesty. Dania, I know wherever you are, there is smile on your face. You are an inspiration, dear one.

Thank you Carol Fregoso for taking time out from your busy schedule to work with the students and me at Downtown High School. The teens and I looked forward to being creative while working the clay each week. Thank you so much.

Karlos Eli, I still remember the day you came into the sacred space classroom meeting and said. "Kenny, I got it!" You have it and it has you. Never apart. What joy it is to know you are out here living happy and free.

Jillian McIlvenna, you are always in my heart. May our creator be kind and merciful to you as you grow in the light of love and devotion. Your prayer for peace and redemption will be granted, that is the law.

274

My friend Manon Pretre wanted her son Adrian Peter Trevino to be happy so she gave him my book to read. He had not read in years. After reading The Last Hustle he called me and said, 'Kenny, Thank you. After reading this book of yours, for some reason, I am just happy. Life is good right now. Keep sharing your light wherever you go. Adrian.'

Right when we started this book I moved to Sonoma, CA, and it is there that I found Baba Harihar Ramji and the Sonoma Ashram. At the time, I needed a form of spiritual practice to support me, and there was Baba saying, "Stop, take a step back, and breathe." Thank you so much Baba.

I never thought I would need a coach, but Emily you showed me differently. Thanks for your generosity and straightforwardness. Perfect advice at all times.

Now I would be remiss if I did not include these two players who have remained true to the spirit of the game. My partners, Warren "Silver Wolf" Morse and Shantam Nityama "Roaming Buffalo." I must give honors also and all due respect to my Native Americans brothers and sisters of Mt Arafat Embassy Clan of the Yamassee Nation. Hotep.

My deepest gratitude to Rupam Heike Henry. You taught me how to listen and to see the true beauty of a woman. What a joy it is to be with you. Thanks for being there in those hours of revisiting the dark side of Kenny Dale. It was your light that guided me safely home. Many Blessings to you Rupam, my friend.

To Eli Jaxon Bear, you gave completely of yourself in so many ways until I can only say "thanks brother" for the helping hand that is still giving of this unconditional love.

Gangaji, at the date of this writing, it's been sixteen years since I first met you in prison, and since that meeting, I've traveled to many places, met many people, and everywhere I've turned, I've been met with your presence. Your grace, the grace of this lineage, has always been one step ahead, preparing the way, reassuring me that I am always in exactly the right place. Without you this life of true freedom would never have been possible. Your prison program was the only vehicle that could turn me and so many other lost souls around and point us toward the true light. Thank you so much for hearing our call and visiting us in our darkest moments.

To my mother, Ms. Geraldine Scott, here is your dream come true. I made it out, and Mom, I know that it was your prayers that honestly did it. The Lord heard you and sent someone to me in prison that I could hear. I know all those lonely days of going to the front window and looking out into the streets trying to make sense of my wild life was frustrating, but all is well now. Thanks for holding love in your heart when I was doing all I could to flee this love. I love you Mom.

Reggie, Maurice, Lemeul, Cynthia, LaChanda, and Robin, God bless you all and thank the Lord you did not have to travel that lonely and treacherous road with me.

A special shout out to my daughter who maintained an attitude of "Dad, you will get out and stay out" long before I met my teacher and found real freedom. You believed in me when I did not believe in myself. The greatest we have is that we survived the prison years, as father and daughter, and now we are growing together out here. I love you Chanette Coleman.

The most wonderful part here is that I get to say how much I am blessed to have you, Shanti, as my coauthor. This book could not have been done without you. Wisdom, foresight, vision, and patience, patience, and more patience are some words that come to mind. You poured your love into each letter and each space between the letters. My dearest Shanti my heart is cracked wide open in deep appreciation and gratitude. There is no end to this love I have for you. I love you sincerely dear Shanti.

There are so many more whom I could thank whose love has been showered upon me over the years. The list is endless. You know who you are. I take this moment to acknowledge you and your contribution to this continual healing process. May God bless you and keep you in this eternal grace.

I have learned something over the years as a member of a

spiritual community. It takes all sorts of situations and circumstances to bring about healing. It may not look like roses all the time. Sometimes thorny situations appear as we are on the road to recovery. Thank you my spiritual family for the sweetness, the bitterness, and those thorny moments in this game of life.

Finally, there is the vessel who held me all of those years while incarcerated. When at my lowest you would come and whisper in my ear, "Read the word my child." Your gentle voice guided my steps and my heart to a sacred space inside where I found comfort and solace. That divine entity was the Church. Thank you Mother, thank you Father, for your infinite love. Without you would be no me this day.

About the Authors

KENNY JOHNSON is the founder and director of This Sacred Space, a nonprofit organization that facilitates meditation and emotional healing for men and women behind bars and upon their release. The programs of This Sacred Space (www.thissacredspace.org) support inmates in the personal changes necessary to live successful lives far beyond prison walls. Kenny currently resides in the San Francisco Bay area and is available for speaking engagements, book signings, and television and radio interviews. Kenny can be contacted at kenny@thissacredspace.org.

SHANTI EINOLANDER is a freelance writer and book editor residing in Ashland, Oregon. She is currently seeking additional true-life stories that have the capacity to inspire lives and awaken hearts. She can be reached at Clear Light Editorial Services, www.clearlight-edit.com.